I'LL SCREAM LATER

I'LL SCREAM LATER

MARLEE MATLIN

with Betsy Sharkey

Simon Spotlight Entertainment

New York London Toronto Sydney

Simon Spotlight Entertainment
A Division of Simon & Schuster, Inc.
1230 Avenue of the Americas
New York, NY 10020

First Simon Spotlight Entertainment hardcover edition March 2009

SIMON SPOTLIGHT ENTERTAINMENT and colophon are trademarks of Simon & Schuster, Inc.

For information about special discounts for bulk purchases, please contact Simon & Schuster Special Sales at 1-800-506-1949 or business@simonandschuster.com

The Simon & Schuster Speakers Bureau can bring authors to your live event. For more information or to book an event contact the Simon & Schuster Speakers Bureau at 1-866-248-3049 or visit our website at www.simonspeakers.com.

Designed by C. Linda Dingler

Manufactured in the United States of America

10 9 8 7 6 5 4 3 2 1

Library of Congress Cataloging-in-Publication Data
Matlin, Marlee.
    I'll scream later / Marlee Matlin.
        p. cm.
    1. Matlin, Marlee. 2. Actors—United States—Biography. 3. Deaf—United
States—Biography. 4. Authors, American—21st century—Biography. I. Title.
    PN2287.M54285A3 2009
    791.4302'8092—dc22
    [B]
                                            2009004809
ISBN-13: 978-1-4391-0285-5
ISBN-10:   1-4391-0285-6

I don't need you to worry for me 'cause I'm alright. I don't want you to tell me it's time to come home. I don't care what you say anymore, this is my life. Go ahead with your own life, and leave me alone.

"My Life," Billy Joel

I'LL SCREAM LATER

Libby and Marlee, ca. 1968

Marlee and Sarah, 1996

1

FEBRUARY 2, 1987, it's nearing dusk when my plane lands in Palm Springs. No one in my family is there to meet me. No friends. Just a stranger, an old man with a face that looks as if it has traveled a thousand miles of bad road. He smiles and waves in my direction. I'm sure he's seen countless like me before.

He seems kind, tries to be reassuring, but it still takes all of my strength to move toward him and his aging station wagon. He is a volunteer, the transportation of lost souls now one of his missions in life—maybe a way to direct a little good karma back in his direction. I understand, I could use some myself.

I have never, ever felt more alone or more frightened in my life; it's as if sadness and despair have seeped deep into my bones.

He doesn't try to talk to me, and I wonder if he knows I am Deaf or just senses that I'm too emotionally fragile to talk. Either way he's right. I have no words right now. I am as close to broken as I've ever been. We head out into the fading light for a fifteen-minute drive that feels endless, the one that will take me to the Betty Ford Center, specializing in treating alcohol and drug addiction, in nearby Rancho Mirage.

My name is Marlee Matlin, and at this moment I am twenty-one years old and at the very beginning of an unexpectedly promising acting career. I've also managed to pack a few other things into those years—among them a serious addiction to both pot and cocaine. Then there's my two-year relationship with actor William Hurt, which has gone from passionate and troubled to dangerously difficult and codependent.

The sun sets as we pull up to the front of the center, BFC to anyone who's spent time there. The building looks imposing, not welcoming, but I can see through its expanse of windows that a light is on inside.

It SHOULD HAVE been the best time of my life. And in a surreal way it was. Almost exactly forty-eight hours earlier and a world away in the bright lights and red-carpet glitz of the Beverly Hilton Hotel, I had won a Golden Globe as Best Actress for my performance as Sarah Norman, the profoundly Deaf and profoundly angry young woman who finds herself and love in the film *Children of a Lesser God*.

I stood on the stage that night in a simple black dress I'd found a few days earlier, no speech, looking down into a sea of faces. So many of the actors whose careers I'd been awed by were applauding me. I had won in a category that included Anne Bancroft, Sigourney Weaver, Julie Andrews, and Farrah Fawcett—all Hollywood veterans. I was dizzy with happiness. I felt humbled, unable to quite believe this was truly happening. To the rest of the world it must have seemed that everything was going my way. My very first film had come with a celebrated costar in William Hurt, who quickly became my mentor and my lover, and not in that order. For the most part the critics had been exceedingly kind to the film, it was doing good business at the box office both in the United States and overseas, which always makes the studio bosses happy, and now the Golden Globes had officially launched the movie, and me with it, into the Oscar race.

Though much of my life was falling apart, for that one night I was able to put all the problems and the pain aside and let the extraordinary evening wash over me. I don't know whether it's fate or karma or just me, but for every momentous time in my life—good or bad—it seems the gods always throw in something for comic relief. On the way up to the podium to accept my Golden Globe, I looked down and realized that one of the Lee press-on nails that I'd glued on and painted bright red earlier that day had come off. Instead of thinking about what I would say, my only thought was how in the world could I sign and hide that broken nail!

But once I hit the stage, that thought flew from my mind. All I could think about was how grateful I was to be recognized in this way. And that is essentially what I signed. Short, simple, heartfelt.

The walk backstage to the pressroom, Golden Globe in hand, was amazing, overwhelming. My heart was pounding, I swear I could feel each beat, hundreds of strobe lights were going off in my face, photographers were screaming my name until Whoopi Goldberg flung her arms around me, gave me a squeeze, and said with no small irony to the crowd, "Hey, guys, she's Deaf, she can't hear you."

But photographers are a hungry bunch—a really great shot puts steak on the table and a Mercedes in the driveway—so it didn't take long for them to figure out the trick to getting my attention. So the shouts were replaced by waving hands, and I twisted and turned and smiled as the hands in front of me waved wildly.

That night I went back to my room at the L'Ermitage hotel and closed the door on Hollywood—at least for a time.

On the other side of that door, the Oscar campaign for the movie was getting ready to kick into overdrive. I had no idea how Oscar season worked in Hollywood, all that it entailed. There was publicity to do, photo shoots to line up, magazine covers to consider, TV talk shows to book. There were calls from the studio, the media, old friends, new friends, agents.

The calls would go unanswered, the interviews would all be turned down, the photo shoots nixed. I had decided I was going to quietly disappear, leaving it to Jack Jason, my interpreter and increasingly the person I relied on to help with the business details of my life, to run interference for me. I told him to say no to everything—though I was pretty much oblivious of how much that would be—but to tell absolutely no one where I was or why I wasn't available. No exceptions.

I was lucky. Today in the world of rabid paparazzi and TMZ such discretion wouldn't be possible. But in 1987, only a handful of people knew where I was going—my immediate family, Jack, and, of course Bill, whose own stint at Betty Ford was barely finished by the time I checked in.

It was hard enough to go into rehab, it was harder still that I had virtually no support for my decision. Bill was the only person encouraging me. Everyone else thought whatever problems I might have with drugs weren't all that serious, and, besides, didn't I realize my career was at stake?

In a seven-page letter that was typical of the pressure I was under from those closest to me, my dad wrote:

> So you smoke pot—big deal—do you understand you are just starting a career and by checking into a hospital, can ruin your life. . . . Don't go to the Betty Ford clinic. You have something going for you—don't throw it away—don't waste it.
>
> You missed a lot in life but maybe this little bit of fame can make up a small portion of what you missed.

This letter came as a follow-up to a huge fight my mother and I had over my decision to go into rehab. Even Jack, who was spending hours a day with me interpreting interviews and meetings, thought the timing was wrong and the problem wasn't that severe.

But it was. Consider January 9, 1987, one particularly memorable day of my life on drugs.

I was in Chicago at my parents' house and due to fly to California the next day to be with Bill at Betty Ford during Family Week as part of his rehab therapy. I knew deep inside that during the counseling sessions they would bust me about my drug use, so I tried to finish everything I had.

Here's an inventory of that day: I had a gram of coke, a half-ounce bag of pot, a pipe, rolling papers, and a bong. All by myself, I finished the coke but couldn't finish the pot; though I really tried, there was just too much. That doesn't even touch the emotional issues I had that were fueling my drug use.

I remember cleaning up my desk in a haze, finding anything that I could that was drug-related and throwing it all away. It was in my gut that this would be the last time I would ever use. But I knew, no matter how determined I was to keep drugs out of my life, I needed help.

Looking back on it now, I realize everything in my life up to that point—my childhood, my family, my deafness, the obstacles, the opportunities, the friends and lovers, the molester and the abusers, the doctors and the teachers, and always the acting—had all meshed to buy me a ticket on that forty-eight-hour roller-coaster ride in 1987. Forty-eight hours that delivered an amazing, drug-free high at the Golden Globes and an immeasurable low as I faced the entrance to Betty Ford and the hard work I knew I had ahead of me if I was to build a life of sobriety.

The intersection of these two events would change the way I would navigate life—and the life I would have to navigate—forever.

2

I⊤ ALL BEGAN for me on August 24, 1965, at 12:03 a.m., when Marlee Beth Matlin came screaming into the world. I was not then, nor was I ever, a quiet, retiring child. As my mom describes it, "None of my kids were quiet, they cried, they screamed—they were anxious to get grown, Marlee most of all."

My family lived just outside of Chicago in Morton Grove, one of a string of upper-middle-class suburbs filled with newly minted bilevel homes to accommodate the growing families with disposable incomes who wanted a comfortable lifestyle, separated from the poverty of the city. My mom and dad, Libby and Don Matlin, definitely wanted to put the grit, grime, and hard times of their childhoods growing up in Chicago behind them.

When my mother talks about her early years, it is a story of abandonment and disappointments. An aunt and uncle had helped Libby's mother, Rose Hammer, and Libby's older sister, Sara, and brother, Jack, who changed his name to Jason, emigrate from Bledow, Poland—a village about halfway between Warsaw and Lodz—in the late twenties, saving them from the almost certain death they would have faced as Jews had they been there for Hitler's invasion in 1939. Libby, the family's last child, was born in 1930 in Kansas City, Missouri. It was a new world full of possibilities. But the family would soon begin to fracture.

By the time Libby was nine, her family had moved to Chicago, where her parents ran a small baked-goods store, though that didn't last long. Libby's father, Paul, diagnosed with tuberculosis, soon moved into a treatment facility in Denver, her brother eventually left to live with the aunt and uncle in Yakima, Washington, who'd helped the family emigrate, and Libby's sister moved in with another family as a boarder. That left Libby and her mother to make their way alone.

Rose, who spoke Yiddish and little English—barely enough to get by—mostly found work in the Chicago sweatshops sewing dresses for little money and long hours each day. Rose and Libby lived in rat- and roach-infested tenements in the city's worst areas, a life that Libby remembers as "soul-destroying."

Her one good memory is of an uncle, a shoemaker who one day put taps on a pair of her shoes. She loved to dance in them for hours, but worried that her overworked mother might take them away or see them as frivolous in their hardscrabble life. Libby would sneak off and find a little bit of bare flooring away from the apartment where she could make the tap shoes sing.

She says she had no real dreams for herself as a child, it wasn't a life that allowed for dreams, but there were those tap shoes and somewhere along the way the hope that maybe, just maybe, she could be the next Shirley Temple.

More disappointments followed. When Libby was twelve, her mother found out that her husband, by then getting his TB treatment in San Francisco, was involved with another woman. Rose divorced him and Libby felt she had lost her father forever. I never knew any of this until after Grandpa Paul passed away.

He would come into Libby's life again when she was nineteen. By then, her sister had tracked him down and reconnected him to the family. He was living in Los Angeles and running a small dry cleaner's on Vernon Avenue, and the next time Libby was in town she went to see him. Maybe it was more out of curiosity than anything else; she said she could never forgive him for emotionally devastating her mother.

A few years later he came through Chicago and asked to stay with our family, but it was awkward and tense. My mother remembers one day going downstairs to the basement with a knife in hand to retrieve some ribs from a fridge down there. On the way down the stairs she stopped and, unable to shake off the rage she felt for the father who abandoned her, rammed the knife into the wood paneling along the stairwell. They rarely spoke again, and when he died in the nineties, she didn't go to the funeral. I was in L.A. then and went to the service, the only one in my immediate family there.

MY DAD'S CHILDHOOD was just as bleak. The Matlin family traces its roots back to Russia, where my great-grandfather was a blacksmith in Gomel, which sits on the banks of the Sozh River in what is now Belarus. By all accounts it was a thriving city in the early 1900s with a large Jewish population. But wars would transform it.

Five of six sons in the family were lost to the fighting during World War I. My great-grandfather died in 1908, before World War II would claim his wife and six daughters along with more than 2 million other Jews during the German occupation of the region.

Edward, my grandfather, the youngest child, was around twelve in 1914, and his mother knew if he stayed, he would have to go into the army like his brothers. She refused to lose another son. So with little more than the shirt on his back, he headed for the United States.

My grandfather made his way to Glenview, Illinois, just outside Chicago, where some other families from Gomel had settled. He went to work for a family that owned a barbershop/pool hall and soon started to learn the barbering trade, sleeping on the pool tables at night.

By the time my dad came along, the real business at the barbershop was a backroom bookie joint my grandfather ran. Eddie was a heavy whiskey drinker—my dad would pour him shots throughout the day. The legend in our family was that Sammy Davis Jr. showed up one day for a shave and a haircut, but Eddie wouldn't let him in because he didn't cater to blacks. I wonder what Eddie would think when years later I would count Sammy as a friend and mentor.

By his count, Eddie gambled away four barbershops over the years with a string of bad bets on the horses. He became a Chicago character, leaving more than a few customers with towels steaming on their faces while he ran to make a last-minute bet before post time. When a reporter asked why, after forty years, he kept betting when he kept losing. Eddie just shrugged and said, "I'm trying to get even."

The relationship between my grandfather and my grandmother, Ann, was just as sketchy. My dad hated to talk about it to me no matter how hard I tried. My grandparents would marry and divorce four or five times over the years and have one more child, my uncle Steve, who is nineteen years younger than my dad.

When times were bad, and they mostly were, Don was passed around from aunts to grandparents. He never knew where he would be living from one day to the next. He never made it out of high school—"I never took home homework, nobody was there to say I should or shouldn't." With an alcoholic father and a mother who was easily distracted by the other men in her life, at sixteen my dad tried to join the Marines, a decision that his mother approved. But after three months, the Marines found out that he and two other boys in the company were all underage and sent them back home.

Don kicked around at odd jobs for the next few years. He had a serious girlfriend that he lost tragically that we would hear about over the years. Near Christmastime, they had argued, leaving things in a mess. That night she went out with another guy. As they were driving back home from their date, another car plowed into them. She was instantly killed. To this day, when Don says her name—and he rarely does unless pushed—he still cries. Another twist of fate; who knows what would have happened had she lived, my brothers and I might not exist.

My dad and my mom dated off and on, from the time they were fifteen, though as my mom says, "We did a lot of breaking up, too."

My dad tells this story of why they finally got married:

"We'd been engaged quite a few times, and Libby finally said she didn't want to hear from me again unless I wanted to get married. I knew she was out visiting relatives in California and heard that there was a big earthquake. I called to make sure she was all right and she said, 'I suppose you want to marry me since you called . . .'"

So the Kern County earthquake in July of 1952, a 7.3-level shaker that would twist highways, crumble buildings, and do more than $60 million in damage, triggered what would become my family.

THE WEDDING ON November 2, 1952, was at noon on a Saturday at the Belmont Hotel in Chicago. Around a hundred guests were invited. On their wedding day, my dad was in a dark suit, and my mom wore a powder blue dress that she bought at a department store for $17. The veil she borrowed. With a rabbi officiating, they said their vows, Don crushed a wineglass, and they both dared to dream a little.

The couple settled into a nice, bright apartment on Chicago's north side, furnished with $5,000 that Don's bosses had given him as a wedding present—a fortune at that time. My mom was soon pregnant with my brother Eric, and four years later my brother Marc was born. Not long after, the family moved to Morton Grove, to the house I would grow up in.

My dad, by then, was selling used cars, a business he would stay in for the rest of his working days. It was hard work, long hours, but the money was enough to afford us a comfortably solid middle-class life. My parents developed an active social life—Wednesdays and Saturdays they always went out. Thursdays my dad played cards with the guys . . . all night.

Over the next few years, my parents would try without success to add to the family. My mother had one miscarriage, and more devastatingly they lost a baby, a boy, who was premature, born the day President John F. Kennedy was assassinated.

By the time my mom was pregnant with me, Libby and Don were hoping for a girl, but like most parents, what they really wanted was a healthy child. Eric had just turned twelve and Marc was eight when I came home in August 1965.

My grandmother Rose is indirectly responsible for my name. She wanted Libby to name me after Molly, her half sister, the aunt who had helped bring Rose and her two oldest children here from Poland. Although my mother really despised this aunt, she agreed— sort of. Sometime before I was born, she attended a luncheon where the speaker was a British woman named Marlee. The woman was attractive, self-possessed, and impressive and was kind to Libby when they met that day. My mother came home and told my dad that if the baby was a girl, *Marlee* would be her name . . . close enough to *Molly* to satisfy my grandmother's request.

For a time there was a nurse—I guess that was 1965's version of a nanny—to help take care of me, although in my brother Eric's memory her main function seemed to be to keep him and Marc away from me. But she soon left and my care and feeding reverted to the family.

To Eric I was just the baby in the background. He was busy becoming a distant teenager, out with friends as often as he was allowed, which was a lot. Marc, though, remembers he was fascinated by the new addition to the household and hung around to help out:

"I remember being intrigued with Marlee's tongue. In those first few weeks when she'd cry, it would curl up on both sides, just a perfect little bow. I learned how to hold her, how to check the temperature of the milk on my wrist, and how to feed her. I remember Marlee always wanted to know who was in the room; even before she could sit up, she'd be lying in her crib but always looking around. I used to think she had radar in her head.

"Oh, and I remember she had regular diapers, I guess it was before disposables. My mother would put them in the toilet to soak and I used to go in there and pee on them."

Just what brothers are for . . .

Life went on and I grew into a babbling toddler—"What's that, Marlee?" "Apple." "And that?" "Dog."

"She wasn't putting sentences together, but she had very clear speech," Marc remembers.

Everything seemed fine. Except it wasn't.

Wearing my hearing aids, age 5

3

THEN THERE WAS SILENCE.

Many theories have floated through my life about why or how or exactly when I lost my hearing. The one that I remember hearing as a child and that has followed me around the most is this:

When I was around eighteen months old, I had roseola, a viral infection common in infants and toddlers. It comes with a rash and a high fever and usually disappears without complications in a week. I would later find out that roseola doesn't cause deafness.

As the story goes, the family was due to fly to California where my grandmother and most of my aunts and uncles now lived. My fever had been particularly high but it seemed to have run its course; nevertheless my mom took me to the pediatrician to make sure I was well enough to travel. He said yes. And so we did.

My brother Marc remembers the plane ride as *Wizard of Oz* scary, rough, with a dark storm he could see outside the windows of the plane. Marc says, "We were waiting for my uncle and aunt to pick us up at the airport, and what my memory tells me is that I said to Marlee, 'What's that?' And she answered, 'Tree,' which it was. Now, looking back, I never heard her speak again, never as a hearing person."

In California everything just stopped. Hands clapped, I didn't hear them. Pots fell, I didn't flinch. People called my name, I didn't look up. My family left me with my grandmother Rose's neighbor so they could go to dinner. When they came home, she told my parents she was sure that I was Deaf. My mom at first chalked it up to the stubbornness of a kid heading into the terrible twos. But the neighbor insisted it was something more.

I don't have memories of before, of a world where I could hear,

I was too young. So I can only imagine what it must have felt like to know that something fundamental has suddenly shifted and you don't know why. The most basic connection we make as human beings is communication, and mine was suddenly irrevocably changed. Over time, I would learn how to bridge this gap, but I still wonder about that eighteen-month-old toddler just learning about life and what it felt like when everything went silent.

The first doctor my parents took me to when we got back to Chicago thought maybe I just had water in my ears and suggested they give it a few days. But there were no improvements. Another doctor identified the problem and handed down the verdict that would change life for me and my family forever: I was profoundly Deaf.

My dad says, "I remember leaving the doctor's office after they told us, just feeling stunned. I couldn't really accept it. I didn't want to believe it. My little girl, Deaf? When we got home, Marlee had fallen asleep, so I put her in her crib. Then I went down to the kitchen and got some pans and stood over the crib, banging them together. She didn't wake up, just kept sleeping, and I stood there, banging the pans, and crying. I still cry when I think about it, one day she could hear, the next day she couldn't. It just disappeared."

Even to this day, when I'm long past wondering what happened, it still chokes my dad up so much he can barely talk about it.

ANGER AND GUILT moved into my family's house along with my diagnosis—something as a child I never felt swirling around me.

My parents wondered if they had done something to cause my deafness, if they had missed some sign along the way. If they'd discovered a problem earlier, while I could still hear, could something have been done? Had the changes in the pressure in the airplane cabin that day as we flew through the storm been too much? Even when they were told no by just about every professional around, it was always there, unsaid, in the background.

Guilt settled in over the years, too, over not learning sign language. My mother did a little, but for me it was soon like talking to someone who knows just a little bit of English—barely enough to get by, and far from enough to have a real conversation. There was guilt that my family could hear and I couldn't—the conversations around the dinner table, the radio in the car, the television sets that were on almost constantly in the house.

And there was anger—at the situation, that it had happened to their baby girl, their little sister, that no one could tell them how to fix things. All their plans and hopes and dreams, everything they thought about what this last child would mean in their lives, in the family, changed.

"I was angry at her being Deaf, that nature played such an awful trick," says Marc. "And I know she wouldn't have wanted it, but I felt guilty that I could hear and she couldn't."

Dealing with my deafness would overtake everything else. For my mother, it would become her obsession. My brother Eric remembers a sea change in the Matlin household; he defines the two stages as the "original family" and then the "Marlee family." Eric says, "My mother's reason to live changed. She poured everything into Marlee. I was older and I didn't need their attention at that point. Marc, I'm not as sure." And I'm not so sure Eric wasn't in some ways hurt that as the oldest, and heading into his teenage years, his needs just fell by the wayside. That's just not right.

Marc remembers that many of the household rules were not just relaxed, but tossed out the window. All of which benefited my brothers as well as me. We'd rarely had treats in the house, but now a cabinet in the kitchen was filled with anything sweet that I liked. Ice cream was always in the freezer. Toys began to fill the house, whereas in the past the boys had made their own entertainment, usually pickup hockey or baseball with other kids in the neighborhood.

From that point on, just about anything I wanted was given to me, as if the toys, ice cream, candy, and an almost complete lack of rules could somehow make up for my being unable to hear. I was definitely spoiled—the baby of the family, the only girl, and Deaf.

Looking back on my childhood, I honestly don't remember ever not getting something that I asked for. By the time I could drive, the toys became cars, with new ones all the time for me from my dad's used-car business. Despite my being a pretty willful teenager, I was only grounded once, and even that was cut from two weeks to one almost immediately.

The message I got from my parents was that their world, and as far as I knew the world at large, revolved around me.

Growing up, most of the time I was happy, I loved to play, I loved having fun. I loved performing, making other people laugh. I had a large collection of friends, a mix of both hearing and Deaf. But as anyone who knows me well will tell you, I also had a temper.

I've thought a lot about that anger, trying to understand the source of it. While it's easy for people to assume I was angry because I was Deaf, that explanation always felt too simplistic. Even when I was completely alone and trying to do a brutal self-examination of my emotions, that never felt like the reason.

I think some of it was triggered by the ways in which deafness isolated me from a world I wanted to embrace and absorb with a passion. Anyone else in the family could pick up the phone and call my grandmother. I wanted to, but I couldn't. Everyone else understood the dramas and sitcoms that played out on TV; someone had to fill in the blanks for me. And too often, no one did.

I had a thousand questions about life, and too many times no one was there who knew how, or would take the time, to explain things to me.

When my mother would say no, in my memory it was always just no, there was no reason why. I wanted to know why, needed to know, but felt lost and too often was left to figure it out—or not— on my own.

Here's how I tried to explain how I felt in an essay I was assigned when I was thirteen. The title: "My Life About Being Deaf . . ."

> I know that it ruined my life from an early age. . . . My brothers had fun with me and tried to talk with me but when they both heard that I was Deaf, they were so shocked and couldn't believe it. And it had depressed them. . . . What I feel about being Deaf is that it is a hard life for myself.

As I grew up, I had to find a way of coping. Whether it was my parents, friends, lovers, teachers, the entertainment industry, or for that matter the deafness itself—anyone who said, "No, Marlee," set powerful emotions churning inside me and I would fight back. Whoever or whatever was trying to hold me back—I would fight against it as if my very life depended on it. And I now believe that it did. That fight, that intensity, that relentless need to break through and connect, has, in many ways, propelled me through this life.

When I was young, Marc, my aunt Sue, and others saw my temper tantrums as a manifestation of my frustration at not being able to communicate. Temper tantrums are common among Deaf children, and I would imagine among hearing children, too, until barriers to communication are broken through. My mother, though, seemed to view it as my punishing her. My father saw these rows as his own private hell, with him caught between the two people in his life he desperately wanted to be happy.

An escalating cycle of conflict between my mother and me would reach its height when I hit my teens, which came around the same time as what I now believe were my mother's increasing bouts of depression. All I knew then is that when my mom closed the door to her room, no one was to bother her, no matter what. I felt closed out, and once again I didn't understand why. I just knew that the moods were dark and we weren't supposed to invade.

One day many years later after I was a mother myself, I was in a grumpy mood and closed the door on Sarah, my oldest child. I suddenly remembered my mom closing her door. . . . I told myself then to try not to repeat what my mom had done to me as a child. To this day, I try to never close the door to my room at home, and if I do, I always explain why to my kids. I don't want them to ever feel that I am shutting them out of my life or, worse, that I'm closing the door to escape from them.

I, too, had a weapon that I would use in fights, my own way of shutting the door—with a turn of my head, communication stopped, all the screaming in the world could not reach me.

As I entered adulthood, I found that, in a sense, I had to grow up all over again—learning how to set limits for myself, whether it was my need for drugs or for attention—realizing that I couldn't control everything, that sometimes I just need to let go and trust; and understanding that just as I wanted to kick down all the doors my mother shut on me, when it mattered most, I needed to find a way not to turn my head away from the difficult moments but to look that problem, that emotion, that person in the eye, and work through it. Essentially I had to unlearn a lot of what I'd been taught as a kid.

It hasn't always been easy, and sometimes progress is slower than I'd like—but I work on it day by day.

4

My PARENTS' DECISION to have me grow up at home, go to mainstream schools, live in and cope in a hearing world, was, without question, the most important of my life, and one that I will forever be grateful for.

At the same time, they wanted to make sure I could navigate the Deaf world as well, so my earliest memories are of moving constantly between the two. Feet firmly planted in both.

As soon as they began to finally accept that I was Deaf, my parents threw themselves into finding out everything they could about how to help me navigate life.

The first group of specialists they consulted suggested that I be sent to a school for the Deaf, essentially institutionalized, which was the most common practice at the time. So my parents packed me and Marc into the backseat of the car and drove to St. Louis, which had two highly regarded schools for Deaf children.

One of the schools specialized in the oral tradition—no signing, you were instead taught how to speak and read lips. The other was more focused on teaching American Sign Language as the foundation for communication and developing an understanding of Deaf culture. Both boarded students through the week, with weekends spent at home.

After the visits, my parents sat in the car in the parking lot of the last school we visited and, once again, cried. They couldn't live with the notion of shipping me off to a boarding school, but they weren't sure what other options were left to them.

Ultimately, they decided that they would find a way for me to attend mainstream schools with Deaf-education programs—that usually meant long bus rides, but allowed me to live at home. They found a doctor in the area who specialized in the oral tradition, essentially teaching the Deaf to speak and to rely on lipreading for communication, and I started working with him several times a week by the time I was three. I was fitted with hearing aids to assist any residual hearing that might be there. I had one for each ear, although the doctors had determined that I had absolutely no hearing in one ear and was roughly 80 percent Deaf in the other.

I didn't appreciate these efforts at the time. The speech lessons were extremely difficult, especially for a three-year-old—sometimes I screamed going in and coming out of them. I did grow to accept them, the lesson learned was not to reject help—I knew at some point in my life I wanted to be able to speak as well as I possibly could.

As a child, I also hated those hearing aids. I was forever trying to get rid of them, tossing them whenever they bothered me, resulting in periodic searches through the neighborhood with a reward of candy or a dollar offered to any kid who found and returned them. One day I threw them out the car window, and my aunt Sue stopped in traffic and retrieved them before anyone ran over them. The worst time was when I was in the fourth grade. I had slipped them into my brown paper sack during lunch. The bag, and my hearing aids, both went into the furnace. This time it truly was an accident, but no one believed me.

My dad was always trying to smooth things over. When people on the street would ask about the hearing aids, my dad had two stock answers. If an adult asked and it was baseball season, he'd say I was listening to the Chicago Cubs on a transistor radio and if they were nice, I'd tell them the score. If a kid was asking, he'd tell them I had bubble gum in my ears, and then I'd chime in, "You want some?"

With my dad working long hours running the used-car lot, my mom shouldered much of the tough stuff—taking me to doctors, always looking for better answers, arranging and shuttling me to speech lessons, as well as dealing with a child whose energy level and interest in exploring the world were extremely high.

∽ ∽

OVER THE YEARS, various theories emerged on why I became Deaf. One doctor suggested that maybe it was genetic. When my mother heard that, she searched for anyone on either side of the family who was Deaf.

She still tells the story of meeting a woman one day at the beauty shop. After hearing about my condition, the woman said she, too, had relatives from the Gomel area of Russia who knew of the Matlins, and that several of the Matlin women were hard of hearing and one was profoundly Deaf. But it always seemed a story born more out of desperation than reality—one that my mom wanted to believe—but no records were ever found. To my knowledge, I am the only person in my family who is Deaf.

Just this past summer I wanted to try to better understand the possible causes for my deafness and I turned to Dr. Patricia Scherer, who is founder and president of the International Center on Deafness and the Arts in Northbrook, Illinois, and was an innovator at Northwestern University for years before that. She and the center have been so instrumental in my life, and she probably knows more about my history than anyone else, having known and worked with me since I was a small child.

As she recalls, about ten years ago a Chicago doctor who was doing pioneering work with cochlear implants approached her wondering if I might consider one.

"When he asked, I said I honestly don't know," said Dr. Scherer. "Part of me was thinking that Marlee would be a good candidate, but another part of me was saying, 'I don't think she would want that.' But I told him her mother was still living in the area, so he got in touch with her."

At a meeting with the doctor and Dr. Scherer, my mother brought all my old audiograms, as well as X-rays of my inner ear from soon after the initial diagnosis. After reviewing the files, the doctor said the X-rays and audiograms indicated that I had a genetically malformed cochlea. That meant that I could likely hear when I was born, but that my hearing would recede over the first couple of years of my life.

Around that time I was giving a speech in the Chicago area, and during the question-and-answer session afterward, someone asked me where I stood on cochlear implants, an extremely divisive issue in the Deaf community. I said that I wasn't opposed to them, but that they were not for me. When my mother heard that, she never broached the idea with me or talked to me about the X-rays.

In some ways it doesn't matter because it won't change anything, it won't change who I am. But it would be nice to get the facts straightened out, just for my own sense of sanity. I'm not so much angry as curious. I want to be able to tell my children about my life and where I came from—why, how, what, and who I am—so that they can tell their children.

When I talked to Dr. Scherer last summer, she took me to a room they have at the Center on Deafness and the Arts, where I started acting. It had all the various displays of the body so you can see how everything works, including an ear with all of its intricate pieces identified. She walked me through an explanation of what likely happened—from the initial malformation of the cochlea to how it would cause me to progressively lose my hearing as a child.

And so at forty-two, I think I finally learned how I lost my hearing. But what I realized is that all that really matters is that this is the life I've been given, with all its many aspects. I am proud to be a Deaf person and wouldn't know life any other way. Yet, I have never wanted my deafness to define me as a person, or as an actress. I am many, many things, and only one of them is Deaf, and I'm at peace with that. But it wasn't always so.

5

NINETEEN SEVENTY WAS a significant year for me—it could have been the end of everything; instead it became the beginning.

Most summers we had a college student come and stay with us, essentially as a summer nanny. The program was designed to give students who'd grown up in rural areas exposure to the city. This year, our summer girl was a University of Michigan student named Jean.

One day Jean was driving me and my brother Marc in a convertible with the top down. We were headed somewhere none of us can remember anymore. She made a left turn right into the path of an oncoming car, which slammed into us. My brother Eric was at a friend's house and remembers getting the call to come home, there'd been an accident, and we were in the hospital. He was the "adult" in charge. My parents had flown to San Francisco just that morning. When they walked into their hotel to check in, they were given a note at the front desk to call the hospital. They did, but the hospital refused to give them any details over the phone. They flew right back immediately. My mother still avoids San Francisco because she associates it with bad news.

Of the three of us, my injuries were the most severe. My nose was bleeding—a man was holding me and I helped myself to the handkerchief he had in the front pocket of his suit. My pelvis was fractured. Marc hit his head near his eye, and Jean had cuts requiring stitches. This was before seat belts were the first thing you thought of when you got in a car, and it's a miracle that we weren't badly hurt.

Marc and I shared the hospital room for the few days we were there. Neither of us was happy about the interruption in our summer vacation—why couldn't it have happened during the school year! Marc was given a box of Bazooka gum, and I kept wanting some. But sharing wasn't easy—he couldn't move, so he kept tossing pieces of gum into my crib!

He still remembers the nurses going insane from a whistling noise they couldn't identify. They would pop their heads into the room, scout around, but they could never discover the source of that irritating noise. It was my hearing aids going off, and Marc decided he wasn't about to tip them off.

When we got back home, it felt as if a prison sentence had been lifted! The doctor told my mother that we could basically do anything we felt up to doing. I felt like playing nonstop to make up for the lazy summer days I'd missed out on.

Jean was more traumatized than anyone else. She was horrified that we had been hurt while in her care, and as soon as she was better, she apologized to my parents, then left for home. My family stayed in touch with her for years afterward and we all think of her fondly, though she would never stay another summer with us.

A couple of years later I found out how lucky I was to have had such a short recovery and no cast. My family was going out that night, and just before dinnertime I was ready and bored. I decided to go into the backyard while we waited for my mom to finish getting ready.

We had a swing set with seats made of wooden slats. I must have been standing up on the swing because I got my foot caught between the slats, then fell—snap, that was the sound of my right leg breaking. I didn't hear it, but I sure as heck felt it, screaming at the pain.

So it was off to the ER again. Thankfully it was a clean break, no surgery needed. This time when I was released it was with a big plaster cast. It didn't take me long to figure out how to get around. I was back on the block in just days with all the problems and perks a cast brings with it—getting all my friends to sign it, going nuts when I had an itch underneath it. My mom just remembers I worked it.

WHEN I WAS five, I started taking sign-language classes. I remember my first night class with a Deaf teacher, Samuel Block, who is still alive today, now in his nineties. This changed my world. Communication and meaning flowed back into my life at full force. He was so sweet, so smart, and so full of life.

The temple we went to on Friday nights, B'nai Shalom, catered to both the Deaf and hearing Jewish community and had a rabbi signing at services, so I began to understand my religious heritage. A Sunday-school class was taught by my soon-to-be-aunt Sue, who was majoring in speech audiology and was a fluent signer. In that class was a six-year-old named Liz Tannebaum.

I still remember meeting Liz for the first time. She was the first kid who looked like me and was Deaf like me that I connected with completely. I just knew it in an instant. I walked up to her and asked, "Who are you?"

"Liz."

I giggled. "Hi, Liz, where do you live?"

"In an apartment."

"You are now my best friend!"

No discussion, no debate. And so we have been for nearly forty years now.

The relationship that Liz and I have has been a defining one in my life, and I can't imagine it without her. We were soon inseparable, spending weekends, vacations, any time we could together. We've shared secrets and growing pains—from our first boyfriends, first French kiss, first joint, and the list goes on.

We've been there for the births of each other's children, through marriages and divorces. We've had good times and bad, and we've both done things to each other that have left a few scars. We've weathered it all together, and when trouble comes, I always know that Liz has my back, and I have hers.

WHEN I WAS seven, I would also discover music. You might not think music would be a turning point in my life, but it was.

The summer of 1972 my parents sent me to a day camp specially designed to work with Deaf children and their hearing siblings. Although my brothers didn't go, I did and I loved it. Dr. Pat Scherer, who was running the camp, first came into my life here. She says:

"We were doing things in the camp like music, poetry, memorization, art—activities you would do with normal six- and seven-year-olds. One of the songs they picked to do was 'John Brown's body lies amouldering in the grave,' and I noticed Marlee really liked doing this, so I encouraged her to perform it with the hearing children. And when we had the program for the parents, she really stood out. The love for what she was doing just showed through."

I remember standing on stage, signing as the others sang, feeling the vibrations of the music rumbling up through the floor under my feet and up through my body as I moved to the beat. I remember the audience, the faces smiling at me, watching, the hands applauding. I loved it. I felt at home and knew I wanted to have this feeling again. I was hooked.

This time in my life was the beginning of my education about living in the real world beyond the safety of my Morton Grove neighborhood, where I knew just about everyone and they knew me.

While my mother focused on the schools and the doctors, my dad focused on acclimating me to the world. When we would go out to eat, which was pretty often, he always had me order my own food. He says, "Marlee had some Deaf friends who would not speak yes or no, couldn't speak. I always wanted her to order, to keep repeating it until the waiter got it."

In what would become a tradition for years to come, just about every Sunday my dad would take us on a family outing, to petting zoos, to carnivals, apple picking, strawberry picking—if there was a fruit that could be picked, the Matlins were there—water parks, bumper cars, and on special occasions to the Dells in Wisconsin, a big amusement park filled with rides, anything to make sure I experienced the world at large.

Dad had just one rule when we hit the amusement parks—be willing to try everything once, even if you're afraid, still try it once. There wasn't much I was afraid of—except a massive roller coaster. Liz, who often came with us, and I stood in front of it and trembled. Surely we wouldn't really have to ride this. We were both terrified. But my dad insisted, despite the tears and the trembling.

I had never been on anything so fast in my entire life, with its wild swoops and stomach-churning dips and razor-sharp turns, the wind rushing past my face, our screams trailing behind us. It was amazing, and I blame my love for speed on those early rides.

Later I would graduate to cars that I loved to push to the limit, the wind rushing past, the radio cranked up so I could feel every thud of the bass, every beat of the drum, my laughter trailing out the window behind me.

During one weekend trip to the Dells, we saw a helicopter flying over the park. On the way home, my dad spotted a sign that offered helicopter rides for a few dollars. He says, "I stopped the car and went and got tickets to take Marlee and Liz up in this helicopter. I give each of them a ticket, and these two girls are crying like you can't believe. I told them. 'You've got to be brave and do it once. If you don't like it, you never have to do it again.' And they're crying but they get in, and of course Marlee, she loved it."

Over and over he would demand, try it just once, see if you like it. And I would. And often the "thing," whatever it was, that I feared the most turned into something I would come to love. I have to believe my dad's habit of putting me in those situations, then forcing me to face my fears, to push past them, helped me learn to believe in myself, that I could do anything—including one day tackling Hollywood.

One thing I refused to tackle, though, was an inflatable trampoline that my brother Eric and his new girlfriend, Gloria, got for my fifth birthday. At first I loved it and spent hours jumping on it the day I got it. That night when I went to sleep, I dreamed it turned into an octopus, and I flipped out! I wouldn't go near it, convinced that it would swallow me whole. Not even my dad could coax me into this one. I don't remember feeling quite as frightened by a nightmare as a child ever again. Gloria remembers that trampoline as her introduction to the family—a rocky start to say the least.

The trampoline didn't stay, but Gloria did. She became like a big sister to me, hanging around our house more than her own, eventually marrying Eric, which was such a good thing because I loved Gloria so. There have been difficult moments in my life since then when I've needed someone I could count on, and Gloria has often been the first person I've called.

She was always so patient with me. When I was younger, she would sit on the bed and let me brush her long, beautiful hair for hours. She shared her *Glamour* and *Cosmo* magazines. We even cooked together. It fit that we all soon began calling her Glo—she does. Great catch, Eric!

6

MORTON GROVE, ILLINOIS, and my street in particular, was a great place to grow up. Our house had five bedrooms and three bathrooms.

Eric and Marc and I shared a bathroom with two sinks and a big mirror. I would take over the bathroom for hours at a time acting out stories in the mirror—that girl could understand everything I said!

Though it drove my brothers crazy, because literally hours would go by, it would be my first training ground for performing. I created sad faces, happy ones, angry ones. I told stories to the girl in the mirror, I learned how every part of the face and body could communicate emotions, feelings.

One of the exercises that my acting coach Jim Carrington would give me on *Children of a Lesser God* was to work on scenes in front of a mirror. When he said that, I knew I was home free—that I could do it.

In many ways I was an ordinary kid. I loved Play-Doh, Barbies, Silly Putty, jumping jacks, and balls that bounced—the higher the better. I especially loved a Mrs. Beasley doll, whose claim to fame was that she could talk. Again and again I would pull the string that made the magical Mrs. Beasley sounds. Even though I couldn't hear her, I knew she was talking to me.

There were always crayons and coloring books, though I would get frustrated when I couldn't stay inside the lines. It wasn't conformity I was seeking but perfection. I wanted the pictures to be beautiful.

Every week my dad would bring home comic books—Archie

Me and Mrs. Beasley

comics *Veronica* and *Betty* were my favorites—and candy. I especially loved Marathon bars, a wonderfully chewy chocolate and caramel twist in a bright red wrapper.

For all the hours I spent inside, I spent more outside, roaming a neighborhood filled with kids. There were football games, roller hockey, baseball, and softball. Bob Michels, who'd turn into a summer crush a few years later, painted the bases on the street every year. Our house and Bob's, which was across the street, were on an intersection that was a gathering spot for a lot of the neighborhood kids. My house was one of the main hangouts, anyone was definitely welcome there.

Bob says, "Marlee was confident even as a young kid and she always had a very strong personality. She was the kind of person who looks right through you, got who you were. It was always like she had the upper hand. She was definitely one of the cool kids, someone you wanted to be around."

I think he's just trying to make up for breaking my schoolgirl heart.

My brother Marc and I thought our house was like the *Brady Bunch,* and I definitely wanted to be Marcia Brady.

I had a best friend, Cathy, who lived on the street. She wanted to learn how to sign, so I taught her. She'd soon help referee neighborhood disputes when other kids didn't understand me. It was so great to have someone on my street with whom basic communication was easy, organic, and, best of all, ordinary. I didn't have to think, just talk. She moved away when I was eleven, and I really missed having her there to talk to.

Every year when the weather warmed up, my parents would set up a plastic pool out back, one with a slide. I remember coming home from school in the spring and getting off the bus and being able to smell the water. I'll never forget that sweet smell.

My room had wallpaper with strips of flowers, a desk, a black-and-white TV, and a queen-size bed, which was a big deal to me. My brother Marc described it as a "princess room" because all the furniture in it was white. It felt safe, my little bit of territory. Most of the time when I was younger, it was covered in coloring books and crayons and comics and clothes. And when I got older, *Teen Beat* and *Tiger Beat* magazines, with posters of Leif Garrett, Scott Baio, and Shaun Cassidy covering my walls.

But as much as I loved having my own room—and I loved it even more after Eric moved and Marc and I both traded up for bigger, better spaces—I didn't like being alone. I felt starved for attention, and to get at least some of that need satisfied, that meant being in my parents' room or the kitchen, the two places in the house where everyone hung out.

We had Apples, a schnauzer, who was old by the time I came along. Apples was a little doll and more than happy to take care of any of my unwanted food under the table at dinnertime. Eric had a German shepherd named Solo, who was the sweetest dog. She disappeared one day when Eric and Gloria took her with them to visit my uncle Steve. My uncle believed she'd been stolen out of the front yard. We pasted the neighborhood with flyers and pictures of Solo, but to no avail.

I was crushed when we lost her and couldn't imagine not being able to throw my arms around her and bury my face in her soft fur. One of my favorite childhood photos is of me and Solo—we're both smiling. Years later I would name my production company Solo One Productions in her memory.

JUST ABOUT EVERYONE has a teacher who has such a positive impact that you remember him or her forever. For me it was Jane Endee, now Sister Mary Elizabeth, a marriage and family therapist at the Franciscan Life Center in Meriden, Connecticut. It's no small irony that one of the greatest influences on this nice Jewish girl was a woman who became a nun!

One of the downsides of putting me in the local school system was that I never knew which school I'd be going to until a few days before classes would begin each year. The district couldn't afford to set up special-needs classes for every school, so they would change where those students went from year to year.

Though we never moved, I would go to five different schools before I reached high school. But at one of those I got Miss Endee.

While I was in fifth grade, Miss Endee came to our school as a teacher. She was in her senior year at Northwestern University and we were her student-teaching assignment. The classes were small—state law limited the class size to eight kids at the most—so when you had a great teacher, you noticed and remembered. She always found ways to keep us engaged and challenged, and she made me feel as if anything were possible.

She remembers, "They were all outstanding kids in their own way, but what was outstanding about Marlee was her ability to engage. In special ed classes there are lots of observers. With Marlee, there was no difficulty communicating. She was outgoing with just about anybody who came into her life—very bright, very animated. She had an inner spark that always came through. I do think also she was very intuitive even when she was young. She really knew how to relate to people depending on who they were, she does have that ability to know what a situation calls for, how to respond."

That instinct would serve me well years later in Hollywood, where much of your future rests with making directors or producers or casting agents or costars feel comfortable that you can do the job.

Miss Endee's father was an amateur magician and she had him come to the class to do a magic show. What I remember most about that day is that he pulled a rabbit out of a hat, which had all of us absolutely captivated. Later in the act he used rabbits again, but at the end of the show, I only saw one rabbit. I came up to him afterward wanting to know what happened to the other rabbits. I had kept count. He would tell that story for years after.

I had Miss Endee again when I was in high school. As always, she kept us on our toes, expecting that we could excel if we tried. So in 1994 when I was asked by the Walt Disney Company to be a presenter at their annual American Teacher Awards, I asked if Sister Mary Elizabeth could present with me.

She remembers, "It was in Washington, D.C., and covered live. I was a mess. I went there with my parents, and Mother Sean went with me. It was wonderful. Marlee was totally focused on us. And we had those little scripts that were written for us. It was quite an experience."

Some years later, I was asked to become involved in Target's Take Charge of Education program, including an ad campaign celebrating the important teachers in our lives. I knew I wanted to be shot with Sister Mary Elizabeth. The company flew her to L.A. for the photo shoot. She still remembers the fun of landing at LAX to find a limo waiting for her, not the sort of transportation a Franciscan nun usually has.

She says, "Oh my gosh, Marlee had hair and makeup for me. They asked me what size I was to get wardrobe. But what I most remember is that Marlee made a point of bringing her two children to the photo shoot so that I could see them. It's amazing to me to know that I taught her and to see how she has become such an amazing woman and has impacted so many people, what a powerful presence she is. But for me almost the greater thing is that she has been able to make this wonderful marriage and have these beautiful children."

It was a wonderful chance for me, in a way, to say thanks to Sister Mary Elizabeth for her part in helping me to believe in myself.

I WOULDN'T CALL my parents couch potatoes; they were more like bed potatoes. Some of my earliest memories are of coming home from school and knowing I could find my mom, propped up in that bed, smoking a cigarette and talking on the phone for hours.

My parents had a huge king-size bed, lots of pillows, and everyone would crawl into it and watch TV. Everyone sat and talked in this comfortable room. My dad was always scratching my back or the bottoms of my feet—and I loved it. It was quality time. One of my favorite memories is of my dad cutting up oranges and bringing them to that giant bed. We'd sit there and watch TV and eat the orange slices together—nectar of the gods!

When I was little, we'd always watch *Electric Company* and *Zoom*—I loved them because they were so visual, a lot of singing and dancing. I tried to watch *Sesame Street,* but would get frustrated because I didn't understand the puppets.

As I got older, my favorite shows were cop shows—high on action and low on dialogue, such as *Mannix* and *Hawaii Five-O*. My dad knew I liked thrillers and we'd look for them together in *TV Guide*. They were always the movies that were playing at 1 or 2 a.m. and he'd promise to wake me. The next morning I'd always ask, "Why didn't you wake me up?" "I tried," he'd say, "I tried." Yeah, right!

TV also began my love of sports—something else I could watch that didn't need translating. I'd sit there for hours, particularly with my grandfather Eli, my grandmother Ann's last husband, just watching, not talking.

He'd crack nuts for both of us, and we'd eat and cheer and watch. It was such comfortable silence we shared, it felt natural. If you want to know how deep and unshakable my Chicago roots are, just ask me about sports. All my teams, even to this day, are there— The Bulls, The Cubs, The White Sox, The Bears, The Blackhawks, The Chicago Fire. And, of course, they are The Best.

⏂ ⏂

ONE OF MY favorite memories growing up is when we had absolutely nothing planned and my dad would pile us into the car and head out for Chicago. We lived about twenty minutes from the city, and we'd get in that car and just drive and drive for hours.

My dad was the best tour guide, showing us all the sights, telling funny stories. In his own way, he was incredibly entertaining, with a black sense of humor. My brother Marc always tried to make sure I understood as much of what was going on as possible.

I loved being with my family, was starved for attention. Always wanting to talk. I think that's why it was such a shock for me years later when the Deaf community lashed out when I used my voice to present an Oscar in 1988. I had spent a lifetime talking, it was almost as natural for me as signing.

I also remember trying to deal with the feeling when my family didn't want to talk to me—it wasn't that they didn't want to, it was more that it was never enough for me. I felt hollow, and though I'd try to shrug it off, I know deep down it hurt, just another feeling to try to bury. I sometimes felt they didn't want to make the extra effort it took to understand me or explain what they were saying. But when they did, I loved it. I'd ask so many questions about anything that popped into my mind. Always talking, always asking questions.

MOST OF THE time when I wasn't in school, unless it was really frigid, which it often was during those Illinois winters, I'd be outside playing with the other neighborhood kids. My parents worried that given all the time we spent playing in the street or crossing it, I would get hurt since I couldn't hear approaching cars. So they convinced the city to put up a special caution sign: in bright yellow and black, it read CAUTION: DEAF CHILD CROSSING.

My very own road sign. Sometimes being different came with perks. *Deaf Child Crossing* would become the title of my first children's book, published in 2002, about the adventures of a young Deaf girl named Megan who lived on Morton Street and was, well, a little like me.

7

WHEN I THINK of my childhood, so many days begin with Liz. Long blond curls bouncing, always laughing and smiling, loved bubble gum so much she wrote an essay about it one year.

Just as she was absorbed into my family, I was absorbed into hers. Sometimes it felt as if her father, Ted, had adopted me, and over the years I would often turn to him for advice, and at least once for financial help when I hit rough times in the acting world. Unless Liz was off on a day trip with my family, I'd go with them on Sundays for lunch and a swim at the country club.

The Tannebaums started taking me on many of their family vacations, which opened up a different world to me. I'm sure it helped them, too, since the family never really learned to sign though Liz was Deaf from birth.

Where my family was middle-class, Liz's was not just well off but wealthy. I think when I first dreamed of movie-star houses, I imagined something like Liz's house, a maid who lived with them and cooked for them. When they took me on vacations, it was for two or three weeks to Florida, Palm Springs, or Acapulco, where they bought another home. Most of the time, we stayed at the Princess Hotel on Revolcadero Beach, where Liz had her first French kiss.

We went to different schools until we were in third grade. That was the year I transferred to Wilmot Elementary School in Deerfield, Illinois, and my life changed. A lot of other Deaf kids were there, and I began to seriously learn signing. All of a sudden I had a group of friends who understood everything I said and, more important, all the things I was feeling. That's also where they gave me my name sign.

I guess the easiest way to understand a name sign is to think of it like a special nickname. Instead of your name spelled out by hand, it's a blend of your name, usually the first letter, and your personality in some way. Mine is an *M* but up by the cheek because I have dimples.

I had an identity. Finally! I thought it was the coolest thing. My mother made up Liz's name sign—which takes the sign for "I love you" and blends it with a *Z* in the air, the movement you do when you sign the letter *Z*.

I'M NOT EXAGGERATING when I say that Liz and I spent almost all of our time together. Every Saturday while I went to rehearsal at the Center on Deafness, Liz would sit and watch until it was over so we could go play. One day the director walked over and asked if Liz wanted to take on a role.

She remembers, "I was very shy. The play was *Peter Pan,* and of course Marlee had the lead. But the director, Kathy, asked if I wanted to play one of the Lost Boys. I was nine years old. When Marlee saw that, she was like 'Yes, yes, yes, go for it.' And so I started getting involved not just in that play but ICODA [International Center on Deafness and the Arts]. My first time onstage with spotlights, the moment freaked me out, but I also loved it and I thank Marlee for that."

We were forever getting into trouble together, and as friends do, at times we fought. Our roughest year was our junior year of high school—we didn't speak for almost the entire year.

Now I can't even imagine how we managed that when we couldn't usually stand to go for a day without talking. If we couldn't see each other, we'd spend hours on the phone—using the TTY, a text telephone system that was really the early version of instant messaging today. But both of us can be stubborn, and that year was one of those times.

When I think of what caused our rift, I remember we were running with two different crowds, and Liz didn't want to get involved with mine. As Liz remembers it, the split happened over the rights to share her locker:

"Before and after school all the Deaf kids would hang out in one corner of the schoolyard, near where the bus picked us up and dropped us off. My locker was right there, but Marlee's was upstairs way on the other side of the building. So I was like 'Use mine, use mine.' But I had a friend named Mitch, who was a sweetheart, would do anything for me, that Marlee just did not connect with. He also was using my locker. To Marlee it was a big thing and she got angry and said, 'You're not my friend.' So for a year, even though we were in the same class, we wouldn't look at each other or talk to each other."

But one day we looked at each other and started to laugh. I'm glad I didn't win that argument. I know now I was being manipulative and ridiculous. Liz and I made up right before lunch, so we skipped class and went to her car and got so stoned. We've had our ups and downs since then, but eventually it always comes back to the connection we have that just can't be broken. When I think of it now, maybe that was the first time I felt Liz might like someone more than me, and that would be a loss I couldn't take.

That day, we went back to class still incredibly stoned. Liz ended up confessing to one of the counselors, which immediately meant that I was going to be involved somewhere along the way.

I remember I was in seventh period and the dean of students came into my classroom, looked at me, and motioned for me to come with him. We went to the office of the teacher who ran the Deaf-education program. She sat looking at me, the school's police officer was looking at me. Everybody was looking at me.

"Were you smoking?" the police officer asked, using the universal sign for taking a toke off a reefer.

"No."

"I'm going to ask you one more time, did you smoke?"

My heart was out the window and the school cop just stood there with his arms crossed. I didn't know if he was disappointed in me or if he thought it was no big deal.

They turned my purse upside down and rifled through everything, but no drugs were there. Then the dean came over and sniffed my hair. He was furious.

"Okay, fine, we're going to take you downstairs to the nurse's office, and we're going to see if you smoked or not."

I remember walking down this long hallway, passing all the counselors' offices, one by one. Then finally we get to the nurse's and walk in, and Liz is on one of the cots. She looks at me and starts, "I'm sorry, I'm so sorry, I had to tell, I had to, I'm so so sorry."

I thought, I am so busted. My heart was racing, I was trying to figure out how I could get out of this one. The nurse took my blood pressure and said to everyone in the room, "Yes, she's high."

At that moment I blurted out something that I would have given anything to take back, it still bothers me all these years later.

"My father hit me this morning."

Instantly they dropped the entire pot investigation and instead called social services to report possible abuse. The county workers called my mom and dad, came by and talked to them. It was horrible. My mom and I had had a fight that morning—lots of yelling, nothing else—and my dad had tried to intervene. He never in my life hit me, ever. And I still so regret that day.

While my family was going through that trauma, Liz was suspended from school for three days since she had confessed. Her parents were so angry at me. I worried that they wouldn't forgive me.

But like everything else along the way, we would weather this, too.

FROM THE BEGINNING, having Liz there has always just made things better. A confidant. Someone to talk to who understood me. As I got older and particularly when I began traveling to work on film and TV projects, Liz would often come to stay for a while.

When I went to shoot *Children of a Lesser God* in Saint John, New Brunswick, Liz came and stayed with me for about three weeks. When I would make the talk-show circuit for various projects, Liz often came along—she was there with me in the greenroom, in the audience. When I joined the cast of *The L Word,* she flew to Vancouver, where they film the series, to spend time with me.

We've always been there for the important moments in each other's life. She is a godmother to my children: I am a godmother to hers. I was maid, then matron, of honor at her weddings; she was the matron of honor at mine—and that was just two months after her second son, Luke, was born.

When the doctor told Liz her first baby was about to deliver, she called me in L.A. and said, "Marlee, I'm having the baby tonight." I packed and ran to the airport and got on a plane. Liz has the shortest, easiest deliveries of anyone, so by the time I got to the hospital Morris was eight hours old.

I came a few days early when Luke was due; I didn't want to miss it. She says, "Marlee was with me the whole week before. The night before Luke was born, I was exhausted, but there was such good, positive energy between us we decided to all go out to dinner to one of Marlee's favorite places to eat, Bob Chinn's Crab House. The next morning I knew it was time to go. So I hit the bed and said, 'It's time.' Marlee ran downstairs and screamed for Mark, my husband. She called my parents to let them know. When we got to the hospital, Marlee grabbed a wheelchair for me. She was there with me all the way. And when Luke was born, Marlee was just filled with emotion, holding him and crying."

When Liz's father was dying, once again I was on a plane to be with her. I got to his building—walked inside, took the elevator, walked into his house and past his bodyguard, and began looking for Liz. She walked into the foyer and stopped. One look at her and I knew. We held each other and cried.

We have had sad times, but we've had many more happy, silly times. Going to Club Med together, two bikini-clad chicks who wanted to play. And sometimes we'll just think of the craziest things and we can't stop laughing.

I still have a whole circle of Deaf friends in Chicago who are dear to me—Barb, Wendy, Mark, Phil, Paula, who lives in California now, and many more—and sometimes they'll come out here to be with me for special occasions or just to visit, but the head of that posse is always Liz.

Our birthdays are both in August—me on the twenty-fourth

and Liz on the twenty-sixth—and we try, when we can, to celebrate together the way we did when we were younger. Any significant event in my life she is there for, and vice versa. But it is the little moments, those more organic connections, that I treasure most.

If there's an earthquake, it's hard to know who will text the "You okay? Did you feel it?" message first. BlackBerries have made our conversations across the miles seamless. It only takes a few words, like "I'd laugh very hard if . . ." that mean nothing to anyone else to send either of us into spasms of laughter.

One New Year's Eve Liz was out here spending a few days with me. I had just miscarried my second pregnancy. She was supporting me and doing her best to cheer me up. We engaged in one of our favorite sports—smoking cigars. We sat on my porch as the sun went down, slowing savoring our smokes and old memories. A band was next door, amps outside, lots of electrical cords snaking around. One of us wondered if we touched the electricity, would it turn us into cartoon characters, our hair frizzed out, exploded cigars in our mouths. We didn't stop laughing until tears were streaming down our faces.

Liz is someone who remembers the five-year-old me. I can still be a crazy kid around her and for a few moments let everything else in life—the fears, uncertainties, worries—fall away.

8

A CONFESSION—MY FIRST true love in the world of music was Billy Joel.

I was all of ten and I fell hard. For some reason, what minimal residual hearing I had could pick up his voice—at least a little.

Both my brothers liked his music, so it was on at the house a lot. After a lot of "Please, please, please . . . ," at some point my brother Marc had written out all the words to "Just the Way You Are," "The Stranger," Movin' Out," and "My Life" for me.

I learned the lyrics, seriously studying them. Then I used the lyrics to "hear" the music, the way a person using a cochlear implant has to learn what sounds are what.

We had this old cassette tape recorder, and I remember pressing the PLAY and REWIND buttons over and over, what felt like hundreds of times a day, and at what I'm sure were ear-piercing decibels for everyone else.

I could feel the vibrations, the rhythm, and the words just moved me, especially "Just the Way You Are," which, not a surprise I'm sure, was my favorite.

For hours, I would sign, sing, and dance along, until I could do it perfectly in sync with the song.

One of my favorite memories is of the night my brother Eric and Gloria took me to a Billy Joel concert when he played in Chicago in 1975. Somehow we'd gotten phenomenal seats, in the first row, and I just sucked it all in—the sound, the concert, the performance, everything.

I never imagined then that I would ever get to meet him. But after *Children of a Lesser God,* our paths would cross.

The first time I met him was in 1988. Someone who knew what a fan I was arranged for me and Richard Dean Anderson, who was my boyfriend at the time, to have dinner with Billy at an Italian restaurant in Manhattan. I feel sorry for everyone else at our table, we just talked and talked for hours.

In 1989, I got to do a cameo in his video for "We Didn't Start the Fire." And I still have a funny drawing he did for me, with a piano and his profile, for my thirtieth birthday.

But one of my best Billy Joel memories was a *Sesame Street* segment we did together in the fall of 1988.

It opened with Billy and me pushing an old piano up to the trash can where Oscar the Grouch lived.

The piano was broken, Billy explained, and he was there to give it to Oscar. The only thing the green grouch had to do was to listen to this love song. So Billy played and sang, and I signed and sang, an Oscarized version of "Just the Way You Are."

Signing for Billy Joel

Nearly all of my friends have their own Billy Joel moment—usually it happens in a fast car with the radio blasting. Here's how Carla Hacken, who was my agent for years and remains a good friend, remembers it:

"Riding in a car with Marlee is hair-raising! Hair-raising! At some point she had a convertible of some sort or I did, but I can't tell you how many times I've been with her in a car where—you know, Billy Joel is not somebody you think of in incredibly loud decibels, heavy metal maybe, but Billy Joel . . . at crazy decibels driving at crazy speeds. We're talking or singing or both. It was just freaky, but great."

Although I would love other music and other performers over the years—James Taylor and Garth Brooks top that list—Billy Joel will always be the first musician I love. I wouldn't trade my *Sesame Street* moment for anything, so thanks, Oscar.

9

TURNING POINTS ARE so much easier to see when you look back on your life. For me *The Wizard of Oz* was one of them.

I had started going to the Center on Deafness and the Arts when I was around seven for the after-school and weekend arts programs that Dr. Scherer was developing in addition to the other clinical and diagnostic work she was doing.

Dr. Scherer had realized in working with Deaf children that they were never really asked to think. They were told what to do and what to think—it was a literal and simplistic world primarily concerned with communicating the basics.

But Dr. Pat, which we all called her, believed that nurturing creative instincts could make a difference on many fronts, from encouraging more complex thought to addressing the balance problems many Deaf children have through the use of dance. She was going against tradition, and at the beginning there was little support for her work.

What I remember is Dr. Pat telling me the center was going to put on a play of *The Wizard of Oz.*

"Do you think you'd like to be Dorothy?" she asked.

"I am Dorothy," I told her emphatically. And so I was.

I'd seen the movie and knew the story, and I imagined at first it would be like the skits that I'd seen at summer camp. But Dr. Pat had something far more ambitious in mind and says, "We worked from the book and came up with a script—one with words and one with signs. We would explain the story and act out whatever we had to so the kids understood not just the story, but all the shades of meaning.

"It took us a solid year to produce the play. We asked the kids

Hollywood, here I come

to bring their own creative ideas that we could incorporate into the play. And we added dance. People in the community were saying we were doing things that didn't make sense for us to be doing for Deaf children. I didn't agree."

I worked hard on my performance, learning my lines, practicing at home. The script that they'd created for us was about forty-five pages long—a lot for seven-year-olds to absorb—but I wanted to get everything right and no one had to push me to work on it. Dr. Pat used to tease me that whether it was a rehearsal or a performance, I would always ask her, "Is it perfect?" I was always setting a high bar when something was important to me.

Years later after *Children of a Lesser God* was released, I bumped into Dr. Pat in a Chicago drugstore. We hugged and I asked her, "Was it perfect?"

She smiled and said, "Yes, Marlee, it was."

∽ ∽

WHILE WE WORKED on learning to sign the entire *Wizard of Oz,* our parents made costumes and sets. Finally we were ready to begin our run. Programs were sent out, and on opening night the theater was packed.

The play was a hit, and I knew this was what I wanted to do for the rest of my life. My mother was glad I was happy, but she was anything but a stage mother. In fact, Dr. Pat had to keep convincing her that it was important to keep me involved in theater.

Dr. Pat says, "Marlee was unbelievable as Dorothy, and I started telling her mother that she was really a gifted child in theater. Throughout our relationship, I would tell Libby that, and she would say, 'No, she's just cute.' And she was cute, but Marlee commanded that stage."

My mother remembers that in the performance something fell out of my basket, and she noticed how casually I reached down and retrieved it without missing a beat. "It was just so natural the way she did it, as if being up there was the most natural thing in the world."

The center in time created a mini-museum of memorable productions, and they have a Marlee Matlin exhibit with my blue-and-white gingham dress that I wore when I was Dorothy. I still get a kick out of it every time I see it.

After *The Wizard of Oz,* there would be *Pinnochio, Peter Pan, Mary Poppins,* every year a new production, and every year I got the lead role, which sometimes caused tensions with my friend Liz, who also had dreams of being an actress. The last time we would be considered for the same role was for the stage production of *Children of a Lesser God,* Liz auditioned the day before I did but was told she was too blond. I'm sure that was a difficult loss for her, particularly given what it ultimately meant for my career.

My family was great, always there at the productions to support me. Other friends would occasionally come, too. I remember how excited I was when Bob Michels, my handsome neighbor, the one I hoped would fall madly in love with me, came to see me perform "What I Did for Love," from *A Chorus Line.*

Both my brothers would come, even though Marc was by then a teenager and Eric was in college. Eric would come with his girlfriend, Gloria, and says, "When Marlee started acting, she always was the top person in the show. Everyone else, their performance was very overstated—like they were making up for a lack of sound with exaggerated movements. Marlee was never like that, she just performed."

I began to seriously dream of acting for the rest of my life. The center had an essay contest, and I've saved the one I wrote—it was the winning essay—to this day:

If I Was a Movie Star

If I was a movie star, I would ride in a limousine.

When I go out of the limousine, I would give everyone my best autograph and I would let people take my picture! OOhh, when I am on the stage, I would give everyone my best smile! ☺

I would have a huge house which would have mirrors all over. I would love when people would write me letters. I would love to send them back but it's hard to write to all the people.

I would love to meet all movie stars. They are so nice!!

I want to make movies all my life!

I am the best!!!

Here's my autograph →

Marlee Matlin

Because it's never too early to start work on some of these skills, even then I would always take the time to give autographs—grateful that anyone wanted one.

Then my very own personal wizard would come into my life—and his name was Henry.

10

WHEN I WAS twelve, *Happy Days* was ruling prime time and Henry Winkler as the Fonz was ruling the show. The series had such an incredible international reach that for years he was the most recognized American in the world.

In December of that year, he and his wife, Stacey, were in Chicago for a film Henry was involved in, and Dr. Pat called his agent and asked if they would stop by the center for its annual Creative Arts Festival. Deaf kids from all over the country were in town competing in various art forms through the weekend, and Henry agreed to come for a day.

I was part of a troupe at the center called Traveling Hands, which signed songs. Besides signing as a group, each of us had a solo, and Dr. Pat asked me to do the solo that day.

Henry says, "We saw this little twelve-year-old Marlee come up, and I think she did 'Free to Be You and Me,' and she danced to it. But it was so powerful, and not because 'Oh, isn't that cute, a Deaf girl dancing to music she can't hear.' It was powerful because this human being, whether she could hear or not, she was born to do this. Her power, her commitment, her ability, that intangible whatever that is that makes a star, was radiating off her like heat waves. Stacey and I just simultaneously started to cry."

Stacey says, "Marlee just transformed everything, like she had magic, she was electric, a life force like if you touched her, you would get a shock."

After the performance the couple came backstage to meet me, but before they could, my mom pulled Henry aside.

What happened next was the beginning of the cold war be-

The Traveling Hands

tween my mother and Henry that continues to this day. My mother feels Henry has cast her as the villain in my story, and I know my closeness to Henry and his family has been hard for her to take.

But looking back on that day, my mom was convinced that my dreams of being an actress would only end in a life of disappointment and rejection. To her, it just wasn't a viable job option. She wanted me to get an education—not just first, but instead of pursuing acting. She says, "I didn't look at acting as a profession. I really didn't have those kinds of dreams for Marlee. I just took each thing as it came."

She tried to enlist Henry in a bid to lower my expectations— what would be better than a reality check from the Fonz?

Henry listened politely, then said, "You know, I can't do that, because what I saw was so big that I can't tell this human being not to do it."

That moment still makes my mother crazy angry. "He's telling the mother of a Deaf child that she can be a movie star. I made that one comment and he will never let me live it down."

As a mother, I can appreciate her sentiment, and like my mother I certainly want my children to get a solid education; but I hope when I am asked that sort of question, I never fail to encourage my kids to dream big.

Meanwhile, I was all business—peppering Henry with questions about the industry I was sure I would be a part of one day.

"Henry came to me after that show and told me Marlee has what it takes to become a professional," Dr. Pat remembers. "He said, 'When she finishes school and if she decides to do this, I will be there for her!'"

Even today, this story feels more like a scene out of a movie than real life. Henry was true to his word. Over the years I would write letters to him, just to remind him that I did really want to be an actress. He was always gracious, writing me back, even when I added a PS one time asking him to tell Scott Baio to send me his picture!

A couple of times when I visited my California relatives, I got in touch with Henry. He would always make time to meet with me at his office at Paramount. In 1980, I wrote to him saying:

> I think I am going to California in winter vacation and summer too. I'm going there myself. The reason why I'm going there is because I want to visit my relatives, look around in studios, and especially I want to see you so we can have a long talk about my future!

Even with the threat of a "long talk about my future," Henry made time to see me.

As he always has, he encouraged me to keep going after my dream.

I remember during his visit to the Center on Deafness in 1978 when one of the kids asked him what he would do if he lost his hearing, Henry said, "I would hope that I have the same courage in my body that you have to be in the theater. Just because you can't hear doesn't stop you. It wouldn't stop the Fonz." It was endearing, honest, gracious, and quintessential Henry.

When I dropped him a note in the spring of 1985 to let him know I had gotten my first professional acting job—a small role in the Chicago stage production of *Children of a Lesser God*—he and Stacey sent me roses and good wishes on opening night.

Over the years he would become my most trusted counselor. My Yoda. After I was starting to have a more public profile, one that was followed in the press, he sent me a note with this sage advice: "I know you've been under a lot of stress lately but, sweetie-pie, it is very important for you to deal with your stress privately and not publicly. People will understand for a while and then turn off."

Brutally honest, Henry has always been willing to tell me things I didn't necessarily want to hear.

I think the only project I took on without discussing it first with Henry was *Dancing with the Stars,* which I knew in my gut was not only something I just had to do, but that Henry would absolutely approve. And he did.

But it was more than Henry. Stacey would embrace me, too. In 1987 when I moved to Los Angeles, they let me crash in their pool house for a weekend, and I didn't move out until about two years later. Their kids would become like family. I finally got to be the oldest. I became very much a part of the fabric of the house. I'd even call if I was going to be late or not make it to dinner, which is more than I did at home when I was growing up.

All my boyfriends during that time, and I was dating a lot when I lived at the Winklers, had to pass muster with them first.

"Marlee would never answer the door, either Henry or I would get it," Stacey recalls. "All of these guys, John Stamos, Rob Lowe, Craig Sheffer . . . There was a different guy every few weeks. And we would meet them first. Then Marlee would come down the stairs, with that beautiful smile."

Carla Hacken—now a top executive at Fox 2000 where she develops and produces movies—still remembers having to meet Henry before I would sign with her in 1988. Carla says, "I had just gone to ICM, I was the youngest motion-picture talent agent ever at

Meeting Henry Winkler

that time, and they gave me some clients, but I was pursing Marlee because I wanted to sign her. She told me I needed to come to the house because Henry wanted to meet me. I was like, 'Okay, great, I'll go meet the Fonz.' So I went to Henry Winker's house in the Valley. Marlee came to the door and said, 'Oh, hi, hi, hi. Okay, now Henry's going to talk to you.' I thought, 'What?'

"And he called me into his library and he sat me down—we were in club chairs across from each other—and he grilled me. He grilled me! But in a nice Henry Winkler way. 'Where are you from? Where did you go to school?' And I thought, *Oh my God, he's interviewing me for Marlee.*"

Henry and I would sit around the kitchen table in the evenings and talk about the business, what kind of roles to go after and how—it was like a master class on the ins and outs of Hollywood.

From Stacey I would learn about decorum and sophistication, she always has style and elegance as she moves through the world.

But, as with family, my two-year sojourn at the Winklers wasn't without its bumps. Stacey basically had to send a hazmat team in to clean my room a couple of times when it reached toxic levels, and there would be disagreements along the way, but she was always there for me. I also loved being with their three kids—Jed, Zoe, and Max. My California siblings! That's about how Stacey saw it, too.

"Marlee was feisty and she was murder, very headstrong, it was like I had another child," Stacey recalls. "If you didn't say what she wanted to hear, she could get very angry and very stubborn. She would act as if she hadn't heard me, but I quickly figured out all I had to do was run around in front of her and hold on to her shoulders. I didn't know how to sign, but we never had trouble communicating. I've always felt parental about her and I always will."

When I met the man I would marry, he, of course, had to meet Henry and Stacey, too. When we married in 1993, the wedding was in their beautiful front yard.

I hold both Henry and Stacey close in my heart. Their willingness to embrace a twelve-year-old from Chicago whom they stumbled across in a talent show one frigid December day still amazes me.

11

"Okay, Marlee, take a deep breath. You can do this."

I've been telling myself this for months, to get ready to write this chapter.

Sometimes you want to block out things in life, erase the memories so they can never again slip into your thoughts even for a fleeting second. Things that feel so bad, so wrong, that you don't tell your family, you don't tell your friends, you try to pretend they never happened.

I have two. And more. I choose to share two.

As much as I've tried to forget them, I can't.

I've decided to try to talk about them here for the first time in the hope that if other girls have faced similar circumstances, they will know that silence is not the answer. If my life has taught me anything, it's that silence is never the answer.

"Marlee, go lock the doors, all the doors in the house, make sure you don't forget any."

It's the babysitter, not my usual ones Christine or Lynne, but still a girl from the neighborhood that I know. She is closing all the blinds while I've been sent to check all the doors.

I briefly wonder if it's a game, but she seems strange today, different somehow, and a knot starts building in my stomach. She lives down the street. I know her. Nothing bad is going to happen. Nothing bad.

In those days, both of my parents worked. Marc had a job after school, and Eric had moved out and was in law school. No one would be home for hours.

She told me to come into the TV room. The room with the ugly plaid couch, the one I hate, hate, hate.

She forced me to take off my pajamas. She pulled down her jeans.

Now I'm really scared, confused, something is wrong, my heart is pounding, and I don't know why. In my eyes, she is a grown-up; I'm supposed to listen to her. "Do what she tells you to," isn't that what parents say over their shoulder on their way out the door?

I was barely eleven years old, a thin reed of a girl. She was sixteen and overpowering.

In those days, most people thought child molesters were perverts who lived in the worst parts of town. Not middle-class neighborhoods such as Morton Grove, with its tree-lined streets and carefully manicured lawns.

Not Morton Grove, where the children were "raised right," where the worst thing teenagers did was smoke, drink, and drive too fast.

There were no health classes in elementary schools to warn about things adults should not do to children, ways they should not touch children, and how to handle it if they tried.

Parents didn't have these discussions either. It wouldn't happen to their children. This was America. This was the suburbs. It was safe.

What she did next is unspeakable. She slid down on the couch. She pulled me over to her. She took my hand. "It's okay, Marlee, everything's okay." She opened my hand and grabbed my fingers. I flinched. "Marlee, it's okay. Just do exactly what I tell you." She is speaking slowly. Making sure I understand. I don't understand.

She pushed my fingers up inside her, again and again. I'm trying to pull away, but she doesn't let go. Won't let go.

"Be quiet, Marlee." I can feel her breath coming fast. Her eyes look wild. I'm terrified. What is happening? Why isn't anyone coming home?

She lets my hand go. "Marlee, come here now, come closer." She's sitting up now; her legs spread, horrible black hair there. She has my shoulders. I'm twisting away. I'm shaking. She pushes down, I fall on my knees.

"Just one more thing, Marlee, please, just one more thing. I just need one more thing."

She is pleading. I don't understand. She wants something else from me.

She pulls my face into her. NO. NO. NO.

I can still remember the awful smell of her, the horrible feel of her. Can't erase it. Have tried, keep trying. It never goes away. When will she go away?

"Come on, Marlee, put your tongue inside, just for a second, just a second, then you can go." I try to pull away. She shows me what she means. "Just a little, Marlee, do this, Marlee. Do this."

I am scared. I do this terrible thing she has demanded. Her grip loosens just a little. Just enough.

I am running into the bathroom, slamming the door. Make it go away, make it go away, God, please make it go away. My mind is racing. I grabbed a washcloth and started scrubbing my hands, my face, my body. I brushed my teeth until my gums started bleeding. I felt sick. I wanted to throw up. I couldn't. I wondered what was wrong with me. What was wrong with her? WHAT WAS WRONG WITH HER? I was drowning in that crush of emotions—fear, shame, anger, betrayal—molestation victims everywhere feel.

I never said anything, just pushed it deep down inside. Tried to lock it away forever. Pretend, Marlee, just pretend it never happened.

My parents never found out. The babysitter never came to my house again.

In the years since, I've wondered if she targeted me because I was Deaf. Did she think she could talk her way out of it or around it if I said something? She's Deaf, she doesn't know what she's saying. . . .

Mostly I try not to think about it at all.

But once, when I was working with the acting coach on *Children of a Lesser God,* he wanted me to dig deeper to get the kind of visceral emotion, vulnerability, and rage needed for a scene. He said, "Marlee, think of the worst thing that's ever happened to you. Go back to that moment. Use it." And I did.

The couch I would come to hate

The next time I let it creep into my conscious brain was during my stay at Betty Ford. One of the exercises near the end of my time there was to write down the worst things that had happened to me. Eleven things were on my list. This was number one.

THIS WAS NUMBER four.

When I was in high school, there was a popular teacher on staff. He was charismatic, confident, and both students and teachers were drawn to him.

I was over the moon when I was assigned to one of his classes my sophomore year. I wasn't too interested in academics, but still I became the teacher's pet.

Suddenly I had this attractive older man—he was thirty-nine— paying attention to me. He cared what I was thinking about. He wanted to talk to me. He told me about his life. I told him about mine. I had just turned fourteen.

He found out I hated onions, and one day he said, "I'll make you an omelet with onions that you'll love."

"Okay."

"Come on then, let's go."

"Now?"

"Sure, we have time."

It's the lunch break and we duck out into the parking lot, get into his car, and head over to his town house. He starts fondling me in the car. I let him, I'm afraid to lose his friendship, the attention. He says he really cares about me. I believe him.

We walk into the house and he leads me down to the basement. Once again my heart is pounding and my insides are twisting. I've been kissed, even French-kissed, by a boy who was a couple of years older than me, but that's it.

He asks me to lie down on a couch. He starts kissing me.

"What are you doing?"

"Don't worry, Marlee, I'll take care of you."

He is taking off my clothes. He is touching me.

He pushes inside me. I gasp with pain and stifle a scream. I am hurting. Blinking back tears. I hate him. Hate him. Love him.

He suddenly stops, quickly pulls himself away from me.

"Please stay, I'll be right back."

He heads to the bathroom. I don't know what's happening. What's wrong? What's wrong with me? Everything's wrong.

"No, no, it felt good, I just needed to finish myself off," he murmurs.

I don't know what he's talking about. I don't understand.

"Now let me make you that omelet."

He does, while I go clean myself up. There is bleeding, I hurt. I want to leave.

"Here." He smiles. He sets the plate down in front of me.

I eat an omelet, made with eggs, and powdered onions.

He takes me back to school.

We slip away again on other days to have sex. When his wife isn't there. When his wife is there.

"No, no, no, no, don't!"

"It's fine, it's okay. I'll take care of you."

One time his kids, still babies, are in another room. Several times after class is dismissed, he has me stay late. He grabs my hand and puts it on him. Other students and teachers are still in the halls outside. He feeds off the danger. It's part of the thrill. He gets bolder. I think he's crazy.

This goes on for most of the school year. In the spring, he tells me he'll give me a passing grade though by now I'm failing every test I take in his class.

I don't care. I tell him I don't want to see him again. I have a boyfriend now. He says okay. There is no hesitation, no attempt to convince me to continue seeing him.

I finish the class. I get a passing grade. I don't tell anyone for years.

About ten years after high school, my best friend, Liz, was driving us around. Suddenly she says, "I have a confession to make. I kept this a secret even from you . . . [the teacher] molested me."

I was stunned. "Me, too," I said quietly.

It turns out there were even more of us.

Some years later, when Liz heard that he was still around, still doing this to his students, she got in touch with the school and told them everything.

The school administrators gave him the choice of resigning immediately or they'd turn things over to the cops, she was told.

He left that day. Disappeared. Silently.

12

You never know in life what sustains you, helps you ride out the bad times, until you have bad times to ride out.

By the time I was twelve, I was on the road a lot with the Center on Deafness's Traveling Hands troupe. We signed and danced to music and performed all over. There were trips to Texas, Nebraska, and throughout Illinois. So much fun!

In each city we'd stay with host families, many of them with Deaf children of their own. It was carefree and fun, and Liz and I loved it—the bus rides as a troupe to the cities, on our own, where we could talk for hours and no one cared.

That year I also began working with the rabbi on my bat mitzvah. As with everything else, my parents were determined that I would have this experience just like any other Jewish girl.

I had fuzzy memories of Marc's bar mitzvah when I was four. I do remember that I got a beautiful blue-and-red dress and white stockings, and my hair was pulled up into a ponytail. After the service there was food and dancing, and I got to dance with Marc, then my dad, then the three of us together. It was such a happy time. Way past my bedtime, someone took me home for the night. I couldn't wait to have my own ceremony and party when I could stay until the very end.

For two or three years, I worked with Rabbi Douglas Goldhammer, studying the Torah and working on my speech. I'll never forget learning about my religious history, but more than that, really connecting to my faith. Understanding that it was a very real part of who I am, beyond the Friday-night Shabbat dinners and Hanukkah candles and presents.

My bat mitzvah day

On the day of my bat mitzvah I looked out and felt surrounded by love. My brothers, parents, sister-in-law Gloria, my uncle and aunt from California, it made my heart feel full. Here's a piece of the speech I wrote for that day:

> I am deeply proud that I am a Jewish girl because this re-
> ligion is very important to me . . . because it teaches about
> what happened in the past to our people. . . . When I first
> studied Hebrew with the Rabbi, it was completely different
> because I didn't know Hebrew at all! At first it was hard,
> but then you get used to it and it's easy and I love it.

My cousin Lynne wasn't able to come, but her parents did, my beloved uncle Jason and aunt Norma. Lynne still remembers their telling her about the service: "My mother said it was the most amazing experience to watch this child recite these ancient words. Everyone there was crying as they watched."

When I looked up and saw everyone crying, tears started streaming down my face. I looked down and saw my tears had fallen on the Torah.

"I'm so sorry, Rabbi," I said over and over.

"Don't worry, my child, our history is stained by tears. Your tears are a wonderful mitzvah."

I'll never forget that moment, that day, his kindness. I began to feel whole again.

I HAVE, IN my own way, tried to stay connected to my faith over the years. Many of the speeches I give and the fund-raisers I work on are tied to Jewish organizations that reach their hands out to help. Whether it's to the aging or the sick, I am always moved by their commitment and their sacrifice.

I was reminded of all of this last summer when my aunt lost a hard-fought battle against cancer.

In her final days, the family gathered in her room, all of us taking turns visiting with her. As I was leaving the house for the hospital, my six-year-old son, Tyler, said he wanted to give her a rose, so I found a perfect red one at the hospital's shop on my way in.

When I first came into the room, Lynne was resting on the bed next to her mother. I started to back out, to not disturb them, but Lynne looked up and saw me and waved me in.

"Mother, it's Marlee."

My aunt, so weak by now, opened her eyes and acknowledged me. As I was leaving for the night, my cousin Lynne asked her mother if she could smile for me, and to everyone's surprise, Aunt Norma gave me the biggest smile. It just broke my heart, but in good ways.

I went back to see her two days later and stayed with the family until her final moments. The room was quiet. I was there with just Lynne, her husband, Elliott, and their daughter, Elisa, around the bed. Lynne's son, Brian, who had been with his grandmother every day since she had gone into the hospital, left the room with his wife, Allison, who was distraught. Aunt Norma died two minutes later.

It was the first time I've been with someone when the person passed. It was profound and touched me and connected me to my family, my history, in ways I could not have imagined. I'm grateful to have been there. Brian and Allison walked back in just minutes later and we all held each other for comfort.

It truly was as if the spirit left the body with her last breath. I knew my aunt wasn't there any longer.

Over the next two days more of the family flew in. We cried, we laughed, we remembered the beautiful woman she was, the amazing legacy she has left in her children and her grandchildren.

My twelve-year-old daughter, Sarah, wanted to go to the funeral. At the end, by the graveside, the rabbi asked Sarah to throw a rose on her great-aunt's grave. I told the rabbi that Sarah's middle name is Rose, which made the gesture even more meaningful for my family.

I remember the gentleness and the care the rabbi took with my daughter, whose tears that day reminded me of my own bat mitzvah and how my tears stained the Torah. Our history is indeed written in tears.

13

Fɪʀsᴛ ᴋɪss. Wʜᴇɴ I was twelve, with an adorable kid named Tony. He was African-American and we were in the same grammar school class and the same theater group at the center. We kissed with his sister Paula standing there between us trying to coach us.

That kiss was incredible. It was great.

First boyfriend. Randy—a great gentleman even though he was a junior in high school. Low-key and had a great smile, handsome. He was the only Deaf boyfriend I would ever have. Randy asked me to homecoming that year, which for a freshman was just heaven.

We dated for about seven months, but around this time I was having growing feelings for my neighbor Bob Michels, so I broke up with Randy. Bob, who was also a couple of years older than me, was so nice, always looking out for me, and he was really great at sports, which made him even more attractive than he already was. We both had feelings for each other but more on my part than his, though he says now we had crushes on each other.

Either way, nothing was to come of it. That summer I went away to camp, and when I got back, the day I got back, one of the neighborhood girls asked me, "So how are you and Bob doing? I saw you guys in the car last week." Last week? I was in camp.

My heart was broken as only a fourteen-year-old girl's heart can be, which means madly, terribly, desperately.

I recovered by seeing Rick—he was not good for me. Older, a drug addict, rode a motorcycle. He was twenty-three, I was fifteen and would sneak out of the house at two in the morning to be with him. I did so much partying with Rick. My friends and I would meet up with him and get wasted on combos of drugs and alcohol.

My parent despised him, though they never tried to stop me from dating him. It was a crazy, exciting time that I'm glad I survived. Rick didn't last long because I would, for the first time in my young life, truly fall in love.

I MIGHT NOT believe in love at first sight if I hadn't known Mike. But we just looked at each other and knew, absolutely, that we would be together.

Technically, I guess it was love at second sight. The first time I saw Mike I was in fifth grade when he and a buddy chased me, and Liz, home from the playground.

We bumped into each other again the first day of a driver's ed class. After a few classes we went over to his house with his girlfriend and a dear friend of mine named Dave. I remember we were smoking a lot of pot that day, which was starting to be a habit with me.

Mike—my first love

Mike told his girlfriend to wait at the house, that he would be right back. Then he told me and Dave we were going for a drive. In the car, Mike looked at me and said, "When I come back to the house, I'm going to drop her and you're going to be mine." Dave sat in the backseat and rolled his eyes and shrugged his shoulders.

Mike remembers, "God, she was gorgeous, every guy's dream . . . boobs and a butt, and I liked that she was a smart-ass. We were both kind of troublemakers. We were happy doing anything, we'd walk out the door and do anything, go anyplace and have a good time."

Mike and I would date for four years. I think everyone expected us to get married, and for a while I definitely did. I know it broke his heart when it was over, as it did mine. He will always have a special place in my heart, and I was so glad that he fell in love again, and now Mike and Cindy have a beautiful son, named Sam, just a few months older than my daughter, Sarah.

MIKE AND I started having sex pretty quickly. I remember being downstairs in my house with Mike one night and he said, "You know we're too young to be pregnant, so we need to do something about it."

"Okay, wait a second."

I headed upstairs.

It was about ten thirty at night. My mom was in bed, reading the newspaper and smoking a cigarette. I walked in and said, "Mom, I'm having sex with Mike."

"Okay, I'll take you to the doctor tomorrow for birth control pills."

Then she went back to her newspaper.

The next day, she took me to the doctor's office. I didn't know what was happening, had no idea that there would be an examination and what that would be like. My mom didn't explain anything to me.

I do remember the doctor being extremely caring, and my parents paid for my birth control pills for years, and I thank them for that. I never got pregnant until I had my first child. Never contracted any sort of sexually transmitted diseases. I know now that I was irresponsible and lucky.

The birth control story always stands out in my mind as what is broken in my relationship with my mom.

I hardly ever remember my mother explaining anything to me, whether it was birth control or why I couldn't have another piece of candy. The only thing she would tell me was that she would kill herself if I ever died in a car accident—that was on the day I got my driver's license. I guess she considered that motivation for me to be careful.

The blanket incident has also stayed with me all these years. I had a blanket I got as a baby, my favorite one. Like Linus in *Peanuts,* I carried it around when I was younger. As I grew older, I still didn't want to let it go—I needed the blanket and a thumb to get to sleep at night. It made me feel safe.

One Saturday night when I was eleven (I know, I know . . . I was too old for a blankie!), my parents were out as usual and it was time for me to go to bed. I couldn't find my blanket anywhere. The babysitter and I looked everywhere for it, all over the house, inside the laundry basket, outside, even in the garbage. I was in tears. Hysterical!

When my parents came home that night, I was still up. "Where is my blanket?"

"We don't know."

After many tears—I was close to inconsolable—they finally confessed that my mother had thrown it away. No conversations, no "Marlee, you're getting older and it's time to put this away." Or planting a seed that it was time to start letting go. Nothing, no warning, it was just gone.

WE HAVE ALWAYS had a complicated family dynamic that was often strained in ways that had nothing to do with my deafness. After I moved out, I would get long letters from my dad that were versions of a thousand conversations we had had at home when I was growing up. Here's an excerpt from one he wrote in the summer of 1987 that is pretty typical of the way it would go:

Me and my mom

When you left you must have had a fight with Mom—I really can't understand it. Why do you let it happen? Both of you fight and the one that winds up with all the problems is me!

You know how the smallest things can sometimes upset her—and I catch all of the shit. I don't know what happened Tuesday except Mom was crying all day and night—when I got home all your pictures and personal things were put in boxes and off the walls.

Somehow the entire responsibility for whether my relationship with my mother was working seemed to fall on my shoulders. It was that way when I was a child, then a teenager, and remains that way now.

I still have the photo album that carries the legacy of one of those fights with my mom—about half of my childhood pictures were ripped out and thrown away because she was mad at me that day.

I keep looking back, searching for those moments of guidance, the ones where parents teach their children about life and relationships, where they talk about the future, about what kind of person you should try to grow up to be. I can't find them in my life. Those were not our conversations.

I don't want anyone to misunderstand. I love and applaud my parents for keeping me at home rather than handing me off to an institution. I am so grateful to my mother for driving me to doctors, for keeping me involved in theater at ICODA while I was growing up, for encouraging me to make friends—driving me to meet them in the middle of a blizzard, a hurricane, a hailstorm—if I asked her to. She cooked me great meals, shopped for clothes with me, and I loved to shop.

But so many times in my life I simply wanted to understand more about life, about her life, her interests, politics, the world, anything. Those are the times I wished she had been there for me, too.

I love my dad hugely—he's funny and irreverent and I know that he loves me. I am grateful for all the ways he pushed me—whether it was to order french fries for myself or to ride a roller coaster. But he has spent a lifetime never recovering from the dark days of his childhood. Then he faced the rocky road of family life that my deafness only heightened. At some point, I became the one person that he thought could change the way his life was going. I couldn't.

When I was a child, I think much of my anger was a desperate cry for someone to step up and be the adult in my life who would take my hand and take the time to explain this incredibly complex world for me. I am trying to walk a different path with my children, and I hope that I succeed. And I couldn't ask for a better father for my children than my husband, Kevin. He's an absolute natural at it.

Sometimes I think that all of us—Eric, Marc, and me—were in so many fundamental ways left to fend for ourselves, certainly emotionally. I've watched as we have struggled to mature as adults, to find ourselves and find some peace with the past.

We are, the three of us, in a far better place today—with ourselves, our careers, and with each other. We grow closer every year with our families so tightly connected. There is love and a growing respect and appreciation for each of our lives, our successes, our differences. We are increasingly, in all the best ways, there for each other, learning to cherish each other. And for that I am so grateful, too.

With my parents, for me at least, it remains difficult emotional terrain. My mom and dad both keep waiting for me to write a different story for all of our lives.

They still don't understand—whether it was Marlee the child, or Marlee the adult—I never had that power in my hands. If we are going to write a different story as a family, it can only happen if we do it together. And I worry that we are running out of time.

14

W HEN I WAS in eighth grade, Liz and I decided to try out for cheerleading.

Two Deaf girls . . . the judging panel just looked at us—totally deadpanned.

Liz definitely had the edge here—she was a really terrific gymnast. For one of the routines during the tryouts, we were supposed to do splits—the big finale. No problem for Liz, but me? I'd never even tried to do splits. But I wanted a spot on the cheerleading team so badly that when it came time for us to do the splits . . . I did! Yeowch!!!!

I thought we were pretty good, but I think they rated us a one on a scale of one to five, or maybe one to ten. I guess I've had better days.

High school for me was John Hersey High School in Arlington Heights, Illinois. Go, Huskies! All in all, it was a series of misadventures and a lot of drugs.

I dropped out of ICODA; I was too busy with the social life that came with high school. Parties, dances, concerts, movies, roller-skating at the Axel, just hanging out.

Hanging out meant doing a lot of drugs. I never really liked alcohol, didn't like the taste of it, but early on in high school I definitely gave it a serious try. My friends and I would play quarters with a bottle of rum. We'd finish the bottle and then we'd drive.

I remember once stopping to get some gas and we put $5 in the tank. I had a $5 bill in my hand to pay for it. After I drove away, I realized I still was holding that five bucks. Wow, I was so drunk I had forgotten to pay. I got home and I never drank and drove again. Thank God I came to that conclusion.

Drugs were my thing. I dropped acid, loved quaaludes—714 Lemmon. I loved sleeping beauties, downers, and then speed. With speed, I would cross a line and sell it, too. I had a friend who almost OD'd on angel dust, so I stayed away from that. For some reason I decided that I wouldn't even try cocaine while I was in high school—and I never considered heroin, didn't like the idea of needles.

But pot was a staple in my life. Now I can't believe I ratted out my brothers when they were growing pot in the crawl space down in the basement when I was a kid. I was looking for Hanukkah presents and found the plants and the lights . . .

I could easily smoke twenty joints a day when I was in high school. When I didn't have it, I wasn't a happy girl.

I had my first joint just before my freshman year of high school. A Deaf friend named Dave gave it to me. I felt that I was a part of this special group now. It felt great.

I still remember that first joint, the first taste of it. We were walking along the street, a police car was right there, and I was so high. I lay down in the middle of the street, just laughing my head off. Then I noticed that the cop was watching me and I tried to casually get up and keep on walking. Glad he thought, *Silly girl, go on!*

IN HIGH SCHOOL everything got more hard-core.

I smoked pot before school, on lunch breaks, after school. I would smoke in my room with the windows open, even when it was twenty below, trying to wave the smoke out. Then I thought, *What do I have to lose?* So I smoked, windows closed, pot smoke hanging heavy in the air, and when I was done, I'd walk out of the room. Sometimes my dad would be there in the hallway, and he would just look at me and say, "Stop smoking," then leave.

I'd leave bongs all over my room. No one said anything. My parents never walked in while I was smoking pot, so I don't know if they were afraid to confront me or were just used to it since both my brothers had been stoners, too.

I stole money from my dad to buy the pot and the pills. I knew he played cards every Thursday night, and he'd usually come back with a wad of cash. I'd slip in there around six on Friday morning, before he was awake, and lift one or two twenties. Every week. He probably knew, but he never said anything to me about it.

Maybe it was my parents' way of coping with a situation they felt was completely out of their control. The only time anything at all was said was when my dad would bring home a new car for me and tell me he had dumped the water out of the bong I'd left in the trunk and put it in the trunk of the new car.

FROM THE TIME I had friends with cars, I was hanging out too long and too late.

My way of breaking curfew was to call my parents on the phone and say I was still out, didn't know where, but wanted to let them know I'd be late. Click. Dial tone. My dad says, "It drove me nuts because you couldn't say anything. She couldn't hear you. I'd just be standing there after she called, holding the phone, angry as hell."

But one night my dad told me to be home by eleven. I didn't call. It was eleven, then midnight. My parents panicked. They called the cops.

A friend dropped me off around 3 a.m., drunk. A couple of police cars were still parked outside my house. Oh, this was bad. The first thing my parents heard was a car door slam, then an engine gunning and the screech of tires.

I went in storming. I figured it was the best defense if I got angry before they did. "How could you do this, how could you call the cops?"

A detective was at the kitchen table—he made me sit down. I was still being a wise ass when he slammed his hand down on the table and said, "You think your parents are crazy? Do you know we found the head of a fifteen-year-old two blocks from here in Harms Woods?"

It was not a good night for anyone.

One of the things that sticks with me about that night is that during the fight my mom was yelling at me, "You have no idea how much I love you."

In the years since, I've tried to remember if she ever told me she loved me other than in the middle of a fight. I only remember hearing those words from her when she was angry—for years I connected her love with anger. I guess I still do.

It was never just out of the blue, just looking across and seeing me and telling me she loved me. Never. She never put me to bed or read me a book, that I can recall. She never got me water in the middle of the night—that was my dad.

I think that's why today I hug my kids to distraction, cover them in kisses. My husband and I make time to talk to them every day about what's going on in their lives. Whenever I leave town, just before I go out the door, I have to kiss each of the kids.

It's become a ritual, and it's important to me. I realized how important one morning when I had to leave and Isabelle, my youngest, was sleeping upstairs. I kissed Sarah, Brandon, and Tyler, then got in the limo. We'd gotten a couple of blocks from the house when I remembered Isabelle—upstairs, asleep, unkissed. I had to go back. The driver turned the car around and raced back—there was a plane to catch—and waited while I ran upstairs and kissed my baby.

I never want them to have to wonder for even a second about my love for them. And I never want them to think that love is angry.

MIKE WAS THE best thing about my life in those years. We would smoke pot, and we did have sex, but what overshadowed all of that was a consistent sense of being totally, absolutely loved. We were best friends, too.

I loved being with him, and I loved the sex, because it felt good. But I loved being someone who mattered in his life. I never doubted that for a second.

We just got each other. I understood him and he understood me. He needed as much love as I did. Beautiful guy. Heavy, heavy drinker. But he had so much love to give. I cooked for him, helped with his homework, and if I drove his beloved car, I was very, very careful. He would spend his last dime sometimes to buy me flowers—my favorites were the carnations that were dyed blue. We had pet names for each other. I remember them still, but that's something I'm going to keep to myself. And I hope Mike does, too.

We went through a lot together, growing and struggling through those teenage years. Figuring out how to have a relationship with someone. It was a heavy time. Crazy.

I didn't see my parents as role models for what I was looking for in a relationship.

I don't remember seeing my parents kiss. One time I asked my brother Marc, "Do they love each other?" He said they had sort of a love/hate relationship. I'd see them laughing together and that was always a good feeling. When they would go to parties, they always danced swing. They were good at it and I loved seeing them dancing together. I think I hung on to those small signs to reassure myself that our family was okay, that it wouldn't break apart.

I don't think my mom ever felt comfortable in her own skin. She was always good at putting herself together, dressing with a kind of style, but she was always changing the color of her hair—as if she was trying to find her identity, trying to like herself. When she felt good about herself, she was great. But that didn't happen often.

Whatever ups and downs my parents had, I know all my friends loved them and hanging out at my house. My friends would stop by whether I was there or not.

Mike remembers, "My dad died a couple of years before I started dating Marlee. And I thought her dad was the coolest dad in the world. He'd slip me a twenty or forty and say, 'Go get sandwiches and see a movie.' He helped me buy my first car when I didn't have anything.

"It broke my heart when me and Marlee broke up. I lost Marlee, but I also lost her family."

15

So THE KID who was smoking pot, doing quaaludes, and stealing money from her dad to pay for it graduates from high school and decides to become a cop.

I kid you not.

Up until then, my experiences in the job world hadn't been all that great. One summer I got a job at Allstate typing and filing. Since I had spent hours and hours talking to friends and family on the TTY machine, I could type like a maniac. No distractions. Not many people could beat me.

I would zoom through piles of typing, and it took me a while to notice that the rest of the typing pool was starting to hate me. I'd finish in half a day what it took everyone else a day to do.

Then I got a job at a department store at one of the local malls. They interviewed me and I got the job as salesperson, assigned to ladies' lingerie..

It was a disaster. Every time someone asked me something, I'd pick up the phone and page for help—it would, of course, echo through the entire store. On my first day, I was approached by a large, homely-looking woman—or at least that's what I thought on first glance. As I tried to help her, I realized she was a he, a cross-dresser. An auspicious start.

One day my parents, who couldn't still quite believe I'd gotten the job, came in to see how it was going. You would have thought they were with the CIA, the lengths they went to so that I wouldn't know they were there. My dad says, "We're sneaking in, hiding behind clothing racks, working our way closer until we could see Marlee. We had been trying to figure out for days how she's going to sell something, we wanted to see for ourselves.

"So we're peeking through a rack of clothes when we see a lady walk up behind her and start talking. When Marlee didn't turn around, that lady got so mad."

The job didn't last too long, but only because I called in "sick" too many times.

DESPITE THE DRUGS I was doing, I was attracted for all sorts of reasons to becoming a police officer. I was really serious about it.

I can trace my interest back to a couple of things. My fascination with the criminal justice system probably got its start when one of my cousins married a cop.

He was a great guy, the kind of cop everyone loves and admires. One day he'd just gotten off duty and had stopped to help someone on the roadside, which was just like him, when he was struck and killed by a drunk driver. It was a tragedy for the family and just another thing in life that seemed so unfair—the drunk driver lives, the good guy who stopped to help dies.

The law itself always intrigued me, too, who's right, who's wrong, and why. How our legal system works to constantly draw the line between good and evil. And, I'd been pulled over by more than my share of police officers and saw all the power that they had over ordinary citizens. I was curious about this power thing and wanted to check it out.

But if I dig deeper into my motivations, I also think the job felt as if it would give me control, put me in charge. I had experienced such painful things in my life—the babysitter and the teacher in particular—where I had felt so powerless. I wanted to put myself in a situation where I would never feel that helplessness again.

And so I began on the criminal justice track at Harper College in Palatine, Illinois. I told one of my first teachers. "I want to be a cop, like you."

"Okay, but you know what, we are going to take a field trip, and you are going to see a prison and see if this is really what you want to do."

So the class took that field trip, and I saw only one Deaf prisoner. An important lesson I learned from the experience is that just because we were both Deaf didn't mean we had anything in common or could relate at all.

When that didn't make me quit, my teacher pulled me aside and said, "Get real, you can't be a cop—how would you talk to anyone, you'd put yourself and your partner and other people in danger."

"Well, I could get a dog. A police dog."

"Yeah, I'm sure the dog is going to be able to deal with the police radio, right?"

Then I thought about being a probation officer working with Deaf criminals, but there just weren't that many, and I wasn't looking for a desk job anyway.

I was frustrated, hitting dead ends everywhere, when my brother Marc heard of auditions for *Children of a Lesser God* by the Immediate Theatre Co. in Rogers Park, Illinois.

I HAD BEEN away from acting for four years by the time Marc saw this notice. Besides, I'd always acted in the safety of the Children's Theatre for the Deaf, at the center, where everyone knew me.

This was an actual Equity production, a professional staging, actors would audition and those who were cast would be paid.

Mike wasn't thrilled about my going back to the stage. He had plans for our future. He dreamed of us opening a shoe store together. Marriage. Children. A house in the suburbs. We fought.

"Why can't you just be happy for me?"

All this before I even auditioned.

To my brother I was saying, "I had my stint, I don't want to compete. Let somebody else go for it. There are far better actors than me."

But Marc was extremely adamant. "Acting is what you love to do, it won't hurt you to try."

Then there was Liz; she was auditioning, too. So it became a competition not just with other actors, but between us. Liz auditioned the day before I did.

I was scheduled to audition Saturday morning for the role of Lydia, a secondary part in the play. I stayed over at Marc's the night before, running lines with him for hours.

Sometime late in the evening I told him to forget it, I was just not going to do this. But my brother's persistence helped me change the course of my life.

"You've come all this way, Marlee, you're here, you know your lines. Just go and try. I'll go with you tomorrow."

So he did. Although he got so nervous he escaped from the theater for a while, he was doing his best to support me, just as he had all those years when I was a child playing Dorothy and Peter Pan.

I auditioned and got the role on the spot. That day Marc and I celebrated. Mike was unhappy and kept saying, "What about me? What about me?" Liz didn't get cast in the production at all. They were two very unhappy people—I was sick to my stomach that they couldn't be happy for me.

It was my first Equity job. I made $300 a week. I was officially a professional actor, with a career.

Rehearsals started and I was having the time of my life. I'd come home completely energized by the work—and a line or two of coke—and Mike would be there angry, and often drunk. And we would fight; oh, how we would fight.

When he saw me opening night, that was truly the beginning of the end. He had never seen me onstage before—we'd started dating right after I had left ICODA—and to sit in the audience and watch me in the lights, to hear the audience cheering at the end, it was just more than he could take.

He was irrational, jealous. He argued, wanting me to quit the play, "I don't want everybody watching you. I don't want you enjoying yourself without me. And I'm going to lose you."

"No, you're not, I love you."

But it turned out that he was right.

16

We were all so psyched in rehearsals, and I was in awe watching the work of Janis Cole, who had the lead in the stage production of *Children of a Lesser God,* which was making its way into the heartland after an amazing run on Broadway. A few days before opening night we heard rumors that Paramount Pictures, which was looking to do a film version of the play, might be there scouting for some of the roles.

Instead, a local agent took the initiative and told the studio she'd film different scenes from the production and send a copy along. If Paramount signed any of us, she'd get the commission. So we all went to her office and she filmed several scenes and sent everything off to the filmmakers.

Randa Haines, who was set to direct the film, says, "I first saw Marlee on a videotape a Chicago agent had made; she was playing one of the kids. I remember seeing her in the background and saying, 'Who's that? She looks like a Deaf Debra Winger.' So I asked the agent to make another video that featured Marlee. And that led us to bring her to New York to read with Bill."

When the agent came back to me and said they wanted to see me doing the role of Sarah, I hesitated. The actress who was playing the role of Sarah was my friend and I had the utmost respect for her work.

"What about my friend?"

"Don't worry," they said.

But she was extremely hurt and angry with me. Still, I couldn't let go of the opportunity, and the studio had already evaluated her performance by then. So I read, the videotape went back to Para-

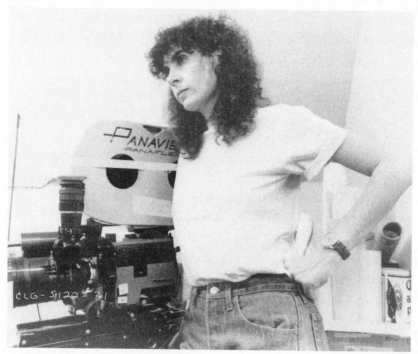

Director Randa Haines (© Paramount Pictures, all rights reserved)

mount and Randa, and the next thing I knew they were flying me to New York to read with Bill.

I will never forget the moment when Bill Hurt, big-time movie star, the actor who had taken my breath away in *Altered States* and *The Big Chill,* walked in. He was late. Apologized to everyone, said hello to me.

He was so tall and so good-looking. I was extremely taken with him; something about him was electric.

Then the scene work began. He was so impressive, so professional, clearly not intimidated or scared reading the scenes with me—I was the one who was intimidated and scared.

Then he looked at his watch and said, "I have to go now and be with my son." He had a kite and I remember thinking, *Wow, look how he cares about his baby boy.*

That was it. They didn't say anything more to me, just flew me back to Chicago.

Meanwhile, Randa thought she had found her Sarah, she just wasn't saying anything to me. Randa recalls, "The moment Marlee walked in the door, even though she looked like a teenager, she is a teenager, in jeans, chewing gum, there was something about her that I went, 'Wow!' And then we did some scenes with Bill, just sitting on a couch, and there is chemistry between them that is already exciting. As a director, you're always looking for that. And I'm already thinking of ideas on how to help her look more like she's twenty-five, which is what the character was. Marlee didn't seem to have the anger and pain that Sarah had, so I started to think of ways to help her develop that emotional context."

BACK IN CHICAGO. More cocaine! Almost everyone around me was doing it. Waiting to hear back, doing the play, fighting with Mike. Our relationship was hanging by a thread—up and down—we were both in denial that we were crumbling as a couple.

Then I heard that the studio had it down to two for the role of Sarah. They would fly both of us to Los Angeles to do a screen test. I was there for a week, rehearsing with an acting coach, Jim Carrington, who was great. We shot the screen test on the last day.

It was the first time I had worked with an acting coach, really the first time I had had any formal acting training. We worked on improvisation, emotions. They were going to shoot three scenes. We worked twelve-hour days that week.

Everything was a first: I'd never been filmed before. Never worked with a crew. Never been on a soundstage, had never even seen a soundstage. Never had a director really directing me before. There was no time to be a tourist in L.A.

The studio put me up in what I guess was a corporate apartment, in a tall, white building near Franklin and La Brea in the heart of Hollywood. I shared the apartment, complete with a full kitchen, with my interpreter—who ironically was the sister of Janis Cole, the same Janis Cole who'd played Sarah in the Chicago theater production.

On the day of the screen test Jim picked me up in his snazzy two-seater convertible. Racy cars are one of my loves, but I could barely enjoy the ride, I was so scared. But in a way it felt as if my life had come full circle—I used to come to Paramount for those summer visits with Henry Winkler, whose office was on the lot.

Someone came up to me and said they were giving me a trailer. *What's that for?* I wondered.

I walked into "my" trailer, which had a bed and a kitchen and a huge chair for makeup. I was stunned, probably one of the few times in my life I was speechless.

So I sat in that huge chair and they started doing my hair and makeup. I started chatting up the makeup artist and said, "You know what I'm in the mood for?"

"What?"

"Pink bubble-gum ice cream from Baskin-Robbins thirty-one flavors, it's what I grew up eating."

The next thing I knew, in walks Bill with a pint of pink bubble-gum ice cream. I was shocked. How had he found out?

He handed it to me and smiled that slip of a smile he can do, his head cocked slightly to the side, his hair falling almost in his eyes. "Hello and welcome."

Suddenly I felt that everything was going to be okay.

THAT DAY, BILL and I did the fight scene that falls near the end of the film, then the bed scene—close and intimate—and another ordinary scene that escapes me now.

And I felt great!

Randa talked me through every step of the way. Everyone was cheering me on. I needed to cry, and I did. I never felt so much love and support.

My director was already plotting strategy: "I kept thinking about how to dress Marlee and how she would look in the movie—she was so beautiful and interesting and sexy, you just couldn't take your eyes off her. There was a real spark."

When we finished. I felt exhausted. It was the first time I had done anything this emotional: it had just sucked up everything I had in me.

I was sent off to grab something to eat, then dropped off at the apartment.

I remember Bill asking me as I was leaving for the day, "What are you doing tonight?"

My brain starts racing. I have a boyfriend back in Chicago. He's waiting for me to call him. So I say, "Nothing really, just packing, I'm leaving for home tomorrow."

"Let me come over at eleven. I have dinner reservations, but I'll come over later and say good-bye." *But for what?* I thought to myself. I needed to tell him no, that I had a boyfriend, I *have* a boyfriend. But being wooed by Bill Hurt was seductive. What would he be like? The curiosity sucked me in.

So I went back to the apartment, nervous as anything. I smoked some pot. I did some coke. I took a shower.

My interpreter wanted to go to bed, but I wouldn't let her. I wanted to make sure she could hear the doorbell.

Bill didn't come at eleven.

At 1 a.m. he buzzed the apartment. As soon as my interpreter heard it, she said, "Good night," and headed off to bed.

Bill was absolutely wasted. I had never seen someone that drunk before.

He looked a little sheepish. "Sorry, I'm late."

I was nineteen, five feet three inches, and all of ninety-eight pounds—there's nothing like coke to keep you slim. He was thirty-five, around six feet two inches, and in terrific shape.

We sat down on the couch, and we just connected. He was wild. The sex was spectacular, and that is the one thing about our relationship that would never change. Sex with Bill was take-my-breath-away fantastic, always.

We completely fit—like a glove. It was extremely intense and crazy, and this thought flashed through my head: *Wow, I'm making love with a movie star, right here in the living room of an apartment a studio is paying for.*

It was surreal.

He stayed for about three hours. We didn't talk much, we didn't sleep. On his way out he smiled and said, "Hope to see you again."

17

I HEADED TO MIKE'S house with a heavy heart. Dark clouds and lightning and a drenching summer downpour only made me feel worse. He was still my boyfriend, though on the flight back from L.A. I knew that whether I got the role or not my life was changing forever and in ways that wouldn't include Mike.

Four years, dreams of kids and houses and loving each other forever were washing away in the gutters. Everything about how I thought my life was going to turn out had suddenly become obsolete. But before I could look to the future, I had to resolve my past.

Walking into Mike's house, I had no idea what I was going to say. He was in his bedroom, still sleeping, such a beautiful boy. I woke him up and he looked at me and I guess my face said everything.

"It's over. I know, it's over," he said, tears streaming down his face.

It was so, so sad, as if my heart were breaking into a million pieces. It was still pouring when I ran to my car. I just had to get out of there, couldn't stand to see the pain I'd caused etched in his face. Couldn't stand the tears.

I pulled out of the driveway and gunned the car—it skidded out of control, barely missing a tree that would have destroyed the car and probably me.

The car rolled to a stop and I dropped my head on the steering wheel, took a breath, and cried and cried. Took another breath—and cried again. Took another breath. Debated going back in. Tried to think of anything I could say to Mike to make it better. But I couldn't.

I drove away, slowly this time, the rain coming down in sheets, my face wet with tears. That was the last time I saw him, my first true love, for a while. Even now, every time "Just the Way You Are" plays, I always think of Mike—without fail—because that was our song.

It was back to a waiting game for me. I was hoping for a call, from the studio, from Bill.

Not long before, my family had left Morton Grove for Northbrook, a more affluent suburb. The house was nice. I'm sure technically nicer than Morton Grove, but it never felt like home. I was nineteen, but adrift in my life and so uncertain about my future that I was content to live at home for now.

About a week after I got back from L.A. I got a phone call from my agent, Harrise Davidson, who had a TTY.

"I'm talking to Paramount."

"What are they saying?"

We must have gone back and forth four or five times with questions. Each time the phone rang both my mom and I would jump.

In one of the calls Harrise asked, "How does $50,000 sound?"

Here I am, not yet twenty, having had nothing but minimum-wage jobs and my one short stint at $300 a week for the run of the play. So $50,000 sounded very, very good. I'm thinking, *That's a lot of money.* I quickly said okay.

The next time Harrise called it was with one final question: "Would you do a nude scene?"

"I'm an actress, so, yes."

Two minutes later she called back: "You got it!"

I looked up and my mother was standing by the doorway with an address book . . . weeping. Ready to call everybody.

"I got it! I got it!"

I had no sense of how my life would change. I didn't even think about whether this was just a one-shot chance or if it would lead to an acting career. But my mind started working overtime. It was starting to feel real. I want to see the script. What am I going to pack?

Then I got the second call I'd been waiting for. From Bill.

"Congratulations. Can't wait to see you."

ne of the rare early photos of my dad's
rents: Grandpa Ed and Grandma Ann.

The only picture I've ever seen of my
parents Libby and Don Matlin's wedding,
unearthed as I was writing this book.

e of the earliest pictures I have of
mother accompanied by her lovely
te to my dad.

I love this picture of my Grandmother
Rose and her salamis. I'm glad they're
kosher!

Growing up, I loved all our family pets but Eric's dog Solo held a special place in my heart.

Everyone says that I drive very fast and as you can see, I started very early!

This is my favorite picture of my dad, taken when I was four. You can see the hearing aid in my ear, which my dad told me to tell everyone was just a big glob of bubblegum.

"I am Dorothy!"—my stage debut at eight years old in the *Wizard of Oz* at the Center on Deafness.

One of the moments that changed my life: me and my best friend Liz with wonderful Henry Winkler at the Center on Deafness.

From my personal pictures from *Children of a Lesser God*: This is the moment where director Randa Haines asked me to improvise in sign what a wave sounded like.

The pool scene from *Children of a Lesser God* looks like love but it wasn't that easy. I remember very clearly Bill and me fighting during this scene. *(Credit: © Paramount Pictures, all rights reserved)*

asn't sure how Bill would react to my
car win but he was very sweet and
cere. (*Credit: © Academy of Motion
:tures Arts and Sciences*)

I never expected to win a Golden
Globe for *Children of a Lesser God*.
Two things to look for in this picture:
the missing Lee Press On Nail and
the beautiful Paloma Picasso bracelet
Bill had given me. (*Credit: Bettmann/
CORBIS*)

Backstage at the Oscars in 1987. To this day I have no idea how my entire
family and Liz made it backstage amidst all the security. But I was so glad to
share in the moment with them. (*Credit: Ron Galella/WireImage.com*)

One of my favorite photographer Greg Gorman, captured this shot Jack and me: one of the few time Jack and I are not looking at each other! *(Credit: Greg Gorman)*

(Below) At the 75th Anniversary bash for Paramount Pictures, Rob Williams was hilariously signing dirty words to me and Tom Cruis and all I could say was "It wasn't my fault!" (*Credit: Time & Life Pictures/Getty Images*)

bove left) At the 1987 premiere for *Walker,* Jennifer Beals and I were practically *—*n sisters with our identical curls and horn-rimmed glasses. (*Credit: Time & Life —tures/Getty Images)*

bove right) This picture belies the fact that I felt like it was 190 degrees in this *—*ss made of heavy wool, but it's one of my favorite candid moments taken by *—*k on the set of *Walker.*

Me and Jean Reno on the set of the French film *The Man with the Golden Mask.* We will remain friends forever.

(Above) He was beautiful then and he is beautiful now; Rob Lowe and I had some great times together. (Right) Richard Dean Anderson and I shared a love of hockey. He was great fun and sweet as could be.

Two different but very dear men in my life: David Oliver, on the left, whom we lost to AIDS, and my surfer boyfriend Darrin Pappas on the right.

18

REHEARSALS FOR THE film would start in August of 1985 in Saint John, New Brunswick. Most of the film was shot in the village of Rothesay just outside Saint John at one of the local landmarks, the Rothesay College School. It was a beautiful old campus. Victorian-style buildings, sitting right on a bay, which I found could generate icy winds even in warmer months—freezing me to the bone during shooting on more than one occasion.

Randa wanted to get the cast—a mix of hearing and Deaf actors—in sync before shooting began. The technical considerations of filming are considerable when not all of the actors will be speaking. It was a logistical challenge—or nightmare—depending on the day. She had blocked out three weeks of rehearsals to make sure there were no nightmares.

Walking into the hotel where the production was putting us up, it started to feel real that I was actually going to be in this movie, complete with a starring role.

My mom had come along and planned to spend a couple of days helping me settle in. When we walked in, Bill was waiting for me. I was nineteen and had never been away from home or my family except for short trips with the Traveling Hands troupe and vacations with Liz's family, which was almost like being at home.

My mom couldn't believe this new life I was stepping into, and I think she was torn between happiness for me and a little bit of envy that she would be leaving and I would be staying.

The front desk handed me a stack of bills—I didn't understand what it was for until Bill explained it to me. So I was introduced to per diem cash—I would be getting $800 a week in spending money in addition to what I was being paid for the movie.

I was in heaven. It only got better. My mom and I ate dinner together that night—fresh lobster caught off Saint John's shores earlier that day, food of the gods!

Bill and I had seen each other one other time between the screen test and the start of production. Liz and I went to Los Angeles in July of '85 for the Deaf Olympics, and Bill was in town. We arranged to meet.

He was looking for us and we were looking for him in the crowds there that day. I first caught sight of him behind the wheel of a convertible. He looked like a movie star. I was trying to play it cool, looking casual, eating a peach. Liz and I jumped into the car and spent the rest of the afternoon tooling around the city, just hanging out. I wasn't sure where it was going with us, but something was definitely happening, and it was only growing in intensity.

We bumped into Randa, too. She'd stopped by to check out the Deaf Olympics activities. A couple of actors who had auditioned for the movie and been passed over were there, too—a few of them definitely gave me the cold shoulder.

Some in the Deaf acting community had been incensed that I had been cast as Sarah. It's a small, close-knit group, and news, good or bad, travels fast. Major roles for Deaf actors in big studio movies didn't come along every day. To make matters worse—at least from their point of view—I came from nowhere, unlike many of them who'd been toiling in theater for many years.

The community of Deaf actors gave me no support, no encouragement, no words of wisdom or welcome. I would face this difficult pattern over the years. One moment the Deaf community at large would embrace me. I quickly became their most visible emissary to the hearing world—a role I never asked for, but tried to take on with grace. The next moment they would castigate me for some perceived slight—most often it was that I wasn't as "Deaf" as they wanted me to be.

Whether it was the Deaf or the hearing community, I've always fought against anyone defining me, stereotyping me, limiting me because of my deafness. At the same time, I've tried to be a strong advocate for Deaf issues—working endlessly for closed-captioning and educational opportunities for Deaf children.

But I decided early on that I had to live my life in the best way I knew how. I had strong opinions and a way of living in both the Deaf and the hearing worlds that made some Deaf activists angry. But I was raised that way, and I wasn't then, or ever, going to apologize for that.

THANK GOD FOR Randa. She had been thinking a lot about how to get me where I needed to be to give her the performance she wanted, the one she believed I was capable of. If I couldn't count on support from the Deaf community, I had a champion in her.

Randa says, "I started working with Marlee in different ways than I normally would. I showed her a film called *Carmen,* by a great Spanish director. It's the story of the opera *Carmen* told through a flamenco group.

"There is fantastic emotion in the dancing and the woman, her carriage, there is such a sense of pain and pride—the way she carried her past in her body and her face. I thought it was a great model for Marlee to use as she thought about how she would play Sarah.

"It was our own private work together. I wore earplugs when we screened it together because we had the sound up so loud—we were working in a physical way to understand the emotions, and the physical manifestation of the maturity and age that Marlee didn't have in her own life.

"The two of us had a sign we created for Carmen, it became a shorthand for us during shooting. A way I could say, 'Remember that part of your character, remember that part of yourself.'"

I BEGAN TRYING to sketch out a blueprint of my character, and Randa and I kept talking things through as rehearsals progressed. Sarah was beginning to take shape in my mind. I knew her moods, I could feel her anguish and pain, her passion.

I made notes on the pages of the script—cryptic references to bad moments in my life that I wanted to use as subtext for how I would handle specific scenes. In one, I tried to imagine my mother's world as a child—she had been deserted by her father just as Sarah had been.

I was also struck by some of Sarah's dialogue. I made a note to myself on one page: *This is a Deaf school, no one knows hearing idioms!* I didn't know the idioms either.

I crossed through a line I was supposed to sign, which read, "But I'm Deaf," and replaced it with simply "Me Deaf," much truer to the stripped-down, direct way that you communicate in sign language.

Jim Carrington, who'd worked with me through my screen test, was back again on set. Another Randa touch. She says, "I knew Marlee needed someone to prepare her for what to expect day to day. To be able to concentrate with a hundred people on the set."

Jim had the bluest eyes I have ever seen—reminded me a little of the way Tim Curry looked in *Rocky Horror Picture Show*—and was as kind as he was demanding. I carry his insights and some of his techniques with me even now.

They gave me my own trailer, which I learned was standard operating procedure, and I started to meet all the many people tied to the production. I thought it was like one giant party. I didn't begin to understand what their jobs were, didn't know what the union was, that everyone there had a job and a specific role.

I spent about half a day one day with wardrobe, and I remember not understanding at first why it was taking so long. There were at least five of us—the director, the producer, and the head of wardrobe and her sister, they were French girls. I was trying on a variety of clothes, and they were explaining which clothes went with which scenes and why. "Oh, okay, this is what I wear here, and this is what I wear there."

When we got to the swimming scene, the sisters said, giggling, "And in this scene you wear no clothes."

"What? No clothes?" Then I remembered the question my agent had asked me about doing a nude scene. "Ah, no clothes, okay." Woo-hoo!

Children of a Lesser God was a crash course in moviemaking, and I wanted to understand everything about it. I watched, I asked questions; I tried to be a giant sponge and absorb everything I could. It was a combination of my natural curiosity and a desire to never be the naive one again.

What I really wanted to do, too, was learn everybody's name. In the years since, I have made it a habit to get to know the crew as well as the other actors. You're just as likely to find me eating with the crew as in my trailer. I never forget they are a significant part of the production; they work long hours for not a lot of pay, and they are always part of my success.

Children of a Lesser God was the only film on which I would manage that feat—two hundred cast and crew, and before we wrapped, I knew the name of every one of them! You all rock!

19

Working on that first film taught me a lot about the nuances I would need to learn to survive and grow as an actor who was also Deaf.

My first scene in the film is at night; I am sleeping. A storm is blowing up, rain starts pelting, a shutter outside my window starts banging, again and again, the curtains rise and fall with the wind. It's a beautiful scene crammed with technical demands; among them, it calls for me to be perfectly still, calm, undisturbed in my sleep.

It was a difficult day for the production—multiple components needed to behave just so—the shutters, the rain, the curtains, the wind, and of course me.

It might sound easy, but when my eyes are closed, I'm cut off. I don't know what's happening, and when you are awake, but unable to use the senses that you do have, that you rely on to fill in the blanks, it can be maddening.

Improvision, too, became a new skill that I could put in my acting arsenal, one that Randa used a lot throughout the production. It requires you to trust yourself and your director and just dive in. For me, the most challenging moment was describing the sound of the waves.

I was struggling and Randa asked me to think of how I would describe it if I didn't know sign language. She wanted something expressive and sensual. Okay, how would I communicate without talking *and* without signing?

I stopped worrying about how and let my mind drift into feelings. I thought about how it feels to be in the ocean, to feel the power of the waves, their rhythm, their movement. I closed my eyes and tried to get lost in the waves.

It was scary and exhilarating at the same time as I stood there and tried to take all those feelings and make them concrete—physical. Using my hands, I pushed up on my body, again and again, the way waves would. I dropped my head back as if they were washing over me.

Randa was pleased with the way the scene was working now. She recalls, "It was such a sensual moment, Marlee has such a wonderful physicality. When she describes the wave, it's such a brave moment. She just put herself out there and went for it. There is a kind of internal freedom she has when it comes to using her body. I saw it again in the pool, she is very at ease with herself."

BEING ON A movie set, you quickly learn—despite being part of an industry that prizes stick-thin figures—that food is never more than a few steps away. I had never been around so much free food in my life!

A scene in a restaurant featured a salad bar, with a really fabulous spread. I went over and picked out a couple of things to munch on.

The food was so, so good that I went back again, but the prop master said gently and nicely. "Hey, Marlee, if you're hungry, craft services is right outside."

I cringed and blushed. I'd been eating prop food. Note to self—prop food is not to be eaten just for fun. Prop food is working food.

Ah, but there is always the magic of the craft services table, changing throughout the day, always filled with the tastiest treats. One of my favorite things was to have a bagel topped with cream cheese and tomatoes. Simple, I know. But I would create the most beautifully cream-cheesed bagels in the world; they were, and I do not exaggerate here, works of art.

One day I was midcreation when Randa came up to me and literally lifted the bagel, that beautiful bagel, right out of my hand. She recalls, "The wardrobe people had come to me and said they were having to let out all of Marlee's clothes. Soon it was going to turn into a problem. She was gaining weight and they said you've got to stop it.

"Right after that conversation, I went in search of Marlee. And I found her, at the craft services table, lovingly layering cream cheese on this bagel. I hated to do it, but I walked over and took the bagel and said, 'Enough.'"

During the production I kept gaining, and I noticed Randa kept shrinking. I guess we each dealt with stress in a different way.

But learning to control my urge to swing by the craft services table would turn out to be useful for many years to come. Thanks, Randa!

One vice I picked up on set was smoking. I have Randa to thank for that, too.

My character, Sarah, had to smoke, actually quite a lot. Though I had spent years smoking pot, I never smoked cigarettes. If anything I avoided them because my mother smoked and I would always give her grief about it.

"Can't I just pretend?"

"No, you have to smoke, it won't look authentic otherwise."

At first I would get dizzy and nauseated; once I threw up. The taste was so different from pot, with no mellow after-haze either. But I got used to it, then addicted to it, and ended up smoking Marlboro Lights—Bill's brand. He smoked a couple of packs a day, and by the end of production I had a pack-a-day habit that I wouldn't lose until years later. So gross. I'm proud to say I don't smoke anymore, ever.

The good news is that I have a strong constitution. I rarely get sick. But at one point I was overtaken by the worst cold. I had a fever, I couldn't breathe, I could barely stand. I guess my body was reacting to too many hours shooting outside in the winds off the bay.

That day was the poker-game scene. I'd never played poker, hadn't played cards much as a kid. Did not know how to shuffle a deck. So I got a crash course in both. Sarah was supposed be a surprise whiz at poker.

With a box of Kleenex and teeth gritted, I got through the day, so glad when it was over. Then I remember seeing the final cut of the film, watching that scene, the moment when I masterfully shuffle the deck. . . . Hey, wait, those aren't my hands!

∾ ∾

SOMETIMES THE STRANGEST things will remind you of home when you're in the middle of a long production and missing all the comforts and safety of your very own space. Two things did that for me in *Children of a Lesser God*.

When I saw the U.S. dollars on the poker table, sick as I was, I was hit with a wave of nostalgia. It just felt so good to see those dollar bills after being in Canada for the longest time. No offense, Canada. Such a beautiful country!

The other was the way they dressed the house that Sarah's mother lived in. It was one of the nicest touches and meant the world to my mother and dad in particular. The walls were filled with my baby pictures—even one of my mom holding me as a child.

When I heard Piper Laurie had been cast as my mother, I remember thinking, *Oh my God, that's Carrie's mother! Will there be blood?*

Seriously, I was excited to be working with her. Piper was nothing but gracious, professional, patient, and beautiful.

20

W HEN I LOOK at *Children of a Lesser God* now, each scene has its own story.

In some, Randa is the main character—a sure-handed director guiding, demanding, pushing, nurturing all of us through incredibly difficult and emotional moments.

In some, it's John Seale, our brilliant director of cinematography, who has gone on to do such incredible work, including winning an Oscar for *The English Patient*. In others, I think of the prop master, or my acting coach, the other Deaf kids in the cast, whom I loved, who were all great.

One particular scene sticks in my mind when I think of John Seale. For the scenes we shot in the pool when I'm completely nude, the crew was kept to an absolute minimum. Cameras were above water and another below. In one complicated scene, I had to dive off the edge of the pool and over the underwater camera. Even more difficult, I needed to do it as smoothly as I could, hitting the water with minimum splash.

I dived over and over, trying to make the entry as clean as possible. I thought I was doing a great job until John motioned at me and said we needed to talk for a second. I pulled a towel around me and walked over, dripping. He hesitated, searching for just the right words.

"Marlee, next time you dive, uummm. I need you to try to keep your legs together." He waited to see if I understood.

Oh my gosh, oh my gosh! I blushed crimson red. Every time I dived in, legs apart, I'd apparently been giving the camera operator an X-rated show!

The nude scenes in the pool were physically demanding and technically difficult with cameras and lights above and below the water. We shot for three days with me spending much of it nude and submerged in ninety-degree water. It was hellish.

In the first scene, I'm swimming alone, trying to move through the water as smoothly as possible. When I was underwater, I was to make as few bubbles as possible, all without it looking as if I were holding my breath. We shot it over and over to get both the physicality and the mood of it.

This critical scene spoke to my comfort in isolation, to the one place I could feel free of all of the limitations of the world and my deafness. Randa was persistent in getting it right, and I look at it now and know she was right to keep pushing. The scene is cinematically beautiful and speaks volumes without a sound. And few bubbles either.

BUT MANY OF the scenes I'm in are defined in my memory by whether Bill and I were fighting that day.

I kept my hotel room, but I spent most of my time at the house the studio had rented for him. We made amazing, mind-blowing love. And we fought. And we worked. I know there were other things—quiet times, ordinary times—but when I watch the movie, my mind swings between those two poles—love and anger, anger and love—a new variation on an old theme I'd been raised with.

Almost everything we did together had an intensity, an electricity, that was searing, in both good and bad ways. I *knew* I was more alive than I had ever been. Life, emotion, radiated off us. It was as if we were our own force field.

On the screen that combustion would bring out some of the best work either of us would ever do. Offscreen, well, that's another story. Bill once said we were two matchsticks who should never be burning at the same time. In that he was right.

ONE OF OUR early blowups came on the day we shot the scene that shows Sarah and James really interacting for the first time.

As it opens, James spots Sarah mopping the floor. He's intrigued, motions her into his classroom, one littered with crumpled paper. She assumes he wants her to clean up, but that's not it at all—James is intrigued by this beautiful, distant young woman. He begins trying to convince her that he can teach her, help her, something she's not interested in.

The scene is supposed to be filled with that tension of a new relationship when both of you are testing the waters, trying to figure each other out. As it's written, it also has humor, sarcasm, and a bit of whimsy.

We were both so angry that when we started shooting the scene, the mood in the room was lethal. In this situation, sometimes after one or two takes everything just relaxes. The tension in the room rolls away.

Not so on this day. Randa eventually had to play referee: "You here, and you there." The production was shut down for about an hour while she first talked to me, then Bill.

Only later would I begin to believe that Bill often ignited the fights specifically to make a scene like this work. He and Randa argued intensely and publicly throughout the shoot, too. But she just chalked it up to his process, knowing that after a few takes, actually usually around take seven or eight, like a cloud in a stiff wind, the anger would blow away.

For me, it was hard not to take things personally. We were immersed in both work and a new relationship, and it felt to me as if the storm clouds kept hanging around.

In the scene where Sarah and James are on their first date—dinner in an intimate restaurant that has a jukebox—people are soon up, dancing on the small dance floor. We'd had a huge fight, screaming at each other, earlier that day.

Most of the time I can't even remember what we were fighting about, it was so inconsequential, but on this day it was about whether I could adopt an adorable orange tabby kitten that was hanging around the craft services truck. I asked the craft services guy if I could have the kitty. Bill thought I was rude to ask.

First Sarah dances alone, slowly, sensually, eyes closed, moving to the music. Then we dance a slow dance together—I'm supposed to be tentative, not comfortable with the closeness. That was an easy place to get to for me; I didn't want to look at him, did not want to let my body relax into his. At one point I rested my face against his shoulder to keep from seeing his face. The texture of the moment is just right.

When I walked into my trailer after we were finished, I saw a litter box, cat toys, and a dish. It was his way of saying he was sorry. We named the kitten Otis—*she* went on to have eight kittens!

So it was another bad day, good day, great scene.

Another of the great-scene bad days began when James has come in search of Sarah. He's standing in a trench coat at the edge of the pool—leaning toward her as he talks. Gravity takes over and he falls in—it is the first time he and Sarah make love. There was the water to tread, the underwater camera, a shoe floating to the bottom, his clothes being pulled off. Extremely difficult physically to choreograph.

At one point I am to open my arms so he can come into them; we embrace. I wrapped my legs around him to help myself balance and to keep from floating away from him as we worked through the scene. It's one of the most natural things to do when you are embracing someone in water.

But Bill became incensed, yelling at me that I was coming on to him. I was shocked. Could not believe it. I had all the intimacy with him I needed offscreen. Did he need the fight to get to that place of vulnerability he needed for that scene? I wondered.

Our other huge fight on set was during a scene when we were making love—again he believed I was doing more than just acting. I kept trying to figure out his anger—was it because he was unsettled by our connection? Afraid our lives offscreen were seeping into our roles on-screen? It all seemed so irrational to me.

Randa came to believe that it was all just part of Bill's process, that he needed conflict, some kind of resistance to fight through before he could get to the place he needed to. She said later that she thought about pulling me aside, telling me not to take it personally. She never did, but I was too emotionally drawn into Bill's world then to have listened anyway.

ᏯᎧ ᏯᎧ

ONE SCENE NEAR the end of the film is particularly difficult for me to watch. We argue, then make awful, violent love.

We'd had an equally awful fight before we got to the set that day. One of our worst. Again, I have no idea what the issue was, I just know it was probably the most volatile fight we'd had during filming.

In that scene after we've made love, we're on the floor and I roll away from him. My dress is pushed above my knees, and down my left leg are a series of fresh bruises. You can see them if you watch that scene now. I never said anything that day, wondering if the makeup crew would notice, would try to cover them. Wondering if Randa would say anything. But no one did. It's as if no one sees.

In the fall of '85 I was trying to understand so many things all at once. Everything was new, including Bill, the first adult relationship I'd ever had. My youth frustrated him—over our nearly two years together he would say again and again, "You are so young, you don't know anything about life yet." I was never sure what he wanted me to do about that.

I think, too, that I was unlike anyone Bill had been with before. I was a fighter, a scrapper, a tough Chicago girl who wasn't afraid to mix it up to survive and navigate this world. If he had expected me to shrink and fold if he yelled at me, I must have been a surprise.

21

AFTER *CHILDREN OF A LESSER GOD* wrapped, I moved to New York with Bill, into his apartment on Central Park West. On the eighth floor, it had huge banks of windows and sweeping views of the park that could just take your breath away.

We started setting up a life together full of hope and passion, still learning about each other, determined to try to make this relationship work.

He was extremely sensitive to any barriers presented by my deafness, immediately adjusting the house to accommodate my needs—lights that would flash throughout when the buzzer rang; a TTY machine for the phone—and he kept working to improve his signing, though we relied more on my ability to read lips and talk.

We were also trying to keep everything below the radar. Bill hated publicity and the invasion that meant into his private life. I was just an invisible girl from Chicago at the time, no one outside the cast of the film and the studio knew who I was.

Not long after we moved in together, Bill had agreed to a *People* magazine article, to talk about his role in *Kiss of the Spider Woman,* which the studio hoped would earn him an Oscar nomination. The interview and photo shoot were going to take place at his apartment. He needed me to disappear for a day.

I was new to the city, had not gotten close to navigating it on my own. What to do with Marlee?

Around that same time, the London premiere of *Kiss* was rapidly approaching. Bill wanted me with him, that was going to be our coming-out party, and had his assistant Robin go in search of a London-based sign-language interpreter to be with me during our time there.

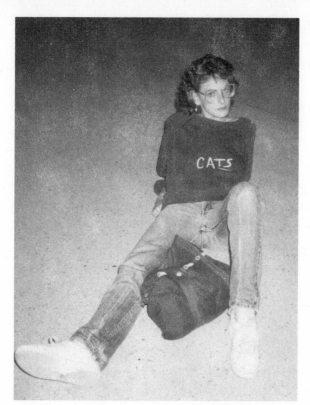

Coked out in New York City

In a phone call that would change my life, Robin was eventually referred to New York University, which sent its Deaf students to England for a summer program each year. Surely they could recommend someone.

At the time, Jack Jason was an NYU graduate student in the film department. His parents were both Deaf, so he'd grown up signing, and he often picked up extra work interpreting for the university's Deaf students. The person who fielded Robin's call knew Jack and his background, and Jack was in the office at the time.

Jack remembers, "Robin, Bill's assistant, explained that they were looking for an interpreter for Marlee in London and could I recommend any there. I told them no, that they would need to bring their own because England has a different sign-language system than the U.S. He asked for a recommendation, and I offered to send them my résumé.

"When Robin called back, he said, 'Mr. Hurt would prefer to have a woman.' And so I did something a little sneaky—I gave them the names of three women who I knew were all out of town. As it turned out, Marlee got an ear infection and wasn't going to be able to fly anyway, but Robin called me back and asked if I could meet Marlee at the apartment. It was December second, 1985."

That day Bill and I were just walking back to the apartment when Jack arrived. I saw this petite man with about two hundred layers of clothing on. He was wearing a suit and a tie with a sweater underneath, and a long winter overcoat down to his calves. It was way too big for him.

He says he had no idea what we were going to be doing so he was trying to dress for any possible occasion.

Clothes aside, the memory that stays with me the most is how well he signed.

He was so fast I had to ask him if he was Deaf. I'd never seen a hearing person who could sign like that. Then I asked him three totally politically incorrect questions.

Number one: "Are you Jewish?" Number two: "Are you gay?" Number three: "Do you smoke weed?" He said yes to one of the three—he was Jewish. Why did I ask? I have no idea—so dumb!

We got into the car Bill had gotten for the day, and while he did the *People* interview, Jack and I drove around Manhattan. I had no idea where I was and Jack asked me what I wanted to do. Shopping was always good entertainment.

So he took me to Trump Tower Mall, a lavish indoor mall on Fifth Avenue. I guess he assumed since I was with a movie star that would be to my taste. I saw it and said, "No, no, no, this is not for me."

I was more interested in learning about him and his Deaf parents than shopping, but Jack was on a mission to make shopping work.

Next we hit Bloomingdale's. I had never heard of Bloomingdale's either, and after I was doused by the perfume ladies spraying anyone walking by, all I wanted to do was escape. I'm from Chicago, that's my point of reference. It was still pretty pricey and I didn't know if I wanted to spend that much. At that time in my life, my fashion sense was, give me T-shirts and jeans and I'm happy.

Then Jack, who was so patient that day and many days since, thought of Macy's. Another store I'd never heard of. But at Macy's I fell in love. It reminded me of Marshall Field's back home.

At the end of the day, Jack dropped me off back at the apartment and I asked for his phone number. I needed someone I could talk to, someone I could sign to. We started seeing each other a lot after that. He was my only friend in New York.

I'd bombard him with questions about his childhood, his parents. We'd meet for lunch, for dinner. There were no barriers to communication between us; it opened up the world there for me. Before long, Jack asked if I wanted to see a movie.

"I can't. I can't read the lips on the screen and there's no captioning."

"Oh. I'll interpret."

"What, you'll sit up there next to the screen?"

"No, silly, next to you."

So we went to see *The Color Purple,* the three of us—me, Bill, and Jack. By that time, Jack was also tutoring Bill in signing.

During the film, I was amazed and fascinated by Jack's ability, how he was able to deliver the subtext of the movie as well as the dialogue.

It was a long movie, and at the end he was crying while interpreting it all for me. I couldn't believe he could do that. I thought to myself that he had to be the best interpreter in the world.

Jack and I have worked together now for almost twenty-four years, and it is an extremely complicated relationship. He interprets for me, and he runs my production company. He develops projects and generally is the middleman between me and the public. If you've seen me on a talk show or an awards show, generally the person by my side explaining what I'm saying, or thinking or feeling, is Jack.

He is also like family. Jack's been there for my wedding and the births of my children. He's like an old shoe. We're comfortable. If we haven't seen each other in a week or a month, it's like old friends catching up.

To the business he brings creativity and can be ambitious, aggressive on my behalf. He brings good ideas, large and small—he's created movie scripts for us to produce, and it was his idea for me to sign the national anthem at the Super Bowl in 1993 when Garth Brooks sang, and again at the Super Bowl in 2007.

In fact, he even fought to have me on-screen with Garth. When Jack was told by one of the show's producers that Garth would be center stage, but I would be offscreen on the edge of the stage, he was incensed. He found Garth and told him what the producers intended to do. Garth had a word with them, and suddenly I was standing right next to Garth.

While Jack's always protective of me, usually a good thing, sometimes he's overly protective. Not so good. In fact, that trait is often where we've had the most conflict. In the early days, if he didn't agree with what I wanted to tell someone, he'd refuse to interpret. Here's a classic example.

An executive at a big studio had done something that really ticked me off. I knew him and wanted to talk to him right then. We were in my Porsche at the time, I was driving, and Jack was in the passenger seat. I had a speakerphone and told Jack I wanted to call the executive. No time like the present!

Jack said, "No, I won't interpret." He was worried about the politics of it.

I remember we were on Wilshire and I said, "Give me the number."

"Fine," he said, then crossed his arms across his chest—in case I'd forgotten that he wasn't going to give me any help on this call at all.

I dialed the number, it rang, a secretary answered. I said, "Hi, this is Marlee Matlin." She understood me and said, "He's not in, may I take a message?" There was silence and Jack glared at me. I glared back at him. Finally he interpreted what she'd said, but he wouldn't speak for me.

So I said, "Please tell so-and-so, 'Shame on him,' and thank you very much," and hung up.

I looked over at Jack and said, "You're fired."

"Marlee, the car is moving, I'm not getting out."

"Okay, so, where do you want to go for lunch?"

Jack was appalled. But I felt better. As far as I was concerned, it was finished—my beef with the studio exec and my disagreement with Jack.

But later I told Jack he could not deny me access to communication, ever. To me that was just incredibly unfair, taking advantage of my being Deaf to force an issue. And he agreed, though we've had this fight a few more times over the years.

Our relationship is such a combination of professional and personal, and we are always trying to figure out where to draw the line. At the beginning, it was about me—I wanted him to support me, agree with me about everything. I can be strong and stubborn, and Jack just can't handle it sometimes.

But over the years, he's gotten stronger and I've seen a lot of changes in him, in good ways—and hopefully I've changed, too.

We can absolutely crack each other up, and at times people have probably thought we were crazy, laughing until tears were streaming down our faces. Show us a photo of a shih tzu in a bow and a tutu and we're gone.

We've also had huge fights along the way, and I'm sure he's come close to leaving a couple of times. That would be the saddest day for me. I cannot imagine another Jack who would put up with me, who would understand me so well and who knows so much.

But as angry as he's gotten, Jack always says, "This is for life." And I believe him.

DECEMBER 1985 WAS one of the lowest points in my life. The fights with Bill kept escalating, and I had no idea how to deal with them. Liz whisked me away for a Club Med vacation in Ixtapa, and I started to feel stronger with Liz by my side and the sun on my back. But those beach memories died all too quickly.

I flew to Spain to meet Bill in Málaga. We were to meet his father, who lived there. One evening, after we'd fought through lunch and as the argument raged on, I felt my will to live just slip away. I felt lost, helpless. I realized I didn't care whether I lived or died. As we walked away from the restaurant, I walked out into the street,

Liz and me, Ixtapa, 1985

dazed. The screech of tires, the smell of burned rubber, the blaring horns, all the chaos was muffled. I couldn't hear it, but more important, I couldn't feel it.

Then I saw a huge truck barreling toward me; the driver had no escape route. I knew if I didn't move, it would be the last thing I would ever do in my life. In that split second, something inside me changed and I darted out of the way. It is a hard thing to admit that I was ever that low, ever so much on the brink. But I know that no matter how tough or how strong you are, the moment might come when you wonder not if you can make it, but whether you want to make it. I'm so very glad I chose life.

22

In March of 1986, I went to the Academy Awards for the first time. The trip to Hollywood was magical. Bill had been nominated and would win an Oscar that night in the lead-actor category for his performance in *Kiss of the Spider Woman.*

We stayed at the legendary Chateau Marmont. Stars were everywhere—and I was starstruck. Even now I can turn into such a fan when I see someone whose work I admire.

It was my first red-carpet event—I walked it with Bill and I loved it. Jack was there to interpret for me, Liz was there for moral support—and so that I could have a girlfriend along to hang out with.

I had an incredible feeling when they called Bill's name, knowing how much it meant and how many years he'd worked on his craft. I loved being there to share it with him, including the Governor's Ball, then a round of after parties.

That trip was just about perfect, except for what Liz and Jack and I refer to as "the Jessica Lange incident."

The day after the Academy Awards, Bill was hurrying us to get in the limo and get out of there. We were leaving town, with packing to be done, and Bill had to check out of the hotel. Liz and I had gotten pretty stoned, pretty giggly, and were not moving all that fast—but then we were in the limo and driving around to the side of the hotel so he could check out. He jumped out of the car and said he'd be right back. When I saw him spot someone and stop to chat.

And so we sit. And we sit.

I ask Jack to look and see whom Bill is talking to. He ducks his head outside and tells us, "It's Jessica Lange!"

Now before I go on, let me just say I think Jessica Lange is terrific—great actress, beautiful woman, always has been nice to me.

But that morning, I admit I had a huge flash of jealousy, and I was really tired of waiting.

When Bill got back into the car, I casually asked him, "Who were you talking to?" Both Jack and Liz shot me a look like *What in the heck are you doing?*

"Jessica Lange."

"Woo hoo, Jessica Lange. Woo hoo, big movie star. *We* were all waiting for you while you talked to the big movie star? Woo hoo."

Bill swung around and got right in Jack's face and said, "Is that true, Jack? Were you waiting?"

Liz and Jack didn't know whether to break into laughter or run for cover. They opted for trying to look completely innocent.

Bill didn't see any humor in the situation—we could almost see the steam rising from his ears! I was *so* stoned.

MEANWHILE, PARAMOUNT HAD been doing test screenings for *Children of a Lesser God,* and the audience reaction was strong— except for the ending. The studio execs were pressing for a rewrite and reshoot to come up with something that felt more as if Sarah and James might have a "happily ever after."

The timing I think worked to my advantage. In the story, I'm a year older and stronger, and in truth the months had left me in many ways more self-assured. The reshoot went well except for the icy winds that blew through what was supposed to be a springtime night, leaving my nose red and runny—which kept the makeup artist busy.

I was anxious for the film to come out or at least get to that point where you're getting some kind of buzz in the industry about your work. I hadn't gotten another serious offer since the film wrapped, and I was anxious to have a career. Living with Bill was feeling increasingly isolated, and without work I had no financial independence.

Still, so many things about Bill were wonderful, and sometimes it felt as if our love was strong enough and passionate enough to carry us through anything.

The notes he'd leave just to let me know when he'd gone out running were beautiful, poetic. The cards that would come with his flowers. Messages left when he was on location. Letters—filled with love, commitment, his hopes for the future, worries about the present. Also, letters filled with his frustration, jealousy, and anger, but mostly he wrote to me of extraordinary love.

I often thought he was working through his feelings for me in these long, stream-of-consciousness rambles. They clearly meant something long after our breakup. I have saved every scrap, whether it was an eight-word note or an eight-page letter. The photo album of those treasured times we spent with his son Alex. I think on some level I wanted to have a record that would stand as witness for both the good and the bad times.

In August I was turning twenty-one. Bill had gotten me the most beautiful Paloma Picasso bracelet from Tiffany's that she had designed and signed. The wide, gold bangle had my name spelled in full-cut diamonds.

If that wasn't special enough, I went home to Chicago and *People* magazine came to my birthday party!

The publicity team was trying to generate interest in the movie, and they saw me as a fresh face with a compelling story that could only help the film. After screening the film, the folks at *People* decided to do a profile on me.

So with a writer and a photographer in tow, we celebrated my twenty-first birthday in Northbrook. One of my favorite pictures was taken in the garage of our house—I'm in jeans and a white T-shirt with a giant peace sign painted on it, one of my favorites. I've just broken open the piñata, the ground is covered in candy, and my family and friends are all laughing.

I had a homemade cake that day, and I was surrounded by love. I felt better, freer, more me than I had in ages. It was a great way to officially ring in adulthood!

IN THE FALL, Bill went to Yugoslavia to film *A Time of Destiny* with Timothy Hutton and Stockard Channing. The separation was brutal and our correspondence from that time was filled with love and yearning. In September, Bill flew me over for a few days and added a ticket for Jack.

The trip was rocky from the start. We flew first to Rome, then to Trieste, near Italy's border with Yugoslavia. Bill was to meet us there with a car for the drive back to Portoroz on the Adriatic coast, where they were shooting the film.

But he'd accidentally left his passport at the hotel, and the border patrol wouldn't let him through, so he sent his driver, Gorky, on to meet us with a handwritten note. Along with many apologies he said for us to go with Gorky, that I could trust him, he was a "good man." Bill said he was "desolate" not to be there, and I know that was true. You can even feel it in the intensity and frustration of the scrawl—he'd written the note on the back of the September 5 shooting schedule that was one of the few bits of paper he had with him.

When I finally saw him, we were both so happy, we just melted into each other. I had bought seven new sets of lingerie—something different for every night I was going to be there. For a while, it was pure bliss. But then things went dark. He was at war with the production over creative issues, then at war with me.

Jack remembers, "I was taking a shower when my friend Joe, who'd flown in from Italy for a couple of days, knocked and said, 'You've got to come out, there's something going on next door.' I got out and I could hear the most horrific sound. I had never heard anything like it before. Two people screaming, throwing things. It was like that nonstop.

"Joe and I debated what to do, and we finally decided to knock on their door. But just as I came out of my room. Marlee came out of theirs. She had bruises on her face and the start of a black eye. I could see Bill behind her, and he had a split lip.

"Marlee wanted to go home or to call the police. I didn't see how we could do either. Bill had the tickets, none of us had any money, and I didn't know how to contact the police in Yugoslavia, and given its politics then, I wasn't sure that would be safe anyway."

The storm blew over. I spent the next day eating fried chicken, french fries, drinking Cokes, and hanging out with Jack and Joe.

Jack asked me why I didn't leave Bill. I couldn't, I loved him and he loved me. It was going to get better.

By the time I left for home, things were back in a good place, or at least a better place. Bill wrote me the most amazing letter, which he started just moments after I left. In it, he worried his old worry, that I was so young I would lose interest in him, there would be younger men to catch my fancy—as I read back over his writings, it is everywhere.

I CAME BACK to the States and started a round of publicity for *Children of a Lesser God,* finally due to be released in September. It would premiere at the Toronto Film Festival, one of the major stops for movies with Oscar hopes. It was such strange new terrain for me to be walking.

By now, thankfully, buzz was starting to build, and I was getting good notices. Add to that, I was the new, exotic flavor of the month for the media. However, apparently few of those who interviewed me had ever talked to a Deaf person before in their lives. At times it was awkward, to say the least.

They would look at Jack, ask him questions, and avoid looking at me. Everyone wanted to know what my world sounded like—I don't know how to compare what I experience to your world of sounds . . . I can't hear! I learned quickly how to get control of the situation—first rule, look at me, talk *to* me. I can communicate. Pretty soon both sides got the hang of it.

I remember seeing the film for the first time, seeing my name on the screen—that moment was unlike any I'd ever had, butterflies inside. My family went to a special showing in Chicago, and when I came on the screen, my mom couldn't help herself and yelled "That's my daughter," and the audience cheered and applauded.

The reviews were exciting, generally the critics loved the movie, and most were moved by my performance. Interest in me—who I was, where I came from—began to build. I started getting requests from the morning shows and *Entertainment Tonight.* I found those TV talk shows so easy and comfortable. I loved settling into a couch and talking about the film, it didn't feel like work at all.

As I got more critical attention, that only upped tensions at home. I lived my life walking on eggshells, probably both of us did, but certainly me. We increasingly wanted different things from our relationship. It often felt as if Bill either wanted intense togetherness or he was pulling away. Wanting hours of solitude in his office to work on whatever the next project was, and he was working a lot. But it was never a comfortable distance; I found myself tiptoeing around the edge of a volcano that could erupt at any time.

There were other differences, too. Our childhoods could not have been less alike—he was born into an affluent family that held education to be a sacred trust and expected him to grow up conversant in politics, literature, the world. He attended top schools, ones that pressed their students toward academic achievement. The prestigious Julliard School was his last stop.

By contrast, the expectations for me were more blue-collar, pragmatic. Basic skills so that I could eventually get through life and find a job that would provide me a living wage. When Mike, my first real boyfriend, and I dreamed, we had small dreams, though they seemed big to us at the time.

For Bill and I, conversation was sometimes difficult because I didn't understand, had not been taught about, the world in the same way as him.

No matter what triggered our fights, they were made far worse by his drinking and my drug use. To this day, my stomach knots when I'm around someone who smells saturated by alcohol.

Sometimes, as I look back, it seems that we were always in some stage of warfare. One night he'd been invited to go to Glenn Close's for a game of Murder. He told me that Glenn didn't want me to come; maybe they thought I was too young. I got angrier and angrier as the night went on. So angry that I went into his office, which was off-limits to me, and started rummaging around in his desk. I found some coke there.

When I saw the coke, I thought, *Bingo, it's my party now*. I snorted most of it. But that wasn't enough. He'd taken the TTY with him, so I called and remember saying, "Guess what? I'm high on your coke."

He slammed the phone down and was back at the apartment in fifteen minutes, raging mad.

November was a truly volcanic month. One night he was out doing research—or maybe not—for his upcoming film, *Broadcast News*. He finally came home around 4:30 a.m., drunk, and woke me up. I looked at the clock, then asked where the hell he had been. I suspected he was having an affair with his research. . . .

The next thing I knew he'd pulled me out of the bed, screaming at me, shaking me. I was scared, I was sobbing. Then he threw me on the bed, started ripping off his clothes and mine. I was crying. "No, no, no. Please, Bill, no." The next thing I remember is Bill ramming himself inside me as I sobbed.

Another night, we'd been fighting for hours and he called Jack to come pick me up, at one o'clock in the morning. Jack took a cab over and he recalls, "I could hear yelling as I was riding the elevator up and I kept thinking, can't anyone else in this building hear this? When I got to their floor, I saw Marlee sobbing on the floor in the hallway, her clothes thrown in heaps around her. Bill came out in the hall, angry, and just kept saying, 'Don't believe anything she tells you.'"

I wanted to go to a hotel, but I was so upset, Jack insisted I go home with him. About an hour later, when I was calmer, I called Bill on the TTY and asked, "Anyone there?"

"Just us ghosts," he replied.

I took a cab back to him that night.

On November 8, Bill wrote me a long, formal letter telling me our relationship was over. He said in that letter that he was guilt-ridden about what he called his "physical anger." But he blamed me for doing things that made him crazy angry. In one moment he said I was emotionally Deaf; in another, he complained that I was too emotional.

The letter pains me to read even now and reminds me of the great chasm we faced. We interpreted everything that was going on between us from opposite banks of that growing divide. Still we were always back together again in days.

On, off, on, off, our relationship was like a light switch gone terribly wrong. If only I had understood him better, his way of thinking, I wonder if things might have been different. Maybe. Maybe not.

On December 26, he told me he was going to check into the Betty Ford Center for rehab, to get his drinking under control. I didn't understand what he was doing. I didn't even know what rehab was. I knew, though, that I didn't want to be alone. Selfish me.

He left that afternoon. I was scared, unsure of what this would mean for us, what it would mean for me. But I was also hopeful. Maybe this would be the start of a new chapter in our lives. It was, but it turned out to be completely different from the one that I expected to be written.

23

J ANUARY 10 IS the other birthday I celebrate every year. I've had twenty-two of these celebrations so far, and I intend to keep having them for as long as I'm around.

I officially stopped using drugs on January 10, 1987. Cold turkey. All the cocaine and pot had either been consumed or thrown away the day before.

The tenth was the day I was flying to Palm Springs to spend a week in joint counseling sessions with Bill at the Betty Ford Center. Whatever the future would hold for us, I wanted to be drug-free, and for some reason I just wouldn't allow myself to walk into Betty Ford high. I knew if I was going to survive in this relationship, if I was going to have a career, I had to turn my life around.

The week was difficult. In one of the first sessions, there were four of us: Bill, his counselor, one of the women's counselors, Jane, who would later be involved in my recovery, and me. I was seriously frightened going into that session, literally shaking. Jane promised me that I would be safe.

As the session started, Bill seemed agitated, looked at me hard, and said, "Go on, tell them everything." It was difficult, I had no interpreter with me, but I did tell them everything. It was the first time I had talked about some of the really dark times to anyone else, the violent depths of our arguments. In my reconnecting with Jane not long ago, she remembered it as I do.

My mother had come to California with me, and everything between us was fine until we went to the center one day to discuss my plans to check into the rehab program. We went back to the hotel, both very much on edge because the session hadn't gone well. My mom felt they weren't listening to her insisting that the center cover the cost of providing an interpreter for me. My family was increasingly opposed to my going to rehab at all. I was on TTY talking to Bill when my mom picked up the phone, disconnecting us, and threw the phone on the floor.

What happened next ended up as number five on my inventory of the worst moments in my life. It was January 12, day two of my new, self-induced detox program, and my body and emotions were a long way from understanding how to cope without drugs.

We fought, my mother and I, terribly—or, as she says, "We fought like idiots." At one point I pushed her, she fell on the floor and started crying. I was horrified, scared, apologizing, could not believe what had just happened. I thought I could never forgive myself for that moment. She left the next day. It would take a long time for me to forgive myself. And for her to forgive me. I don't ever expect her to forget this incident, and I don't blame her.

THE NEXT FEW weeks were a blur. I was packing for the Golden Globes; planning for a four-week, under-the-radar stay at Betty Ford; and spending a lot of time on the TTY with Bill, as his stint at the center was winding down. Next up for him was *Broadcast News,* which was going to be filming in D.C.

The tabloids had picked up that Bill was in rehab and that I had visited him there. He sent me a note on how he was going to handle it, and ultimately his publicist confirmed that, yes, he was at Betty Ford.

In those days, it wasn't considered such big news; there were a couple of brief mentions including one in the *New York Times* and a story in the *Star.* For the most part, though, he was able to handle it quietly. Internet gossip sites have changed the rules of engagement so radically in the years since that these sorts of stories have now become a staple for even more-celebrity-friendly magazines such as *People* and *US.* I am thankful it was a quieter time.

My parents came in for the Globes ceremony, which has been held forever at the Beverly Hilton Hotel. It's one of the looser awards shows with film and TV all under the same roof and more of a party atmosphere. The red carpet is short, crowded, and fun. I was wearing a simple black cocktail dress, with spaghetti straps and covered in sequins. It was beautiful and I felt beautiful in it.

Fans were crowding to get as near the red carpet as they could, and as I made my way along it, my mother remembers them chanting my name.

Happier times for Bill and me, Golden Globes, 1986

Tables at the Globes are always hard to come by, and the Hollywood Foreign Press uses just about every available inch of space so there is little room to move around. I sat with Randa and Jack at one, with my parents not far away.

We were definitely not at one of the prime tables—I remember because the walk to the stage when they announced my name was like making my way through a maze. That was a good thing; it gave me a few minutes to collect myself. I was truly shocked, just kept saying over and over to myself, I can't believe this, I can't.

Others in the room couldn't believe it either.

As Jack and I made our way past one of the tables near the front, at least one big-name celebrity was saying to his companion, "Who the fuck is Marlee Matlin?" I'm just as glad I couldn't hear that. Instead I felt completely surrounded by support. I could feel the applause. I could see so many faces smiling encouragement.

Jon Voight and Whoopi Goldberg were the hosts that year, and Jon had pulled Jack aside before the show started to ask him how to sign "We love you," in case I won. When I did, Jon delivered it with gusto!

When Randa leaned over and told me that they were calling my name, everyone at my table jumped up. "Oh my gosh!" were the first words out of my mouth.

When I say that I hadn't written a speech beforehand, I really mean I hadn't written a speech beforehand. All the way to the stage, I kept saying over and over, "I can't believe it!"

Jon handed me the Globe statuette and kissed my cheek. I held on tight and hoped that would help steady me as I said one more time, "I can't believe it!" I needed to buy myself a few moments more to collect my thoughts. As I looked out at the audience, this popped into my head: "Thank you, thank you so much. I'm not much of a speaker—he is," I said, pointing to Jack. The crowd roared.

I managed to get out a few thank-yous, to Randa, the producers, Paramount, my parents, Liz, and the cast and crew. It was short, simple, and truly all from the heart.

Backstage in the pressroom, it's just a crush of photographers and reporters, with a short window for questions and photos before you're whisked off and the next winner is marched in. It's fast, live, and you really don't want to make a mistake—a slip of the tongue can easily land on one of those endless video loops that haunt you forever.

One of the advantages at times like these of having someone interpreting what you're saying is that you have an extra breath between your signing and the interpreting, so meanings and words can be smoothed out. Over the years, Jack and I have done it so often that we have it down to a science.

It was a wonderful night and I never wanted it to end. Of course, it did, and Betty Ford was looming on the horizon.

I WOKE UP to a bright California morning not wanting to crawl out from under the covers. Even when the decision to go into rehab is completely and totally yours, as it was in my case, it's not easy. Even if you're stone-cold sober and it's been twenty-two days since you've used any drugs—me again—it's not easy.

No one else in my life was there that day. No one offered to take me, no one offered to go there with me. I was hoping that I wouldn't just crumble and disappear.

A late-afternoon flight to Palm Springs had been booked for me. My parents, and my Golden Globe, had headed back to Chicago; Jack had caught a flight back to New York where he was in graduate school still. I took a car to the airport alone with doubts and endless worries running circles around my brain. I spent most of the flight trying to rip off the rest of those damned red press-on nails.

When the plane landed, the old guy in the blue vest and the smile met me. It was late enough that I would soon have to go to sleep by myself in a strange place. That thought was terrifying. I felt empty.

I knew when we passed the Eisenhower Hospital that we were there. As I walked toward the entry, I kept telling myself, "Don't cry, don't cry."

Two counselors were waiting inside for me—Bill's, who to this day reminds me of Rock Hudson, and Jane, short with dark hair, pretty, serious. I remembered them from Family Week, and when I saw them, I just lost it.

I was crying, sobbing, shaking—then I stepped back. I must have looked as if I were planning an escape because they both came to me, reassuring me. Both of them said it was okay—to just let it all out. So I sobbed until there was nothing left.

From there I went to the nurse's office. She opened my suitcase in front of me. "What are you doing?" She was looking for drugs, but also Tylenol, mouthwash—she looked at everything. There was the urine test to take. I told them I wasn't high, but they'd heard that before. And medically, they needed to know whether to put me through detox first. I tested clean.

Then I went to my room. No frills, just two beds and a bathroom. I met my roommate, who hugged me and said. "This is your bed, the one by the door." No one gets a private room, but I didn't want to be alone anyway.

I felt like a little girl who was so lost. I remember thinking that I was going to let them help me, yet that was terrifying, too.

I was enough of a celebrity by then that I was getting recognized on the street, but I was hoping no one here would know who I was. I wondered if I would be the only Deaf person. I wondered if there would be anyone I could relate to—communicate with. I didn't have Jack with me; instead I had two total strangers—one during the day and the other at night—interpreting the most painful and emotional experiences of my life.

That night was my first AA meeting, too. An older woman was in the hallway outside my room, and Jane told her it was my first night there. The woman took my hand and said, "Welcome to the Betty Ford Center. I was a patient here once twenty years ago, and I've been sober since." I remember telling myself that I was going to do that, too—stay sober more than twenty years, just like her. And I have. Now I'm *working* on doubling that figure.

On that first day, late as it was, I was given a journal, and one of my assignments was to write about what I was feeling every single day—no exceptions. I flip through the journal now and can feel the ups and downs in my emotions as I moved through the treatment program:

"Today was a beautiful day . . . when I received a telegraph from Bill I felt elated. Made my day." On another day: "I was feeling a little worried about myself . . . will I understand all the things happening (and those that have happened) to me? I feel anxious, very anxious."

One frustrating day, I had to read aloud some of the work I'd been doing on the 12 Steps, the foundation of Alcoholics Anonymous, which anchors the treatment approach at Betty Ford. I felt Jane, my counselor, was being hard on me during that session. In my journal I tried to explain my feelings—it was not just a window into that moment, but my past:

> When I was asked to do the reading of my first step, I felt anxious, but concerned mainly about my speech. . . . All my life, when I want people to understand me, I have made a huge effort to speak clearly. I know you told me not to worry about the group . . . but I don't quite understand how I cannot worry about people when they're listening to me. As a child, I've been made fun of, teased, and pushed about my speech. It's not easy.

I also don't want to minimize the pull of drugs. Although I quit cold turkey, that doesn't mean it was ever easy. At my worst, I was probably doing an eight ball a week—that's three grams of coke.

I had nosebleeds. My heart would race, would beat so fast it would terrify me. When I couldn't sleep, I'd stay up all night, then the sun would come up. I hated, hated that part. That was the worst, seeing the sun come up and thinking, *Shit, I've been up all night.*

I still remember the taste of pot. I loved that taste. I loved Thai sticks, black hash, Red Hair, pot in any form. If you are an addict, you are an addict. It's not that you're never tempted again, you are. I am. But then I look at my life, my children, all the people I love, and I get through that hour, that day.

ᥫᩣ ᥫᩣ

MUCH OF MY time in rehab was spent dissecting how and why I feel the way I do. That constant examination is never easy, but I was learning things about myself. I was also finding new ways to cope with situations that had hurt me in the past.

One day a group of us were talking, and everyone else dissolved into laughter. I didn't get what was said and asked the woman next to me what was so funny. "Nothing." Whoa!

I asked her again, to see if she would hear what she was saying. Again she said, "Nothing."

I told them, "I've taken *nothing*s almost all my life, and I will not take that anymore." When I wrote about it in my journal, I went on to say, "I hate my deafness, but I've learned to accept it. Of course, not totally, maybe seventy-five percent or so. That took a lot of courage for me to speak out today."

I would begin to build on that courage from that day on.

THE WEEKENDS AT Betty Ford were hard for me; that's when visitors could come and I didn't have any.

Broadcast News was keeping Bill in D.C. I asked, but my brothers didn't come. Gloria didn't. Liz didn't. Only my dad would come, and it wasn't too successful. He started breaking down in the counseling sessions, crying and unable to go forward.

My mom, still reeling from our fight during Family Week with Bill, refused to come. Here's some of what she wrote me about her decision in a letter dated February 16, 1987:

> Just a little while ago, I talked with Jane, your counselor, and told her of my reasons for not coming. . . . I'm not feeling well and also your "sudden fame" has taken a toll on our family and the adjustment has been tremendous and also something I didn't tell is that I or I should say "we" meaning Dad and I, cannot afford to just pick up and come because you say "Come now!"
>
> I have bowed to you for too many years and I know now that I haven't been fair to myself or you. . . . I have

lived through your deafness far too long. It has given me some importance. Now is the time to get on with my own life and stop trying to live it through you.

I tried too hard for you—I should have relaxed and tried to enjoy you more and while I'm at it, given you more discipline, a good swift smack in the "behind" would have taken care of a lot of things.

I love you no matter what.

There is more. What this letter represents is the longest, most honest, in-depth discussion my mother has ever had with me. I wish that we had been able to use that as a starting point to create a different and better relationship with each other. It saddens me greatly to say that we haven't.

24

It seemed that a new face was showing up at rehab every day. When it happens, it feels as if you are starting all over again—a new round of someone else's pain to share, someone else to share your pain. More stories of the awful struggles people go through, the bottom that they've hit—often many times. It will all live somewhere in your subconscious forever. I tried to embrace it, but some days I was frustrated.

On day three, everything changed. Ruthie had arrived.

I remember the first time I saw her. Into the cafeteria walks this regal, tall, tall, tall, beautiful black chick, just scoping out the room. She had attitude—I liked that. She looked about my age. Finally, somebody I could maybe relate to.

Ruthie remembers, "I noticed Marlee was by herself and she seemed sad, really sad. I think I'm always drawn to underdogs. We just started talking—I was still bouncing—but the vibe from her was all this positive energy, and she was also very sure of herself, even in the sadness. I felt that energy, and I thought, 'This is someone I want to know, someone I can confide in.'"

Ruthie would become one of my best friends for life—we consider ourselves soul sisters and that's truly what we are. So many times she's just looked at me and known exactly what I was thinking, and I can look at her and decode her thoughts in a second. We got each other almost immediately.

The days at Betty Ford were structured—every minute is scheduled from 6 a.m. to 9:30 p.m., with lights out at 11:30. One of the best parts was the time after breakfast—7:30 to 8:30—that was set aside for the morning meditation walk.

The grounds are beautiful with a creek running through expansive, manicured, green lawns—you could mistake it for a country club. February was a perfect time to spend outside—the meditation in the summers must make you feel like you're in a sweat lodge.

Most mornings Ruthie and I would walk together—that is when you really get to know someone. You start telling them your stories, the gritty parts that you might not ever reveal in group sessions, and they tell you theirs.

We've always said it's a good thing we didn't know each other when we were doing drugs—we would have been dead! We are very, very influenced by each other to this day. If I ask her to do something, she does it. If she asks me for anything, she's got it.

And a really deep mischievous streak lives in both of us.

In the years since, we've done crazy things together. Mooned Sting and his wife Trudie on a winding Italian highway when our car passed theirs on the way to meet them for dinner. Spent two crazy weeks in St. Bart's one Christmas in which the "Maa-Ruu" song, blending our names into one crazy rap, was born:

> The Maa-Ruus, the Maa-Ruus, the Maa-Ruus are on the island.
> We don't need a mule, let the motherfuckers rule.
> Rule, Soul Sisters, rule!

We sang this at the top of our lungs a million times in those weeks as we cruised around St. Bart's outer reaches. Pure craziness! I'm sure everyone loved us!

There was the David Copperfield–paparazzi incident . . . more on that later. And during rehab, we helped one woman escape—sneaking with her into her husband's rental car, we all took it for a spin around the block. That was all she needed, not to leave forever, just for a little bit.

A SHORT NOTE near the end of my journal from February 10 reads, "I'm feeling anxious about the announcement for nominations for Academy Awards tomorrow. Then I hope to 'forget' about it during my stay . . . I want to put it away."

I knew the nominations were coming, but I didn't know what to expect. I had no idea how the process worked—between my näiveté and my seclusion from the real world at Betty Ford, I was completely oblivious of the industry's Oscar craziness. For that month, I was just Marlee Matlin from Morton Grove, Illinois, trying to get better.

Just after five thirty the next morning, my counselor Jane came in and woke me up. I remember I was startled: my first thought was that something had happened to my family. You know, that phone-call-in-the-middle-of-the-night feeling. My heart was beating so hard. "No, no, no, your family is okay," she said. "You have a phone call from Jack."

Getting through to me was no easy matter. A strict procedure governed phone calls—and random phone calls for residents at off hours were simply not tolerated. This is one of those times when I was grateful that Jack refused to give up. He says:

"I was watching the announcements on the little thirteen-inch TV in my dorm room at NYU, and they called Marlee's name. No one else knew where she was. I knew I would start getting flooded with calls from the studio, her publicist, the media. I had to get through to her.

"I called Betty Ford and said I have to talk to Marlee. They said, 'You can't.' I kept trying to convince them this was really an emergency. Finally, I said that she had just been nominated for an Oscar and I really had to talk to her."

Jane motioned for me to come with her. I put on my robe and walked over to the pay phone. The TTY was ready, and Jack and I had this short conversation—I have the fading roll of TTY paper still. Jack says:

"Is this Marlee?"

"Who else?" (Sorry, Jack, it was early, I was still half-asleep.)

"Well, I was looking for the actress in *Children of a Lesser God* who was nominated for Best Actress. Is that you?"

My heart just stopped.

Jack went on, "The actresses in that category are Jane Fonda, Sissy Spacek. Sigourney Weaver, you, and Kathleen Turner. The picture got five nominations."

"Thanks for calling. I'm gonna scream later. I have to go, we're not allowed phone calls. . . ."

This was the first time Jack and I had communicated since I'd checked in.

"Marlee, Lois [who was handling publicity for me] said there's something very important. She needs a comment from you. She's gotten around thirty calls already. How did you feel when you were informed?"

"I feel great, oh, God, this lady is telling everyone. . . . I feel great and elated and honored being in the same category with the other great artists. I feel good."

"You should, honey, you deserve it. . . ."

"I'm glad you're the one to tell me. I think Spacek will win."

"You already won, Marlee, you already won."

That is one of the reasons Jack and I have worked together for so long—at times he knows exactly the right thing to say.

Jane was standing right there and I looked at her and smiled, and she smiled. Later she wrote "Congratulations" in my journal.

After I'd hung up, Jane asked how I was feeling—emotional moments, even good ones, can be tough on addicts, even recovering ones. I said, "Pretty cool, pretty cool."

"Great," she said. "Now go back to your room, it's time to get ready for breakfast."

I told Ruthie, and thanks to the woman who had overheard some of the morning back-and-forth, the news was out and others offered me congratulations.

But it really slipped into the background pretty quickly.

My February 11 journal entry is filled with feelings, but it's all about rehab—the great group session when I was finally able to talk about the conflict I was having with someone else in the group; grief and sadness at one woman's painful story; frustration at how work on the Valentine's Day skit was going; more frustration at the AA lecture that night: "I'm so tired of hearing about alcohol. I'm a drug addict! I'm really looking forward to the NA [Narcotics Anonymous] meeting tomorrow."

∽ ∽

OUTSIDE, THE PRESSURE to reach me was reaching a boiling point. Everyone was calling and yelling at Jack. He stood firm. Day after day, he fielded calls.

"No, you can't talk to her. I'm sorry. She's away. She's not reachable. I can't help you." He must have used variations of that a hundred times. The studio was livid. Among the things I would miss was the London premiere of the movie—Princess Di and Prince Charles made it, but I couldn't?

Finally the pressure was too much. My publicity people told Jack I had to do at least one interview, for the *Los Angeles Times Magazine*. Everyone at the studio and on my publicity team was convinced if I did the interview, I would win the Oscar. It was critical; they demanded I agree. The cover story would feature Paul Newman and me—the actors the magazine was predicting would win that year.

Long negotiations took place with my counselors at Betty Ford to get them to agree to let me leave for a day. Thankfully none of them involved me; Jack handled that, too.

It was not just a matter of saying, yes, I would do the interview. Any number of logistical issues had to be dealt with to accommodate the interview and the photo session without letting anyone— especially the writer and the photographer—know that I was in rehab. And my counselors didn't want to see the progress I had made go up in smoke either.

Finally, we agreed that on February 21 I would be at the Palm Springs Marriott for the interview at 10:30 a.m. I got up and showered, then put on a nice outfit that I'd borrowed from Pattie, one of the women in my group. No designer duds that day. Jane, my counselor, was going to be with me to make sure I didn't stumble. Jack was flown in to handle the interpreting.

So the masquerade began.

My little plastic hospital bracelet was cut off. I would get a new one when we got back. I asked Jane who she would be. "Your girlfriend." We laughed at that.

I was scared—I didn't want to be found out. In a strange way I felt like a fugitive, too. I was outside, I could easily have just walked away. I wasn't even tempted. I wanted to go back, it was too much freedom, more than I was ready for.

Suddenly, you are all on your own and there is no one to hold your hand.

Still, I was so happy to see Jack. And the interview went well. I felt calm and good about myself. It amazed me that people wanted to know about me, who I was, where I'd come from. The toughest part was waiting for the photographer, who was two hours late. I was angry with him, but it did give me a chance to get a sense of how I would live outside Betty Ford.

When it was over and I got back into the car, I remember breathing a sigh of relief—all I wanted to do was get back to the center.

Walking back in felt like walking into a safe zone; it was like sucking my thumb and having my security blanket, too.

25

Twenty-six—the number of days I was at Betty Ford.

Fifteen—the number of letters Bill wrote me.

Two—the number of telegrams he sent.

At least this is what I've saved. There is even a note one counselor jotted down on a strip of paper torn from a legal pad: *Marlee, I called Bill, he also left a message—he said: Our love is more important than the nominations.*

We were apart while I was in Betty Ford, but far from disconnected. I tried not to, but I lived for any word from him. The letters usually left me feeling better—loved and optimistic—our TTY conversations often dissolved into fights. Old habits die hard.

As I read through the letters now, I can ride the waves of his emotions that month. And my own. I think back sometimes to the moment Randa asked me to describe what waves are like. I would describe them differently now—capturing the way they endlessly pound, over and over, eating away at whatever shoreline they hit.

Sometimes Bill would write a letter in the morning and another late at night when yet another thought would strike him. Mostly he wrote of love and support for my recovery. Sometimes he wrote about just ordinary things—how our cats, Otis and Bully, were doing, about the house he was living in during the *Broadcast News* filming in D.C., the weather. Sometimes he sent me prayers or meditations that had moved him, insights he was finding from his own recovery that he thought would help in mine.

In some of the letters he was trying to work through his feelings of jealousy and resentment at all of the critical notice I was getting for my performance in the film. In one, dated February 4, he finally congratulated me for the Golden Globe win. Apologizing that it was so late in coming. Amen.

On February 10, the day before the Academy Award nominations, his letter was filled with concern that he might not be able to handle it if I won an Oscar. That at twenty-one I was walking away with so much so fast while he had worked for so many years to get that sort of recognition. If the Oscar was awarded to me, he mused, it would serve as his ultimate humiliation, the innocent making him face his arrogance and pretension.

On February 10 he wrote again at midnight. It had just occurred to him that because of his *Kiss of the Spider Woman* Oscar as lead actor the previous year, he would be presenting the Oscar in the Best Actress category, which might be me. He was struck by the irony. He hoped he could be gracious.

On February 11 the nominations were announced. He tried to get through to my parents and finally got through to my sister-in-law—his conversation with her and his letter to me were all about how we were going to have to deal with this frightening time. Why did it have to be frightening?

On February 13–14, he wrote just at midnight, just a few words, asking me to be his Valentine.

On February 14 we talked by phone—he referred to it in his next letter as our own "St. Valentine's Day Massacre." The letter is dripping with sarcasm and bitterness—words underlined with instructions for me to "go look up" the definitions.

On February 17 he compares us to Cinderella and the prince going to the Oscars. The tone is light, the love is back. And I wonder how I did not go insane.

Though Bill and my first boyfriend, Mike, could not have been more different, the conflicts in the relationships in some ways boiled down to the same thing—what my success as an actress would mean for them. How would they bear that burden? Though I hadn't yet admitted it to myself, in my bones I knew my days with Bill were numbered.

ᏩᎤ ᏩᎤ

ON FEBRUARY 28 I left Betty Ford, which was harder and sadder than I had expected it to be.

I started that day's journal entry on a flight to Paris for the French premiere of *Children of a Lesser God*. My month of rehab was bookended by my new celebrity life. Here's what I was feeling:

> I'm scared about this. Going out to the crazy, zombie world. I want to function well. Will I? Will I go to meetings? I need them. . . .
>
> Bill and I had a terrible fight on the phone last night. My heart hurts . . . I'm tired of fighting. I love Bill, but he emotionally drains me. I'm scared of him.

In Paris, right after my stint at Betty Ford

In the phone call, he had told me I was prostituting myself for going to Paris to do publicity. I could never reconcile these particular rants since he did more than his share of high-profile interviews. But I was just so tired of trying to understand things like this.

I would go to AA meetings in Paris. I wanted to hold on to my sobriety. I wanted to reclaim my life.

Paris was cold, and sometimes rainy. It was hard for me to focus on much beyond trying to figure out how to be a normal human being again without losing all that I had learned during rehab. The premiere itself is a blur.

Jack, who went along as my interpreter, had spent days before the trip getting lists of all the expat AA meetings in the city. The one I attended was in the shadow of the Eiffel Tower, the room choking with thick smoke, a table filled with pastries, a bottomless pot of dark coffee, and generous people who wrapped me in emotional support.

26

THE FIFTY-NINTH ANNUAL Academy Awards. Monday, March 30, 1987. Dorothy Chandler Pavilion in downtown L.A. And I had an A-ticket to the show.

It was like stepping into an imaginary world that I'd seen at a distance for years. Suddenly I'm there and it's all turning out to be very real. Pinching yourself on these occasions helps, too!

In addition to my nomination, I'd been asked to be a presenter—for Best Achievement in Sound.

I thought that was funny; thank goodness someone attached to the show had a good sense of humor. Besides, I've never wanted to be treated with kid gloves.

Of course, some around me thought it was insulting and encouraged me to decline. No, no, no, no, no! The Academy wanted me to be a part of the pomp and ceremony, and I wasn't going to miss out on that for anything.

Theoni Aldredge would design my dress for the Oscars that year. It was the first time I'd worked with a designer, and Theoni had created many remarkable clothes over the years. This jeans-and-T-shirts girl was meeting a designer who'd already won three Tonys for her work on Broadway and an Oscar for her costume designs for *The Great Gatsby* in 1975.

I was so happy that she took on the project and so anxious to get started that I don't think I ever thanked Theoni properly. My time at Betty Ford, then the trip to Paris to promote the film, had left us with little more than three weeks to get everything done before the show. Luckily, Jennifer Beals was helping me with all the Oscar prep, too . . . I love that girl.

Famed Hollywood and Broadway costume designer Theoni Aldredge has won numerous honors in her long career. This is the drawing she gave me of the dress she designed for me to wear to the 1987 Academy Awards when I won an Oscar for Children of a Lesser God.

Whatever Theoni designed, I knew I wanted to use my favorite color—purple. From the palest whisper of lilac to the deep richness of eggplant, it's a happy color for me, a good strong color; it can feel tough and feminine at the same time, maybe a little like me. Theoni envisioned a lace dress and sent me samples in different shades—I went with soft lavender—along with lovely sketches of long, fitted sleeves, a tight bodice disappearing into a cummerbund of lavender ribbons that opened into a sweeping skirt with lots of swing and swish to it. The design had a blend of romance and elegance that I loved.

(If you're wondering how I stacked up in the celebrity constellation at this point in my career, I should mention that the sketches she sent over were addressed to Marlee Martin . . . oh, well.)

Meanwhile, back in New York I stayed busy. I was trying to hit a lot of AA meetings, and the studio wanted to make up for lost time on the publicity front. I also made frequent trips to D.C. since production on *Broadcast News* was in full swing.

Bill and I seemed to have reached a sort of détente in those weeks, tentatively stepping around each other in our newly sober lives. He had gotten his son, Alex, a dog, a big furry beast, a border collie name Maggie, one of the sweetest dogs ever and a great distraction whenever the tension would start building between us.

I was also trying to arrange for my family to make it to L.A. for the Academy Awards show—and I defined family as my mom and dad; my brothers, Marc and Eric; my sister-in-law, Gloria; my nephew, Zach; my hairdresser, Dennis; and of course Liz. Plus Jack was coming to interpret, and he wanted to bring his mom and dad, Sarah and Benny, and brother Sam, too. That meant a request for eleven extra tickets. We got them all.

Getting ready for the Oscars, 1987

Bill and I were booked into the Bel-Air Hotel, and on the morning of the awards show my family came over so we could get ready together. At the last minute I decided to wear my hair up, with curls on top, and at the last second my hairdresser, a dear friend who has since died of AIDS, put in a sprig of baby's breath. I had a new pair of oversize, black, horn-rimmed glasses that I'd just picked up that week. When I debated ditching the glasses, Bill looked at me and said with more than a little sarcasm. "You're not a model." So the glasses stayed.

The look would land me on a few Worst Dressed lists. Cringe, I hate that. But if you try to overthink the fallout from fame in Hollywood, it will drive you completely crazy. Besides, there will always be another dress, another show.

As the day wore on, tensions between my family and Bill were rising. As Gloria put it, "No one can suck joy out of a room quite like William." My mom describes his angry eyes as "shooting daggers," with long silences broken by uncomfortable attempts at conversation.

The cloud lifted for the red-carpet walk into the Dorothy Chandler Pavilion. We were the couple of the moment. The media was in love with the plotline—couple meets and falls in love on film set, now they arrive on this day each with an Oscar nomination, and, as Bill had long ago figured out, if I won, he would be presenting the award to me. The three of us—Jack was interpreting—made our way along the crush of reporters, photographers, and a long string of bleachers overflowing with fans.

It's hard not to feel your spirits lift in moments like these. There is such a connection—the feeling that it takes all of you together, the combined energy of the stars, the crowd, the photographers, the reporters, to make the moment electric. I have always been so grateful to my fans, they have extended such sincerity to me through the years that never ceases to touch me. I keep waiting to get tired of all of it, but I never do.

Inside the auditorium my family and Jack's were tucked away in the farthest reaches of the balcony, but at least they were there! Chevy Chase, Goldie Hawn, and Paul Hogan were cohosts for the evening. Everywhere I turned, major stars were greeting one another. I wanted to be a part of that club.

A CONFESSION. WHEN you're up for an award, try as you might, it's hard to concentrate on the show. The Oscars usually runs a bit over three hours—the longest three hours of my life, not counting labor and childbirth.

But finally it was time. Bill was behind the lectern, reading the names of all the nominees. There was the envelope. Snap, the seal was broken. I couldn't hear it, but I swear I could feel it.

And the winner is . . . he said my name, then used my name sign. And that's when I knew for sure. My stomach dropped. I had, against all odds, won.

The other nominees in my category were all established stars, and the performances that year were extremely strong. The odds-on favorite to win going into the night had been Kathleen Turner for *Peggy Sue Got Married.* I had thought it might go to Sissy Spacek for *Crimes of the Heart,* in a performance I'd loved. The other nominees in the category were Jane Fonda for *The Morning After,* and Sigourney Weaver for *Aliens.* To be standing in the company of these women was amazing.

The applause erupted as I got up and made my way to the stage. The camera panning the other nominees focused on Jane Fonda, who was smiling and saying, "Isn't that wonderful," and looking as if she absolutely meant it. When you work in Hollywood, you collect memories like these, or at least I do—those moments of spontaneous kindness that feel absolutely real.

I wasn't sure how to approach Bill. I tried to block out all the time he'd spent in recent weeks examining and reexamining the emotional toll my winning would take on him.

Play it safe, Marlee, keep it professional. I stuck out my hand to shake his—he took it, then pulled me in for a quick, gentle kiss. I breathed a sigh of relief. Maybe everything would be okay.

Meanwhile Jack had quickly and as discreetly as possible gotten to his position, too, just a little below the podium. At first the producers had wanted Jack to stay in his seat with a microphone in hand. That was crazy! Jack explained why that wouldn't work—we actually have to be able to see each other to communicate—so he and the producers came up with a compromise that put him on the steps leading up to the stage.

Emotions were welling up inside me as I looked out at what felt like the entire entertainment industry. I wanted to savor this moment. Just two years ago, almost to the day, I had been onstage in a small Chicago theater with a minor role in an independent production of *Children of a Lesser God.* Now I had an Oscar in my hand. Dreams do come true.

Once again the speech was simple—I thanked my family, Randa, the producers, the cast and crew, though this time I singled out Bill for the quality of his artistry, his mastery of the craft, which is exceptional still to this day. I ended with two signs—for "Thank you" and "I love you"—then made my way backstage, where Goldie Hawn grabbed me and gave me the biggest, warmest hug.

In the chaos backstage I felt a tap on my shoulder and whirled around. It was Elizabeth Taylor. I had to keep my jaw from dropping to the floor. Talking to her even just for a moment was mind-blowing.

Great moments like that were sprinkled throughout the night. *Variety*'s celebrity columnist Army Archerd learned to sign "Congratulations" before the show in case I won, then used it when he saw me. Later that night at a party, both Sissy and Sigourney were so gracious and generous in their good wishes, too.

That didn't mean everyone was on my side—the New York *Daily News* film critic Rex Reed wrote a scathing piece telling Academy voters that they would be wasting their vote on me. I wasn't "acting," I was merely a Deaf girl playing a Deaf girl. He predicted that if I won, it would be a fluke, there would be no career for Marlee Matlin.

I've got to be honest—that hurt like hell. You try not to take that sort of criticism to heart, but it's not easy. But by the way, Rex, I was not even close to giving up on Hollywood, and it wasn't through with me either.

I am still the youngest woman to win an Oscar in the category Actress in a Leading Role, and one of only a handful to win an

Kiss my ass, Rex!

Oscar in their debut performance. I love the precision of the Academy on this: I was specifically twenty-one years and 218 days old on Oscar night.

The next youngest was Janet Gaynor, at twenty-two years and 222 days, when she won hers, the first year the Academy Awards were held. Most of the rest of the younger winners were in their midtwenties, and among my contemporaries I'm pleased to be counted with Hilary Swank, who was twenty-five when she won for *Boys Don't Cry,* and Jodie Foster, who was twenty-six when she was recognized for *The Accused.*

I also remain the only Deaf person to have won an acting Oscar. In the more than twenty years since I won my Oscar, with so many talented Deaf actors, I had hoped other Deaf actors would have joined that league. The talent is there, the opportunity should be.

When you're standing up there in the lights, heart pounding, Oscar in hand, there's always someone you fail to mention. I think it's just the nature of these awards shows. Everyone has their story; mine is Jack.

Although we met after *Children of a Lesser God* had wrapped, by then we'd been working together closely for more than a year. He was a great, steady presence in my life and in my work, but I didn't think to mention him that night. His father, who until then had pretty much adored me, was deeply hurt that I had overlooked his son. It would be a couple of years before he completely got over it. Thankfully Jack didn't expect it. He was completely focused on being a part of the Oscars, his voice playing to an audience of millions; he was having a blast.

Meanwhile, despite incredibly tight security, somehow my entire family managed to talk their way into one of the pressrooms backstage. My publicist at the time, Alan Burry, looked at all these milling Matlins and said, "What is this? Ma and Pa Kettle go to the Oscars?" Hey, I loved having them there. Their love and support has always been important to me, but on this night it meant the world.

BACKSTAGE I WAS also waiting for word on who would win Best Actor. Bill was nominated, as well as Paul Newman for *The Color of Money,* Bob Hoskins in *Mona Lisa,* James Woods in *Salvador,* and Dexter Gordon in *Round Midnight.* I know, looking back now, that Bill's chances of winning back-to-back Oscars in the same category were small. As many had predicted, the Oscar went to Paul Newman. I don't think he was there that night, and I'm sad that I never had a chance to meet him.

Oscar night is always a long night for winners. There are the mass interview sessions, where you face a huge, hungry pack of reporters asking questions. There are hundreds of photographers—so many bulbs flashing that you can literally feel the heat they generate as you get close to the room. Then you hit the television press. There's the Governor's Ball and the round of parties after. All in all it's exhausting, but in a terrific, this-really-rocks kind of way.

The interviews and Governor's Ball over, I slipped into the back of our limo, kicked off my shoes, laid the Oscar by my side, and finally relaxed, letting it all sink in. Though it was late, we were headed to Spago's on the Sunset Strip to catch the tail end of Swifty

Lazar's annual Oscar bash. Bill got in and sat across from me, and what happened next will forever be etched into my memory.

"Well, you've got that little man beside you," he said, nodding at the Oscar.

"Yes."

"What makes you think you deserve it? There are hundreds of actors who have worked for years for the recognition you just got handed to you. Think about that."

My face just fell. I was stung, crushed, hurt. A churn of emotions was running through me.

I had hoped for better from Bill, that he would have had enough love and empathy on that day to allow himself to be happy for me, just this once. When Jack got in the limo, Bill turned to him and asked him to start looking into getting me enrolled in core classes at NYU right away. This was crazy. My head was absolutely spinning. I didn't have the energy to analyze what that implied.

I got little sleep that night. I had an early interview poolside at the Bel-Air with *Good Morning America.* When we'd wrapped that, my mother arrived, purse in one hand and toting my Oscar like a dumbbell in the other.

"What do you want me to do with this, Marlee?" she said just as she walked past Kathleen Turner. I cringed, figuring Kathleen would probably have a suggestion or two about what she could do with it. . . .

The next day, Bill headed back to the East Coast, while my family and the Oscar headed back to Chicago. Gloria, seven-year-old Zach, and Jack all stayed over an extra day, and we celebrated by going to Disneyland. We checked out of the Bel-Air Hotel that morning and stayed in a Howard Johnson motel that night.

At Disneyland, I think we rode all the rides at least once, screamed on the Matterhorn, giggled through Pirates of the Caribbean, ate junk food until we were ready to explode, waited in line with everyone else, and laughed all day long. It was one of the best days ever. I'd highly recommend it to any Oscar winner postceremony; it plants your feet right back down on the ground.

27

In 1987, HOLLYWOOD wrapped me in its embrace. On January 30, the day before the Golden Globes, Paramount Pictures and *Life* magazine came together to do a photo shoot celebrating the studio's seventy-fifth anniversary. More than sixty of the studio's stars of film and television came to participate, and I was invited to be a part of it. I was thrilled. I headed to JFK Airport for the flight to L.A.

There's always time to kill in an airport, and while Jack and I were waiting, I noticed a girl about my age with her head buried in a book, and a stack of more books beside her. She was striking—with a mass of dark curls, a fantastic leather jacket, and jeans. I looked harder. "Oh my gosh, Jack, it's Jennifer Beals from *Flashdance*. I've got to meet her."

She was going to Yale at the time, and I didn't know what she was majoring in, but I knew she was a photographer and the book she was studying was about photography. I was hesitant to disturb her, but I wasn't going to pass up this chance.

I walked up and said, "Hi, I'm Marlee Matlin." She looked up, smiled, and said. "Nice to meet you," then went back to studying. After we boarded the plane, she slept most of the flight.

I was starstruck, really starstruck.

When we saw each other again at the big bash for Paramount, somehow we connected like old girlfriends, as if we'd known each other for years and years. She's from Chicago, too—I think if you have those Chicago roots, there's just something about the city that binds you together. Although Jennifer will razz me that she's really from Chicago, I'm just from the burbs.

The stars that Paramount assembled that day were unbelievable, from Robin Williams to older stars such as Fred MacMurray, Jimmy Stewart, Bob Hope, and Elizabeth Taylor. It was crazy. Robert De Niro, Danny De Vito, Al Pacino, and Gregory Peck were milling around. And of course, Henry was there. He'd just about grown up on the Paramount lot for years along with the rest of the *Happy Days* cast.

There I was, one moment talking to Olivia Newton-John, and John Travolta walks up, and I thought, *Wow* Grease *and* Saturday Night Fever*! Right here, talking to me.*

"Don't I know you?" John asked.

"No," I said, knowing that was something I would have remembered.

"Are you sure we don't know each other?"

"Yes, I'm sure!"

Then Olivia stepped in, playfully telling John to get over it, accept it, we had never met!

Life magazine was doing lots of smaller setup shots, and they took a photo of me and Buddy Rogers, who had starred in the 1927 film *Wings,* the first Best Picture winner ever. He could finger-spell and told me about a friend of his from back home who had attended the Kansas school for the Deaf. I saw Karl Malden from *Streets of San Francisco* and thought about how my dad and I used to watch it when I was growing up.

It was so high wattage when it came to Hollywood royalty in the room that everybody was meeting someone he or she was awestruck by, so I didn't feel alone. Robin Williams and Tom Cruise were talking and teasing each other up on a podium and motioned to me to come on up. I was trying to breathe, thinking, *My goodness, Tom Cruise! My goodness, Robin Williams!* In front of *everybody* they asked me to teach them a few cuss words in sign language.

So what's a girl to do? I showed them how to sign a couple of the juicier ones, and they just broke up laughing, and of course Robin immediately began trying to use them in a dirty joke. And me, I was on cloud nine—I mean, I'm this girl from Chicago, I was nobody, I was one of the people who paid money to see these people work, and now here I was standing in between them. It was unbelievable.

When it was time for the big photo of everyone, we were each given a number, and I think it was random. I got number fifty-three and I went to check out my chair and found I was in the front row! Jennifer came up and said, "Oh my God, we're almost next to each other."

She was number fifty-five. We had no idea who was sitting in between us, so she sat down next to me and we were like girls in high school gossiping about everyone. "Oh, look at them. Oh, he's so cute. Oh, *he's* not so cute. She's so nice, but *she's* not so nice. . . ."

Then we looked up and there was Harrison Ford, holding his number in his hand, staring down on us. "I'm number fifty-four."

Jennifer just smiled and said, "Oh, you know what, we wanted to sit next to each other. Do you mind if we just switch seats?"

He looked at us and said again, "I'm fifty-four."

We just looked at each other, then back at him, and said, "But we really want to sit together."

He just kept standing there, staring at us, and said again, "I'm number fifty-four," completely calm, but not budging.

Then Danny DeVito, who was sitting on the other side of me, chimed in and said, "Oh, let the girls sit together."

So in the photo that *Life* ran in its big Hollywood issue in April 1987, on one side of the front row you'll see Danny DeVito, then me, Jennifer, and finally Harrison Ford, all smiling.

Tom Cruise was great to me that day and has always been so every time we've seen each other. He takes the time to make sure I understand him word for word when he speaks. I went up to him years later at the Santa Monica Airport's Barker Hangar, which is a popular space for events. He was there with his family and his two kids, and I was there for a birthday party. I wanted to say hello, but I didn't want to intrude on his family time.

Finally, after much debate, I walked over with my husband, Kevin, and said, "I just wanted to say hi, I'm Marlee." He gave me one of those big Tom Cruise smiles, said, "Hey!" and hugged me. He immediately turned around and introduced me to his mother and his kids. He's always been genuine. I've never seen him as the "big movie star," just decent and kind and absolutely focused on whomever he's talking to.

APRIL WAS A whirlwind month. I flew to Chicago to make an appearance at the Center on Deafness and the Arts. What a great reunion that was, and I loved talking to the kids about their hopes and dreams. If I could give even one of them the kind of encouragement Henry gave me all those years ago, I wanted to do so.

Things were looking up on the career front. A number of projects were being sent my way to consider, and I had already signed on to join the cast of *Walker,* starring Ed Harris. At the end of the month I was headed to Nicaragua, where production was getting under way.

Before leaving, I was part of ABC's *Happy Birthday Hollywood* extravaganza, a massive show celebrating the industry's first hundred years, with movie clips and dozens of huge Broadway-style production numbers. Hundreds of stars from over the years were featured, so many that it dwarfed the Paramount party, and many of them were performing set pieces that were seeded throughout the show.

I was asked to be a part of the segment they did on Hollywood heroines through the years. We were all dressed in these Victorian-style, white, floor-length dresses, posed in and around an old-fashioned gazebo. Ally Sheedy introduced the group, and after everyone had been highlighted, she walked center stage and said, "And now I want to introduce the latest addition, Marlee Matlin, this year's Academy Award winner."

I took a deep breath and I spoke as I signed, "There's one actress who's a heroine to all of us . . . Miss Katharine Hepburn."

I was so nervous about how I sounded, but I know from friends who've watched the show that I sounded pretty much like anyone else. When you're a Deaf person speaking aloud, that's exactly what you're going for—normal, ordinary, anything but different.

28

Nicaragua—so much beauty, so much poverty, and a war was going strong in 1987 when I landed there for *Walker.*

Sandinistas, teenagers really, with AK-47s casually slung over their shoulders, were always around. Kids and dogs, equally skinny, roamed the streets. Remnants of houses and buildings, half-crumbled by the 1977 earthquake, were still visible in the city and the countryside.

I hadn't really realized until then how much we take for granted in America. Children were living on the street, begging for money. The people were so impoverished. So much sadness was there, but a lot of pride, too.

We stayed in Managua at the Intercontinental Hotel, and buses and taxis shuttled us back and forth each day to Granada, a little town of about four thousand where director Alex Cox had chosen to shoot the film. The route was so choked with traffic that a horse pulling a cart, women carrying baskets, men crowded on a flatbed truck, were not uncommon sights. The road was a nightmare, pitted by potholes that looked like craters. It usually took more than an hour to make the drive there with our driver dodging the holes and the people like an NFL running back.

The country was still suffering under a U.S. embargo, with ongoing skirmishes between the Sandinista and U.S.-backed contra rebels, mostly to the north of us. Two of the production's drivers lost sons to the fighting while the film was being shot.

In a bizarre way it was the perfect setting to film the story of William Walker, a renegade American who was a bit crazy, who'd invaded the Central American country around 1855. He ultimately declared himself president and ran the country for a couple of years before being kicked out. After two failed attempts to return to the country, he was finally executed in Honduras.

I had been intrigued by the idea of working with Alex Cox; his film *Sid and Nancy* was one of my favorites. *Walker* was a smaller independent film with a $6 million budget, but in addition to the appeal of Alex, Ed Harris was starring, and he was on my short list of actors I really wanted to have a chance to work with.

Alex and I first met in New York to talk about the movie when he was still casting the film. I should say, we tried to meet.

He walked into the hotel lobby, all coiled intensity, glanced at me, but then started running around, searching for this mystery actress he was supposed to meet. It was before *Children of a Lesser God* had come out, so I was a long way from recognizable.

He'd spotted someone who looked about the right age and remembered thinking to himself, *That can't be her, she seems to be talking on the phone, but I wish it were. The woman is just so tremendously sprightly and interesting and beautiful.*

What he didn't see, at least initially, was that I was on the phone with a little help from Jack.

I wasn't sure what to expect either. I noticed a tall, skinny guy with long red hair and a droopy handlebar mustache. He was running around the lobby, wearing an old T-shirt, a bandanna, and a floppy hat. I thought, *That cannot be him.*

But then we locked glances and it clicked for both of us at exactly the same time—Oh, *you're* Marlee! Oh, *you're* Alex!—and we both started laughing.

I immediately felt comfortable with him. Alex was so passionate about the project, but also very much an actor's director—despite all that intensity—patient, working from something deep inside him. I knew I could trust him. As for the running around, well, I would see a lot more of that on set.

Alex has more energy than I've ever seen. No wonder he stays thin, he would race around the set talking to this person, checking on that shot. One of my favorite memories is when he was really pleased with a take, his face would just light up and he'd tell us,

"Brilliant, now *that* was brilliant!" You couldn't help but catch that enthusiasm.

My character was based on Walker's fiancée, Ellen Martin, who had actually been Deaf. Ed and I would be signing during my scenes, but unlike in *Children of a Lesser God,* where Bill's character essentially served as the translator, putting words to my signing, Alex planned to use subtitles. I liked that idea.

He had gotten the backing of the Nicaraguan government—some of its high-level officials had read and approved the script. That backing made just about anything possible. When Alex asked if the telephone and power lines could come down for the duration of the production so that the town would look much as it did a hundred years ago—down they came. Many of the streets were still unpaved, but a layer of dirt was trucked in to cover the central square.

Just about everything for the production had to come from outside the country, and because of the embargo, nothing could be shipped directly from or through the United States. The guns the soldiers carried in the film came from London via Russia. Even things as basic as toilet paper and the nails used to construct the sets, including a huge one that replicated San Francisco Bay on the shores of Lake Nicaragua, where Granada was nestled, were shipped in.

The days were long and hot, and the costumes were authentic—that translated into heavy wool. Some days I thought I would melt into nothing by the end of the day. The production was long, but my role as Walker's fiancée was small—she dies unexpectedly in a cholera epidemic. So in the end, I would spend less than a month there.

The character as written is feisty and significant to the story. She is Walker's moral compass, the one adviser he truly trusts. I liked that she was strong, smart, and outspoken with Walker. Her death becomes a turning point in his life and triggers his spiral toward obsession. The script was one part historical drama and one part black comedy—I hoped we could pull it off.

I spent a week filming, then went back to the States for a week for an event in New York I couldn't miss. When I came back to Nicaragua, I was armed with a bunch of baseballs to give out to the kids that hung around the set every day—baseball was a national passion there—and $20 bills to buy food and other necessities from one of the few stores in Managua that was well stocked and only took U.S. dollars.

The per diem money came in giant stacks that were incredibly hard to handle. At the end of my time there I gave my remaining per diem to my driver—a stack of the local currency, córdoba bills, that was about ten inches high. He broke down in tears, and someone told me later that I'd given him the equivalent of a year's salary.

It was a good thing we were all passionate about the film because the creature comforts were few. There were no trailers; we all changed clothes in the back of the same trucks that were used to cart in supplies. The people were wonderful, but the food . . . well, it wasn't great. A lot of the cast and crew were hit with bouts of intestinal viruses from the food and water there. I was spared. Jack wasn't.

One day we were shooting in the forest and Jack told me he was dying, really dying; he had to get to a bathroom right away. The Porta Potties set up for the production were, I'll admit, pretty disgusting. "I can't even go in there," he said.

His face was pale and getting paler. He was drenched in sweat and not just from the heat. I looked around and pointed a little deeper into the forest. "Just go in there, I'll come back for you in five minutes."

Jack is an incredible trouper in many ways. He can face down huge crowds, hostile reporters, angry studio execs. He cannot, however, use the bathroom in the great outdoors. I came back in a few minutes. He looked even more miserable and said, "I can't. I just can't."

So Jack went off in search of better facilities, and I fended for myself that day. Luckily the people of Granada had embraced the production. A family took Jack in for the day, gave him the use of their bathroom, which was modest but clean, fed him Pedialyte to keep him from getting more dehydrated, and let him sleep there through the afternoon.

ᘏᗢ ᘏᗢ

On set with Ed Harris

ED HARRIS—WHAT CAN I say? He is the ultimate professional, always working on the craft, absolutely disappearing inside his character. And in case you haven't noticed—great, expressive, beautiful eyes, and an amazing smile. I adored working with him.

I can look back now at the scenes we had together and they feel completely organic. He didn't have to sign extensively, but he handled it so naturally, nothing ever felt forced.

In one scene Walker comes back and finds that Ellen has died. I'm laid out in a coffin, a rosary in my hands. I remember lying there, sweating in that wool dress with its long sleeves, high collar, and floor-length skirt, eyes closed, rosary clutched in my hands, and praying, *praying* that none of my Jewish forebearers were looking down and seeing me!

Without meaning to, I got caught up in international politics for a brief flash while I was there. Whenever I shoot in other countries or visit them, I try to take a trip to the local schools, and Deaf schools if they have them.

On my second day in Nicaragua, I spent some time at a school for the Deaf in Managua—La Escuela Centro Especialidad. I came to see the children, who were so sweet and put on a terrific performance for me.

I learned two lessons that day. One, never forget that sign language is different in different counties—I found out that the way we in American sign a *T* is an obscene gesture there. And never underestimate the power of mixing Hollywood and politics.

I went to the school to meet the children, but Nicaraguan president Daniel Ortega also came by to present me with an award. Suddenly the school was a crush of reporters and photographers, and no one wanted to shoot pictures of me with the kids.

A simple visit had turned into a political event. By morning, photos of Ortega and me were splashed across newspapers both in the United States and throughout Mexico and Central America. I'm at my most informal—wearing a *Walker* T-shirt, my hair in a ponytail—smiling and talking to the leader of a country with nothing but bad relations with my own. Suddenly everyone wanted to

Who would have thought that an innocent visit to a school for the Deaf would trigger an international incident with President Daniel Ortega of Nicaragua an me? (Credit: Julio Donoso/CORBIS SYGMA)

know my politics, what I thought about the embargo, Ortega. I was getting hounded by the press; requests for interviews were piling up.

It got so crazy, the production organized a press conference. I agreed, hoping to be able to talk about the film and my character, but no one was interested in *Walker* or Ellen Martin. What they wanted to know was why an Oscar-winning actress was meeting with the president of Nicaragua. There had to be something more to the story than that I wanted to visit a local school for Deaf children.

The day of the press conference, the room was packed not by entertainment journalists, but by political reporters from all over. I was hammered with questions. What were my politics? Did I support the Sandinistas? How well did I know Ortega? What did I think of the U.S. position on the war here? It was crazy.

The entire time, photographers' flashbulbs were going off. After a while, I simply couldn't take it anymore. I threw up my hands and asked Jack to end it. Just end it.

29

Random question—why do they call them Secret Service agents since you can pick them out of a crowd in a heartbeat?

In May 1987, I was in Los Angeles at the Four Seasons Hotel at a fund-raiser for the Jewish Home for the Aging, where my grandmother Rose was now living.

I spotted these guys with close-cropped hair in crisp, blindingly white shirts, dark suits, ties, and black earpieces with cords snaking down and disappearing inside their coats, milling around in one of the hallways. I looked at Jack and said, "I bet the president is here. I want to meet him."

"You can't do that, you can't just walk up and say, 'I want to meet the president!'" But that's exactly what I did.

I walked over, tapped an agent on the shoulder, and said, "Hi, I'm Marlee Matlin and I'd really like to meet the president and I need to be able to tell him a little story."

After a brief discussion among the Secret Service agents— thankfully one of them was a fan and decided I was not a national security threat—one of them disappeared behind a doorway.

In a flash, Jack and I were escorted into this room, flanked by Secret Service, and there was former president Gerald Ford, smiling.

We shook hands and he said, "Marlee, both Betty and I loved you in *Children of a Lesser God.*"

I was beaming and said, "I just wanted to tell you that I have always been and will forever be grateful to your wife for opening up the Betty Ford Center, because I was there for my own drug addiction. I've been sober now for more than four months!"

"Well, congratulations. I'm proud of you for taking care of yourself," he said. "Betty will be so pleased to hear."

Years later, I would meet President Reagan in an equally random way. I was getting my hearing aid adjusted at the House Ear Institute in L.A. Suddenly they started clearing everyone out of the building. Former president Reagan was due in a few minutes. Dr. House asked if I wanted to meet him and said he'd be glad to introduce me.

Then the hallway was filled with the dark suits and white shirts . . . and I saw President Reagan standing in a dark gray suit, and I remember his hair was as black as night.

Dr. House came out and introduced me, saying, "This is Marlee Matlin, who won an Academy Award for *Children of a Lesser God*."

President Reagan sort of looked at me . . . he was a big, tall guy, then he smiled and said, "Well, I never won one of those."

IN JUNE 1987, I got a call from Jennifer Beals—we had stayed in touch after the Paramount bash and tried to get together whenever our schedules would let us. She'd just finished her final photography project at Yale, with a special exhibition scheduled of her work.

She invited me and Jack up to Westport to stay with her over the July Fourth holiday and see the exhibition. I was vague, maybe I could, maybe I couldn't.

By now, Bill had bought a house in Snedens Landing. This beautiful home was in an even more beautiful area in the Hudson River valley that was a popular enclave for both artists and actors. Snedens Landing was quiet, surprisingly remote despite being just about a half hour from midtown Manhattan. It should have been the most peaceful place, surrounded by nature so that all your cares can just melt away. I dreaded it. The place and its remoteness frightened me.

On July Fourth, Jack went to visit Jennifer, relaying my apologies—plans with Bill that I couldn't cancel. Really, we were just spending the weekend in Snedens Landing. He was never interested in meeting my friends.

The following day was a typical, hot East Coast summer day with humidity so thick you could cut it with a knife. That morning I was watching *Sid and Nancy,* feeling so drawn to the film, and of course it felt different watching it now that I had worked with the director, Alex Cox.

I don't remember when or how the fight started; what I know is that I have never been as scared in my life before or after that day.

The struggle turned violent. I was afraid I might not survive. I pulled myself free and ran to the phone. I called Christine Vericker. She was married to Bill's AA sponsor and had become a good friend. They lived not too far away.

Before I could say anything, Bill yanked the phone out of my hand and slammed it down. I said a quick prayer, thanking God that he hadn't ripped it out of the wall. Minutes later I broke free again, grabbed the phone again, and called Christine. This time the call went through. I sobbed, "Please come get me, please. Hurry, please."

Bill turned on his heel and stormed out of the house.

Christine immediately dispatched her husband, Billy, to pick me up. She thought that if anyone could reason with Bill, he could.

It was a little like what I imagine you do in a fire or a flood or some other emergency when you only have a few minutes to get out. I grabbed a small bag, stuffed a few things in it, got my purse, nothing else. I left almost everything I owned there, including my cat, Otis.

I barely remember crawling into Billy's car or the ride to the Verickers' house. So many emotions were coursing through me. How had the love between Bill and me turned into this? Why were we killing each other this way? How could we ever patch things up after today?

Deep down, I knew the only way to recover from this day would be for me to never go back to him. That was a great, great sadness.

Christine remembers, "It was a hot, hot day, and Marlee came in crying these huge sobs, and she was shaking. She was wearing a jean jacket so she was completely covered up. I thought she should go to a hospital, but she refused. She was worried that someone would recognize her, that Bill would find out."

Christine insisted I see a doctor anyway and called her ob-gyn, Dr. Robert Gallo, and asked if he would examine me right away. He agreed.

Dr. Gallo remembers, "Christine had called my wife and explained the situation. I was going to do an assessment, make sure there was no major trauma. Marlee was upset and embarrassed—she cried during the exam but had clearly been crying a lot beforehand. She asked me not to say anything to anyone, and I assured her I wouldn't and I haven't spoken of it until this day.

"There were fresh bruises on her arms and her face, but no major tissue trauma. I felt my role at that point was more of moral support and to assure them there were no major medical issues."

I felt lost. The kindness of those around me—Christine, Billy, Dr. Gallo—helped. But I did not know how I was going to get through the next twenty-four hours, the next week, much less how I was going to rebuild my life.

I called my sister-in-law, Gloria, that night around ten and said, "I need you, Glo," and asked her to come as soon as she could. She did; she got on a plane that night and landed around 2 a.m.

In the days after that, Jack would go over to Bill's and pack up my clothes, my life. I knew I couldn't let myself go back—ever. I was terrified for two reasons: we would in all likelihood fight again, or just as bad, I might not have had the strength to leave.

In a stroke of luck, Jack had just rented an apartment on Waverly Place in Greenwich Village, but hadn't yet moved over from student housing at NYU. He stayed at the university and let me have the apartment instead.

It was a huge studio loft that Gertrude Stein had once lived in. Right below was the Coach House, the legendary restaurant that got a mention in *Prince of Tides* and was famous for scrumptious American fare and was a longtime favorite of James Beard's when he was alive. The smells that would sometimes waft upstairs were heavenly.

The loft was right across from Washington Square Park. The floor slanted wildly toward the front of the building, and I would sit there, curled up, looking out the window and trying to figure out my new life.

Gloria and Jack helped me set up the apartment and buy all the basics. Gloria remembers, "It was a very emotional time for her and also for me. We did have some fun that week. We did a lot of walking, eating, and laughing. I felt like we had the chance that week to get reacquainted. As I was leaving, Marlee said, 'You need to have another baby, you're such a good mom.' I laughed then, but I got home and a week later I was pregnant with our daughter, Arielle."

It was the first time that I had lived alone ever. I didn't do much to fix the place up—it never felt like home, just a way station to somewhere else.

30

AUGUST BROUGHT WITH it a sense of freedom and re-
lief. No more walking on eggshells. No more trips to the edge of the
volcano. No more volcano!

I wanted to breathe deeply, let the muscles in my body relax,
embrace life in a different way, laugh—a lot. That was my personal
prescription.

Rob Lowe, with his amazing smile and blue, blue eyes, helped
get the party started.

But let me back up a little. I'd got to know Stephen Collins,
who years later became the anchor of the popular family series *7th
Heaven,* and his wife, Faye Grant, through Jack. Stephen invited us
to come see him in *The Three Sisters,* a Chekhov play that was one
of the productions at the Williamstown Theatre Festival that year.

This terrific festival does so much to nurture the tradition of the
theater, and in such a beautiful spot. I fell in love with the Berkshire
Hills of western Massachussetts, which was easy to do.

The festival always attracts top actors—in addition to Stephen
the cast of *The Three Sisters* featured Amy Irving, John Heard,
Christopher Walken, Kate Burton, and Rob Lowe, among others.

We were all hanging out after the show talking with Faye and
Michael Unger, who had just finished appearing with her in *The
Rover* earlier in the festival, when Rob walks up. I thought, *Oh my
god, Rob Lowe, Rob Lowe!*

The always gracious Mr. Unger stepped in quickly and said,
"Marlee, this is our friend Rob Lowe." I'd like to say that I played
it totally cool, that my jaw didn't drop, but it did. I recovered nicely
though.

We hit it off immediately—he was so funny and laid-back and easy to be around. No complications, no tension, no dark moods.

With Rob, everything was easy. We drifted into a comfortable friendship—friends with benefits. One unforgettable night on the beach in Santa Monica we had all the light we needed from the luminescence of the fish swimming near the shore.

I hung out a lot with the sweet, playful, extremely flirtatious Mr. Lowe, who is gorgeous to this day. Together we'd hit concerts—U2 one month. Springsteen another—or parties, and we had a grand time vamping it up on a photo shoot for the cover of the now defunct *In Fashion* magazine. He was described as a Hollywood heart-throb; I was called strong-willed and magical. It was a kick teaming up like that with him, and that cover photo remains one of my favorites—as does Rob.

In Fashion threw a big party in New York for the issue, which came out in the spring of 1988. I'll never forget getting to ride on MGM's private plane, which took us to the party. The plane was so luxe, everything was tricked out to be top-of-the-line. Even the bathrooms were plush, so plush that Jack felt moved to include them in the video he shot of the trip. But then that boy can get crazy with a video camera. He shot a few behind-the-scenes videos of some of the early projects we worked on together that are easily two or three times longer than the movies themselves turned out to be.

Rob and I would finally get to work together years later on *The West Wing*. But more than anything else, Rob introduced me to a new Hollywood circle that included everyone from Demi Moore and Bruce Willis to Charlie Sheen and Robert Downey Jr., to Jane Fonda and Tom Hayden.

Rob was interested in politics and pulled me into that world along with him. I was his date for an Actors Fund gala in D.C. Through Rob, and his assistant Stephanie Matlow, who would become a good friend, I became involved with other young actors who mobilized for voter registration drives and fund-raisers.

I was a guest of Senator Joseph Biden's at the Bork confirmation hearings. I got involved in support of SANE—the Committee for a SANE Nuclear Policy.

The political involvement I was introduced to by Rob would quickly grow into full-blown activism on the issues that matter most to me.

AT THE END of August, I went back to Chicago for a joint birthday celebration with Liz. I was turning twenty-two.

It was a great party; all my family and friends were there. We had a cake with twenty-two candles for me and twenty-three for Liz. It's amazing it didn't set off the fire alarms. There was dancing and much laughing—and karaoke, big-time! It was a happy time and I started to feel that things were going to get better.

Not long after that, I flew to Australia for a round of publicity, and their version of *60 Minutes* wanted to do a piece on me. While there, I visited one of the country's schools for Deaf children and was really bothered by how primitive it seemed. They were providing the fundamentals, but nothing more. But I loved spending time with the children.

When a reporter asked me about their schools for the Deaf, I said it was sad that none of the children seemed to have any dreams for their future—a statement that would cause a ripple throughout my stay. "Actress criticizes Aussie schools for Deaf!" A minor ripple compared to what was to come.

Eventually I stopped reaching out in this way to the Deaf community, both in the States and abroad. It became virtually impossible for me to do so without triggering some sort of backlash or wave of criticism for what I did or did not say or do.

It was a painful time for me. I didn't feel as if anything I did on behalf of the Deaf community was appreciated. I got tired of being used for target practice by the growing number of ringside critics looking to take me down.

So I pulled back and waited for better times, other ways to channel my energy and my desire to help. I would find them.

31

By the time I got back to New York, it was fall. In the first months after Bill and I broke up, we spoke on occasion and a couple of times we saw each other. One of the last times was not long before I was to leave the city for good.

I was taking an afternoon nap in my apartment: in the months after I got sober, I napped a lot during bouts with depression—sleeping to mask all the bad feelings that were still hanging around the edges of my life. I guess I had left the door unlocked for Jack, who was working with me pretty much full-time at that point.

I'm not sure what woke me; maybe I just sensed something. When I opened my eyes, I was startled to find Bill standing next to my bed, watching me.

I didn't ask how he'd gotten in or why he was there. We both made a few seconds of really trivial small talk, nothing more, then we made love.

Afterward, we went to grab a bite to eat and talked a little more. On our way back, he stopped on the street and said. "It's over. It's really over. I just wanted to verify it."

I was stunned, floored, confused. Then I was crying. I didn't think he could hurt me again. I thought I had grown enough by then to say, "I'm my own person now. This doesn't matter."

Later I decided he said it outside because he knew I would get upset; by the finality of it, the abruptness of it. When I got upset, that never led to anything good between us.

But, as I had learned to do long before Bill entered my life, I licked my wounds and dived back into life and work. I did a couple of magazine shoots—I was in *Esquire,* as part of its "Women We

Love" series, and in *Glamour,* answering the question if there was life after Oscar—there was.

I love photo shoots—each is going after its own mood, trying to visually tell a story, and it's fun slipping into characters and the clothes, too. Back then, though, the days were often extremely long with hours and hours of downtime.

All I can say is thank God for today's digital cameras. They have cut the time it takes to do a cover shoot or magazine spread by hours, even days. No more waiting for the Polaroids to dry before the real shooting begins.

Work was picking up, too. Studios and directors were interested in meeting with me—a good thing—but I was spending half my time on airplanes between New York and L.A. to make those connections. I realized that L.A. was where the work was going to come from.

I sat on my slanted floor, looking at the leaves in Washington Square turning brilliant yellows and reds, and decided I had to move to the land of palm trees and sand. I talked to Jack and convinced him to work for me there.

So I embarked on a grand adventure. Headed to a city where I could count the number of people I knew well on one hand, though it helped that I had extended family in the area. I landed on the West Coast with no place to live and not much money in my pocket. But I had dreams. . . .

WHAT IS IT with me and earthquakes!

The flight to L.A. was on October 1, 1987. While we were in the air, the pilot came on and told us that the city had been hit by a major quake. I had no idea what to expect when we landed, was just grateful that we were apparently going to be able to land. Besides, I did not have a plan B if L.A. didn't work out.

The Whittier Narrows earthquake rocked the San Gabriel Valley with a 5.9 quake that day. Eight people died and thousands were without homes, hundreds of buildings were destroyed, including most of what was downtown Whittier.

After the plane landed, Jack and I headed for the safest place I knew—the Winklers' house. Henry took one look at us—I'm guessing we looked pretty pathetic—and said, "You're staying here for the weekend." Whew!

So he and Stacey put us up in their pool house—a beautiful space in the back of the house. I took the bedroom; Jack took the couch in the main room.

Over the next few days, I started settling in, trying to get used to the aftershocks, which were mild, but rolling through steadily.

Then on October 4, at 3:59 a.m., came a huge aftershock—5.6 magnitude—everything was shaking. I jumped out of bed and bolted for the house. I had that sense of chaos you feel when you have no idea what's going to happen next, and with earthquakes you never do.

Inside the house, Henry had grabbed his son Max. He recalls, "It was the middle of the night and I've got on brown socks and I'm in my Jockeys, and I'm running down the back stairway with Max in my arms when Marlee comes running in the kitchen door.

"Just then I slipped, so here I am in my Jockeys and my brown socks, trying to hold on to Max, sliding down the carpeted stairway. And Marlee thought that might have been the funniest thing she had ever seen. I was trying to make sure that Max, who was maybe two or three at the time, wasn't hurt. Marlee was bent over laughing.

"Max is now twenty-five and I think my backside has just recovered."

Nothing like seeing the Fonz in his underwear bouncing down a set of stairs balancing a baby to take your mind off an earthquake!

The aftershocks moved on, and Jack did, too. He found an apartment at the Oakwood in the Valley; it's one of the apartment complexes of choice for people trying to break into Hollywood. But I stayed with the Winklers. For all practical purposes they adopted me.

I ate with the family, went to Stacey and Henry for advice, played with the kids. I did a lot of growing up there. It was such a happy time for me, and my memories are filled with the sound of laughter.

WALKER PREMIERED IN New York in December, and Jennifer Beals donned one of her fabulous leather jackets and went with me.

We were captured arm in arm on the red carpet, looking as if we could be sisters.

The reviews for the movie were scathing. After I'd been overwhelmed by terrific reviews for *Children of a Lesser God,* these came like a shock to the system. I stopped reading them. Here's a taste of why.

Roger Ebert wrote, "Some bad movies are in no hurry to announce themselves, but *Walker* declares its badness right from the opening titles."

Ouch!

One reviewer suggested I get a new agent—that would happen soon enough, though not because of *Walker.*

For me it was another session of Hollywood 101, one of those sometimes-you-learn-the-hard-way moments. My *Walker* lesson: at times a project can seem to have all the right ingredients—director, actors, passion—but even with the best of intentions and hard work by everyone, nothing guarantees success.

Christmas of 1987 was the year Ruthie and I escaped from everything here—bad reviews, bad boyfriends, bad memories—and invaded St. Bart's for the first time. The Maa-Ruus were definitely on the island.

Ruthie and I hit St. Barts

For the first time in a long time, I felt completely free. We talked and laughed and spent endless hours in the surf. I truly started healing.

As Ruthie says, "I could tell she was finally done with Bill."

But I wasn't quite.

IT WAS DECEMBER 1989. I made dinner (with Ruthie's help) for Bill before we headed to an AA meeting in West Hollywood. I think Bill and I both envisioned it as a kind of cleansing. I spoke first, with Jack interpreting and Ruthie there for support. As they encourage you to do in AA, I shared my experiences, all the things that had brought me here, with as much honesty as I could muster.

Jack recalls, "I felt it was the best job I'd ever done interpreting for Marlee. It was so organic, so real, Marlee was very specific about accepting responsibility for her part in the breakdown of the relationship with Bill. She was also candid about all the things that had happened between them—the pain, the violence, her drugs, his drinking—it was an incredible moment of heartbreaking honesty."

After I spoke, Bill pulled me aside. He was furious. I remember him saying, "You never learn, do you. These people can't be trusted not to talk." I was, once again, hurt, but I told him. "You stop pulling my strings, you can't do that to me anymore." I dug deep for the courage to just walk away.

After that, though he would occasionally cross my mind, we lost touch completely.

In September of 1994, just a little more than a year after I'd married, I was given the Innovator Award as part of the annual Diversity Awards, a fund-raiser sponsored each year by the Multicultural Motion Picture Association.

The awards show was held in the International Ballroom of the Beverly Hilton Hotel. Those involved are a mix of studio executives, politicians, and artists drawn from the worlds of music, film, television, and sports.

The recognition was for my work on closed-captioning and my involvement with several children's charities. I was truly moved to be included.

It was a lovely night. Jack was there and flipped through the program, which as part of the fund-raising efforts is filled with paid ads. He noticed a full-page ad next to my name, reading, "Mazel Tov, Marlee Matlin, Recipient of the Innovator Award, from William Hurt."

I've always wondered about that ad. What was Bill thinking when he placed it? Was it an attempt to reconnect? Or to make amends? Was it sincere or sarcastic?

About three years ago, our paths crossed briefly at an event tied to the Oscars. It had been so long since we'd had any contact, but I realized my feelings about him remained so unresolved, I freaked out when I saw him across the room. Thank God my husband, Kevin, was there. He suggested I go over and talk to Bill, make the first move. Just as we turned to head over, Bill was there with his son, Alex.

With Kevin right by my side and his good energy helping to calm me, Bill and I chatted for a while as if we were only casual acquaintances. Then it was over and we quickly moved past each other into our separate nights.

32

I THINK I MIGHT be a sports fanatic. Wait, no, actually I *am* definitely, officially a sports fanatic. I love sports—watching, playing, analyzing. I follow my teams religiously. Hand me a bat and you can count on a couple of RBIs; toss me a basketball and I'm good for a two-pointer.

Some of the best times I've had in Hollywood have been at the celebrity sports events that are generally put together to raise funds for various charities. It's easy for me to say yes to these. I'll take getting dirty running bases instead of a black-tie gala any day.

So when I was invited to a celebrity ski event in Calgary before the 1988 Winter Olympics, I was there!

It was beautiful—clear days, pristine snow, good friends, absolutely carefree. I met Brooke Shields there—*Pretty Baby,* whoa! I taught her to sign the alphabet—such a sweet and genuine person.

There were all sorts of races and competitions; ice sculptures of all sorts of animals seemed to be everywhere you turned. It was crazy. During a slalom race, I watched MacGyver battle it out with Superman.

I don't remember who won the race, but as Richard Dean Anderson and Christopher Reeve finished, I knew I wanted to meet Ricky. I'd loved him as MacGyver, but that was just leftover affection from an early crush I had on him as a teenager when he was starting out his career as Dr. Jeff Webber on *General Hospital.*

He always seemed to play the tough good guy with a heart of gold. That is exactly who he was. Oh, and more than a little hot!

I have to admit, I'm a hopeless flirt—always have been, always will be—thank goodness for an understanding husband who knows he's my one true love now!

With Ricky, though, I was just simply hopeless. In what has to rank as one of the lamest flirts I've pulled over the years, I waited for him at the ski lift after the race and told him I was scared to ride alone. Would he ride with me?

Since he didn't know me yet, he had no idea how absurd that was. We spent the fifteen-minute ride up the slope laughing and talking. It wasn't *love* at first sight, but it was definitely *interest* at first sight.

That night at a banquet we kept exchanging glances. Brooke and I were sitting next to each other, and I was probably driving her crazy talking about him—how cute, how nice. She kept encouraging me: "Go for it, go talk to him." Finally I did.

The banquet tables were big, the speeches were, well, a little dry. So I walked around and said, "Hi, Rick," and he smiled and said. "Let's get under the table." What?

So we ducked under the table like kids in a fort on a rainy day and stayed there for the rest of the night talking.

Later that night he walked me back to my room at the hotel and asked me if I wanted to exchange phone numbers. "Definitely!" Then he gave me the sweetest kiss on the cheek and said goodnight.

He was a big star, one of *People*'s most beautiful people, one of Hollywood's most eligible bachelors. I couldn't believe he'd given me so much of his time. I went to sleep wondering if that would be it.

When I woke up the next morning, a note had been slipped under my door: *Marlee, it was great meeting you and I have a question—do you want to go to Hawaii with me?*

And . . . I declined. Darn it! I was scared and a little intimidated by this handsome, magnetic man.

We would reconnect a few weeks later when he got back and invited me to come visit him in Vancouver, where he was shooting *MacGyver*. I remember spending an evening walking together. It was dark, in a sort of warehouse district, and my heart was pounding, hoping I'd made the right decision to come. We walked and talked and walked some more, for hours. And I started falling in love with him.

He was the sweetest, gentlest, kindest man. Funny, with a dry sense of humor. There was a lot to fall in love with. Not many guys when you've just started dating would take a trip with you to visit your grandmother. But that's exactly what he did—it was one of the most romantic things ever.

While we were there in Reseda, California, at the Jewish Home for the Aging visiting my grandmother Rose, Ricky told me he was falling in love with me and wanted to be in a relationship. That moment touched my heart.

Ricky also had the Winkler seal of approval, always important in my life—Henry was a producer on *MacGyver*. He told me, "Rick's one of my guys, he's a good guy, you'll be safe with him."

We had great times together. He had a hockey fan in me and we would hit the Kings games when he wasn't shooting in Vancouver. I'd always try to make his pickup hockey games on Monday nights. His dreams of becoming a pro player had been dashed when he was a teenager and broke both of his arms in two accidents within a few weeks of each other. But he was still fantastic on the ice.

One of the things I loved about Ricky was his love of life—something was always on the agenda, and it usually involved some sort of challenge. So I wasn't surprised that he signed on to race in the Long Beach Grand Prix. I went with him, and my only regret is that I didn't find a way to drive in the race myself.

Put me behind a wheel and I move at warp speed; my friends still have driving-with-Marlee nightmares. I may be fast, but I'm also, if I do say so myself, pretty skillful. No accidents on my record. I think I could have been a contender!

Then again it is never too late to try something you think you'll love, is it? So don't be surprised if one day you see me down in Long Beach suited up like Danica Patrick, tucking my hair into my helmet, ready to race with the big boys!

Ricky would go with me to the Oscars that year. We'd become one of those "hot couples" all the celebrity mags would watch for a

Hollywood minute. In May, we were on the cover of *Us* magazine, looking deliciously in love. By June it had ended for us.

It was a great six months, but he was fiercely independent, and I know I got too clingy for him. I wanted more, wanted to commit, and he just wasn't emotionally there. Broke my heart because he was such a great guy.

We've stayed in touch over the years; we both left the relationship with no bitterness. It just wasn't right.

Ricky, who has dated so many beautiful, smart, and talented women over the years, has never married, but he does have a beautiful daughter who was born a couple of years after my oldest, who is the center of his life. When we talk, he sounds happy. And that makes me happy—if MacGyver deserves anything, it is a happy ending!

IN LATE FEBRUARY, not long after I had started dating Richard Dean Anderson, I would go with an arts delegation to Russia, then to Leningrad, for the Second American Film and Theater Diplomacy Film Festival.

The first was held in 1959. Seven films were featured, and Gary Cooper came as Hollywood's representative. This time there were twenty-five films, a lot of actors, but also other cultural representatives from dance and music. The idea was that the arts could bridge gaps that politics never could.

The pretty big group included Daryl Hannah, Richard Gere, Michael Douglas, Matt Dillon, Cicely Tyson, and the Muppets' Jim Henson, among others.

Moscow was so cold. (I know, no surprise.) But somehow when you're in a city that isn't merely cold, but that feels so bleak—the faces of the people looked dead, completely without emotion—it can chill you to the bone.

I'll never forget the subway there—people moving along like automatons, no smiles, no eye contact, shoulders drooped as if every single one of them was carrying the weight of the world on his or her shoulders.

But inside the theaters was a different story. People would wait for hours in line, in the cold, to get a seat. I introduced *Children of a Lesser God* to an audience made up mostly of Russians who were Deaf. The process was multilayered—I signed using ASL (American Sign Language), then someone translated my signs into Russian signs. And Jack was interpreting what I signed into English, and someone else was translating what he said into Russian. But in the end, it all worked out just fine.

Leningrad was better, lighter somehow, but I was anxious to get home. It's one of the most consistent feelings I have. No matter where I go—whether my career or my love of travel has taken me there—I'm always ready to leave as long as home is on the other side of that plane ride.

In one of those this-is-a-small-world-after-all moments, I learned years later that Kevin had been in Leningrad at the same time I was there. Imagine, your future spouse—of all times and places!

33

THE 1988 OSCARS were back at the Shrine Auditorium, and ironically I found myself in the same position Bill Hurt had been in the year before.

As the Best Actress winner last year, tradition dictated that I was to give the Oscar to whoever won Best Actor. And the nominees were . . . yes, you guessed it. Bill Hurt for *Broadcast News,* along with Michael Douglas in *Wall Street,* Jack Nicholson for *Ironweed,* Robin Williams for *Good Morning, Vietnam,* and Marcello Mastroianni in *Dark Eyes.*

I have to admit it—I was praying that Bill didn't win. I couldn't imagine how uncomfortable it would be given how awful our breakup had been. I'd certainly moved on in my life, and he had in his, but still.

But what was causing me far more sleepless nights than the prospect of his winning was my decision that I would speak, aloud, that night.

I was tired of people assuming that if I was Deaf, I was also mute, and I wanted to break down that perception. Anyone who knows me well will tell you that's hardly the problem being around me.

About six months before the show, I began working with Dr. Lillian Glass, a noted speech pathologist who'd also written the book *Talk to Win.*

We had no idea who would be nominated, so we came up with a list of all the potential nominees, and I began work on pronouncing their names. And apologies to the late great Marcello Mastroianni, but I was hoping he wouldn't be nominated either—that name was going to be almost impossible for me to say!

There is an art to speech that if you're not Deaf will probably never even cross your mind. Your mouth and tongue must be positioned in so many specific ways to get the sound that you want. And there is inflection, nuance, cadence. When you speak, the emphasis changes with each syllable, again with each word. Entire levels of meaning can be communicated by tone of voice—ask any kid facing an angry mother.

None of that comes naturally to me, or to anyone who can't hear. To learn it is challenging, particularly since most people pick it up by a sort of osmosis. You hear how other people around you sound. You hear dialogue on television, in movies. You hear lectures in class. You overhear others on the street, in the subway. You learn that a certain tone means anger, another happiness. It's a whole science that, as someone who doesn't hear, I continue to study.

The Academy Awards were going to be my coming-out party, but a project was also in the works, *Bridge to Silence,* that called for my character to speak as well. I wanted the entertainment community, from those who created the characters to those who greenlighted projects, to know that I could do more than they imagined.

There was also a new look to showcase.

It's painful to be dissected so mercilessly by the fashion critics; I think that they're at their most creative when they hate an outfit you're wearing. The sarcasm just drips. I wasn't going to have that happen again if I could help it.

This time I wore an absolutely gorgeous, strapless raspberry sheath with a big kicky bow designed by Chuck Jones. It was short and looked and felt youthful. I wore my hair straight—no baby's breath anywhere near, no horn-rimmed glasses, though Stacey Winkler worried that I would blink the night away since I was still getting used to my contacts. Walking the red carpet on Ricky's arm, I felt beautiful. And I got a thumbs-up from the fashion police!

The show started and went on and on. Best Actor is one of the last awards given. Finally it was time.

I walked to the podium. I signed the intro with Jack interpreting. But then it was me, just me, reading the names of the nominees. No Jack, no signs. It went perfectly! Everyone could understand me, including, most important, Michael Douglas, who took home the Oscar.

All in all it was a good night. Until the Deaf community weighed in. . . .

"OFFENSIVE? DEAF ACTRESS'S Use of Speech Proves Divisive Among Peers."

The headline—in huge type—stretched across the entire front page of *Silent News,* the biggest newspaper for the Deaf community. The story took up the rest of the front page, except for a photo of me at the podium Oscar night. Elsewhere around the country the debate was raging.

This is apparently what my speaking, without also signing, the names of the Oscar nominees meant, according to what I could decipher from the media coverage:

Parents of Deaf children should stop teaching their kids to sign.

The only way for a Deaf person to be successful is to speak.

I wanted to insult the Deaf community at large.

I was undermining efforts to have sign language, ASL in particular, considered an original language.

And on and on it went. I was shocked.

Whoopi Goldberg was great, helping me weather this storm. She told me about the time she was on the cover of *Rolling Stone* wearing blue contact lenses. The African-American community was outraged—how could she turn her back on her black heritage?

Her good advice was to stay strong, be your own person, and stop paying attention to anyone who is trying to take you down. Her encouragement meant so much. She could always cut through the BS and get to the heart of an issue. She was as tough as she had to be—I liked that a lot.

I had never intended to become the most famous Deaf person in the world. If anything, I'd worked long and hard to make sure my deafness didn't become a barrier to my dreams. I fought against anyone using my deafness to define me, to limit me. I was a lot more than Deaf.

Still it seemed unavoidable. I was visible, people wanted to interview me. I was invited to participate in all sorts of public functions. Everywhere I went, Deaf people were always in the audience. I had become the public face of the entire Deaf community, which represents about 8–10 million people in this country alone, who are classified as significantly hard of hearing or Deaf.

When *Nightline* did a special segment earlier that year on the uproar at Gallaudet University on student protests over the controversial naming of a new president, who was hearing, over other candidates, who were Deaf, ABC had me on the show along with the Gallaudet student-body president and the new president to debate the issue.

I very much supported the student protest—that the only university for the Deaf had once again given the top job to someone who not only wasn't Deaf, but couldn't sign, was insulting. I refused to believe there were no qualified Deaf candidates. The president would quickly be ousted.

For taking that position, I was widely praised by the Deaf community. Now after reading the nominees aloud at the Oscars, they had completely turned.

I went from being the most well-known Deaf person in the world to the most hated Deaf person in the world, in one night. Apparently when it came to the Deaf community, I had no individual rights. And that I would not accept.

I spoke Oscar night because I can. I spoke because I have a career that would benefit from my ability to speak. I spoke because I always have. In the end, I opted out of the fight. I would hear on occasion that the debate raged on, but it did so without me.

It took me a long time to forgive them for hating me. For not giving me a chance.

Instead, I began to focus on fighting a battle that was truly important to me. And the battleground was Washington.

34

Here is what television was like for me before my uncle Jason got a decoder box for our TV set and a handful of prime-time television shows began offering closed-captioning.

I loved *All in the Family,* but had no idea that Archie Bunker was a bigot. I laughed at the slapstick and tried to read Archie's expressions—I could tell he was always in trouble.

I watched as President Gerald Ford spoke to the country in 1974. I could tell it was important; he looked extremely serious. My mom tried to translate what was happening, but I didn't understand why she needed to. Why couldn't they make television so I could understand it? I wrote a letter to President Ford asking just that question, but never heard back.

Mannix was one of my favorite TV shows because Mannix didn't talk much; he was all about action and I could make up a story to fill in the blanks if my dad wasn't around. Same with *Streets of San Francisco;* it was filled with intense car chases and Michael Douglas was always running.

When *Three's Company* hit prime time in 1977, the world changed for me. You might not think that a comedy starring John Ritter, Suzanne Somers, and Joyce DeWitt as roommates would be revolutionary, but in my life it was. It was the first closed-captioned show I ever saw.

Suddenly, I didn't have to guess what was going on. I could actually read the comic bits in the string of words that now ran across the bottom of our television set.

It wasn't just about the show—it was that I could experience it pretty much like everyone else. I could "hear" all the words, not a truncated translation by my brother Marc, who did most of the heavy lifting on that front. Though I loved him for doing it, closed-captioning brought me an entirely new level of experience.

Over time, more shows would be closed-captioned, but it was far from being adopted universally. Technology would keep advancing—a chip was developed that could be put into a TV set that would automatically provide closed-captioning in real time. It was a minimal cost for TV manufacturers—an average of $3 to $5 a set, but the industry was dragging its feet on adopting it.

Captioning for movies was nonexistent. When *Children of a Lesser God* offered captioned screening in theaters when the movie was first released in 1986—in ten cities and usually at 10 a.m. on Saturday mornings, but still—it was the first English-language movie to do so. It's one of the reasons I've always loved foreign films—subtitles!

The first closed-captioned home videos didn't come along until 1981—there were three, *Close Encounters of the Third Kind, The China Syndrome,* and *Chapter Two.* But it was hardly a trend.

This became my cause.

I knew how it could change a child's world, and I also thought of all those Americans who were losing their hearing—and their connection with the world—as they grew older. When you factor them in, the number of people who could benefit from closed-captioning topped 24 million.

There were other benefits, too—it could aid hearing kids learning to read, immigrants trying to learn English as a second language. There just were no downsides to pushing for expanding closed-captioning.

In 1987 I became the celebrity spokesperson for the National Captioning Institute. I talked to anyone who would listen about how I longed to fully experience popular movies such as Woody Allen's *Annie Hall,* classic movies such as *Sunset Boulevard,* and I could if they were closed-captioned. I set about trying to mobilize Hollywood and created the Friends of NCI. Roughly a hundred celebrities signed on, including Bob Hope, Bill Cosby, Lucille Ball, Robin Williams, Rosie O'Donnell, and Richard Dean Anderson.

Elizabeth Taylor declined, but nicely; she was worried about shift-
ing any focus away from her AIDS charity efforts—which I totally
respected.

In February of 1987 when I went on *Nightline* to discuss Gal-
lauder University's controversial Deaf President Now movement,
the show was captioned for the first time. Anchor Ted Koppel used
most of the intro to explain to the audience about the captioning
they would see—technically, open captioning, since anyone could
see it—interpreters they would hear, signing they would also see.

It was 1987 and the U.S. public was getting its first primer on
how a significant number of their brethren couldn't hear and how
closed-captioning—treated as if it were an exotic bird—could help.

That same year, I would receive an honorary doctorate of humane letters from Gallaudet. I was so honored and I understood
the importance of being given one, especially from the only Deaf
university in the world. I was thrilled to stand there in a cap and
gown and be handed the diploma for, as Provost Catherine Ingold
said, "sharing the message that Deaf persons are individuals who
have pride in themselves, their accomplishments, and their deafness." That doctorate is like another Oscar to me.

But as always, whether I wanted it to or not, controversy seemed
to shadow me. Some of the students protested I was "just an actress," turning their backs when I was given this honor—the ultimate insult in the Deaf world, the one way to close someone out.
Thankfully they didn't disrupt the ceremony, and I didn't even hear
about it until afterward, and I'm glad. Otherwise I might not have
gone. I try to let those sorts of things roll off my back, but back then
I was still just a kid. It hurt.

I remain an avid supporter of all the work Gallaudet does, and
in 2007 I was named to the university's board of trustees—yet another honor that meant so much to me.

OPRAH WINFREY, WHO has been a leader on so many fronts, was
an early adopter. She just immediately got it. She knew all about
barriers, that those barriers have to be broken down—anyone needs
access to live, to make a living, to stay alive.

In 1986, *The Oprah Winfrey Show* became the first daytime talk show in the country to be closed-captioned. I was so pleased to present Oprah with NCI's first Humanitarian/Media Leader Award a few years later. And we also teamed up that day to donate decoders to twenty needy students.

I started pressing for any TV show I appeared on to offer captioning. Others were beginning to step up, too. Arsenio Hall, my great, wonderful friend, made sure his nighttime talk show, which premiered in 1989, was closed-captioned.

Because of my relationship with NCI, I knew about the technology that could dramatically expand the availability of closed-captioning. I wanted to go to Washington. I wanted to talk to Congress, to the president if I could.

On June 19, 1990, I was at the White House, talking with First Lady Barbara Bush, who was active in supporting anything that could advance literacy in this country, and we knew closed-captioning could. NCI president John Ball was going to present her a decoder and demonstrate how it would work. I talked more personally about what it could mean. I knew firsthand.

Mrs. Bush was wonderfully warm and funny. After our serious work of showing her what the technology could do, she took Jack and me on an impromptu minitour.

As we passed a set of windows, she motioned us over, saying, "Come look, I want to show you something." We looked down on a group being led in for a tour of the White House. Mrs. Bush knocked on the windows and waved at them, and they all waved back wildly. I really liked that she got such a kick out of that small spontaneous connection with real people.

The next morning I would be testifying before a Senate committee along with Emma Samms. The aim was to get Congress to pass legislation that would require new TV sets to be equipped with closed-captioning circuitry. Too many of the estimated 24 million Americans classified as either Deaf or hard of hearing—a figure that has now risen to about 30 million—were essentially being denied access to entertainment, news, and educational opportunities because they couldn't afford the expense of the set-top decoders.

Senators Tom Harkin of Iowa and John McCain of Arizona were behind the legislative initiative. The response we got that day was overwhelmingly supportive. On August 2, the Senate, by unanimous consent, passed the Television Decoder Circuitry Act of 1990. The House would follow suit on October 1, and President George Bush, the elder, would sign it into law.

So in 1993, all TV sets sold in the United States that were thirteen inches or larger came with decoder circuitry. Now any remote can, with the press of a button, put captioning on a TV screen. Most DVD releases—of both movies and television series—are closed-captioned now.

Every day, the world opens up a little more for those who can't hear. I'm grateful that I've been a part of making that happen.

David E. Kelley, one of the great men in my life. I am grateful we are good friends to this day and that he found his true love with the amazing Michelle Pfeiffer.

Me and Mark Harmon goofing around on the set of *Reasonable Doubts*. I used to kid him by announcing that the "Sexiest Man Alive" was on the set; he hated that and I loved it.

Never in my wildest dreams did I imagine that I would perform with my idol, Billy Joel. And yet here we are on the set of *Sesame Street* together.

When I asked David Bowie if he liked kids he said no. Then I said "but you were a child onc and he replied, "No, I was borr Rock God." He was hilarious.

I would always run into my friend Lauren Bacall on the streets of New York. Once I told her about my problems with Bill and she saltily replied, "Men, fuck 'em." What a gal! *(Credit: WireImage)*

At Swifty Lazar's post Oscar party in 1986, I was stunned when Bill took me over to meet Hollywood royalty. There she was, Elizabeth Taylor, as gracious as she could be. *(Credit: Michael Jacobs)*

The national anthem that almost didn't happen. When NBC refused to play Garth's video for "We Shall Be Free," he simply walked out. Garth showed up just a few moments before we were to perform when they finally played the video. (*Credit: Al Messerschmidt/WireImage.com*)

I loved wielding Ty Pennington's megaphone when I hosted *Extreme Makeover: Home Edition*. I used this as my holiday card one year with the caption "Do You Hear What I Hear?"

I'm not acting here. I was truly shocked when everyone in my family, led by Jack in a coconut bra came out on stage during a luau to surprise me for my 30th birthday in Maui.

k any red carpet photographer Hollywood and they would say I s pregnant for years—they were nost right. This is one of my favorite ctures of me pregnant. *(Credit: © kael Jansson)*

e Matlin mishpuchah together for mom and dad's 50th wedding anniversary luding my niece and nephew, Arielle and Zach, and Marc's longtime partner, Jay.

I never imagined myself as a desperate housewife but the creator of the series, Marc Cherry, did and I had a blast working with Felicity Huffman and Doug Savant on the show.

Not only is Jeff Daniels a brilliant comedic actor he also has a great talent for drama. I think he deserved an Emmy nomination for his work on Hallmark Hall of Fame's *Sweet Nothing in My Ear*. (Credit: Erik Heinila/Hallmark Hall of Fame)

(Above left) Read my hips: never in my wildest dreams did I think I would be dancing in front of 22 million viewers every week on *Dancing with the Stars*. Here I am with my dance partner, The Mambo King, Fabian Sanchez. *(Credit: © Kelsey McNeal Zink/American Broadcasting Companies, Inc.)*

(Above right) With Jennifer Beals, Cybill Shepherd, and the rest of *The L Word* cast, this girl's club ruled! *(Credit: © Showtime Networks, Inc. All rights reserved)*

(Left) The Academy Awards, 2008. In a Nick Verreos gown; this time the critics loved the dress and I did too. *(Credit: Wirelmage)*

One of the happiest days of my life was when I married Kevin Grandalski. Of course there had to be some fun, and we surprised each other—I wore a pair of crazy sunglasses that my brothers had given me and Kevin and his groomsmen wore hot pink socks.

(Left to right) Sarah, Brandon, Tyler, and Isabelle. This is just after Isabelle came home from the hospital. Kevin is a master photographer; he even got the baby to smile for the camera!

35

T HE NEXT REAL break in my career came with the CBS-TV movie *Bridge to Silence,* which also starred Lee Remick and Michael O'Keefe.

It was scary new terrain for me; a lot of my dialogue was spoken aloud, and this project would first introduce me to the much larger audiences that television routinely draws.

I could relate to the story, but I wanted one fundamental change. *Bridge to Silence* follows the life of a young Deaf woman who loses her husband in an awful auto accident. As she struggles to recover from the grief and depression of that loss, her mother, played by Lee Remick, steps in and tries to gain custody of her five-year-old daughter.

The spine of the story is built around the conflict between mother and daughter. Not only has Remick's character never accepted her daughter's deafness, but, we learn late in the movie, she is actually responsible for it—overlooking a high fever when Peg, my character, was a child. It all felt familiar.

The way the script was initially written, though, Peg's anger is largely tied to her resentment at being Deaf. That's something I pushed to have them change.

As I thought about the character, began working on developing a backstory for her in my mind, that plotline increasingly made no sense to me. The anger, I believed, would come from the loss of her husband, the ridiculously freak accident that turned her nearly perfect world upside down. That would allow the anger to come from an organic place. Then the conflict would naturally shift to the fight with her mother for her daughter.

Yes, Peg was Deaf, but in this story that wasn't the real issue. Thankfully, the filmmakers agreed.

This highly emotional script dealt with death, all kinds of loss, even love. Michael O'Keefe's character was Peg's husband's best friend, but also very much in love with Peg.

The estrangement between mother and daughter was particularly poignant to me. In one scene, not too long after my husband has died, my mother shows up to check on me. There is a fight over an old shirt that still has the smell of my husband, and I don't want to let it go.

We are both extremely emotional in the scene, neither of us understanding where the other is coming from. The disagreement only underscores our emotional distance. I had so many moments from my own life to pull from to add texture and hopefully truth to that scene. But it was also a tough reminder of how my relationship with my mother was so saturated by tension and conflict.

I had great respect for Lee Remick, but it was difficult working with her because she barely moved her lips when she spoke. Even with a script, I was often searching for where we were from moment to moment in a scene.

I talked to the director about it, but apparently Lee felt that if she talked more clearly, moved her mouth more emphatically so that I could better read her lips, she would look foolish—she was worried about how it would play on-screen. So we limped along, finding ways to make it work.

At the end of the shoot she gave me a necklace, the same one she had worn the first time we'd met—I had noticed it and said how beautiful I thought it was. That she remembered and wanted me to have it was such a thoughtful gesture.

She was a lovely woman and a terrific actress, and I'm glad I had the opportunity to work with her. Her life and career were cut short by cancer only a few years later, at fifty-six, far too early.

Bridge to Silence also began my connection to Sammy Davis Jr. We met in Washington, D.C., when I received a Victory Award, which honors, as they put it, "individuals who best exemplify exceptional strength and courage in the face of physical adversity," in part for my performance in the film.

Sammy and I just connected immediately. He kept up with what I was doing over the years and always encouraged me—he knew everything about being an outsider and succeeding against the odds.

I have such fond memories of so many evenings at his house. I'll never forget the night he had me and Jack over with some other friends for a screening of *Tap,* starring Gregory Hines in the lead, and Sammy as Little Mo. Lucille Ball, one of my heroes, came in wearing a white jumpsuit with the words LUCY WHO? stitched on it, and with that red hair and creamy skin she looked absolutely stunning. She spent a lot of time with me that night encouraging me not to let Hollywood get me down, telling me, "I was older than they liked their stars to be, I wasn't the kind of beauty they were looking for, and I'm sure they didn't like my attitude, but I never quit, and you can't either." Those are words that I try to live by even now.

One of the last times I saw Sammy was at his house for a big

Hanging out with Sammy Davis Jr.

party. So many Hollywood legends were there, no one wanted to miss what would probably be his last party. As usual, it was an amazing night; if Sammy was there, you just knew everyone was going to have a good time. He just had an effortless way of creating that vibe.

During the evening, a group of us had drifted into the kitchen and were standing around reminiscing. I met Clint Eastwood in the kitchen that night. I so admire his work, whether it's in front of or behind the camera. But he is also, I discovered that night, one of the most difficult people for a lip-reader. He has the thinnest lips, which always makes it harder for me to follow, and he barely moves them when he talks. I would have loved to know what he was saying; hopefully I didn't miss anything profound, but I just couldn't figure it out.

Sammy was already so weakened by cancer that night, yet still very much his old warm Sammy self, making it such a happy/sad occasion. He was surrounded by so many of us who loved him dearly.

It devastated me that I was on location in Mexico shooting *The Man in the Golden Mask* when he passed away. Had I known how grave his condition had become, I would have flown in to see him one last time. To this day, I miss his presence and his good counsel, but most of all I miss his smile and his love. I know he still keeps watch over me.

36

Fame is never easy. It comes with many fringe benefits, but also has a lot of sharp edges. One of the things I hadn't counted on is just how my celebrity would impact my parents and my brothers.

My mother had written a letter when I was in Betty Ford to let me know that my sudden fame had been hard on the family. Probably the biggest misconception that they had is that along with my fame had come huge amounts of money. Everyone assumed I was rich.

That couldn't have been further from the truth. I definitely made better money than I would have if I'd kept the department-store job, but I was often just barely making ends meet between projects.

At times it was tough, and even impossible, for me to pay Jack. So he was often just scraping by as well. Living with the Winklers for as long as I did helped more than they'll ever know. By opening their home to me, they also helped keep me financially afloat during some lean times.

None of this my family knew. They just saw my life being played out in magazine spreads. Reports from the front line of the parties I was going to. News of me at a premiere, on the red carpet.

My older brother, Eric, was facing his own struggles at the time. He was trying to build a business as a stockbroker and it wasn't going well. He'd asked me to provide some introductions to people I knew in Hollywood. My name could open doors that his could not.

I did. The short version of this story is that it did not go well.

It put me in an uncomfortable position with the talent agency that represented me, and other producers and executives I knew in town. They wanted to help me, but they weren't interested in doing business with my brother. That hurt him.

It caused a nasty rift between us for a while, but we got beyond it a long time ago, and I think our relationship may be stronger for it.

One of the best things to happen to Eric is that along the way he found what he truly loved to do and returned to law, where he's developed an extremely successful legal practice. I am so proud of him. I feel that he is always in my corner these days, and I hope he knows that I am in his, too.

Marc, my sweet brother Marc, the middle child, always the peacemaker in the family, had almost a counterreaction to my visibility. He actually works to this day at blocking out as much of my life and career in Hollywood as he can.

It's all in the cause of preserving the idea of the sister he knows and watched grow up, rather than someone who is also a creature of Hollywood. When he's in town, he'll opt for a trip to the beach with my kids rather than a front-row seat to watch me in *Dancing with the Stars.* Sometimes that's hard for me, I'd like him to embrace all of who I am, but I have never doubted his love for me. He's always been there.

Marc also has made an amazing success of his life, with a life partner of twenty-three years, Jay, whom he treasures, and his own business, Chicago Dog Walkers, which employs a huge staff and walks, by my guess, most of the dogs in the Windy City.

My dad, my dad, my dad. He's spent a lifetime breaking his back to make money to support the family, and another lifetime trying to hold on to the money he made. There have been bad deals, gambling debts. Good times, but a lot of tough times, too.

In the spring of '89, he wrote asking me to front him $100,000 to underwrite his car dealership. That was an impossible request. He'd done so much for me over my life, but I didn't have that kind of money. It was painful for me to have to say no.

I remember in 1994 doing a Screen Actors Guild conversation tied to the TV film *Against Her Will: The Carrie Buck Story,* which my friend and costar Melissa Gilbert hosted. One of the questions from the audience came from a young woman who described herself as a struggling actress. She asked, given my success, what advice did I have for her.

I told her, "Today, I can tell you I'm a struggling actress. I'm not working, I'm not shooting. Anytime you're not working in this business, you're struggling. You have to have an aggressiveness in you, a desire to get yourself out there even when it's tough."

Here's how I think of it: There's a wall, and you know it's there, and you know your strengths, and you have to find that one place in the wall where you can use your strengths to push through. You keep going at it until you find that spot in the wall—you never stop looking for it.

That's how it is every day in the acting life. No one has a guarantee that there will be another project, that there will be another paycheck. You have to really want to be doing this. To keep searching for that spot in the wall.

So many times I'd pick up the phone and call my agent, Carla Hacken, and say, "Help me find work, help me find a movie." You always want to do the best work you can, to be able to carefully pick each project along the way, but the hard reality—at least for most of us—is that if you get offered a job, you take it.

Keep yourself working, keep yourself in the game, put everything you can into every project, and walk away from it having learned something new. What happens when it hits the screen or the critics get hold of it—well, that you have no control over.

So I took work where I could find it. Often small, independent films that were struggling to find a voice, to say nothing of financing.

One of the crazier ones for me was called *The Linguini Incident,* and I mean that in a good way. It originally came out in 1991 and was at some point auctioned off by SAG (along with six other films) after the owners defaulted on residual payments. Now living in DVD-land, it's been retitled *Shag-o-Rama,* I'm sure in an effort to plug into any remaining nostalgia for the seventies.

Carla helped pull together and populate this painfully small movie with a number of clients on her roster. It wasn't art, though it aspired to be, and the cast, crew, and the director did everything we could. But it was a heck of a lot of fun.

A lot of people thought my agent Carla Hacken and I were sisters.

The movie starred David Bowie and Rosanna Arquette as the would-they-or-wouldn't-they-fall-in-love couple. It was shot in downtown L.A. in an old Buick showroom that the set designers converted into the restaurant where most of the action took place.

The premise was sort of like *Green Card*'s, as David Bowie's character has just a month to get one, crossed with an Austin Powers–heist kind of vibe—the waitstaff would conspire to take the restaurant's money and run.

The set matched the zaniness of the story—going for a Salvador Dalí–inspired look that took surreal to the extreme. Rosanna and I wore sexy, shimmery, silver lamé minidresses. Almost everyone else wore short, dark go-go-style wigs. My hair was sculpted into a—it's hard to describe, but think of big swaths of hair fashioned atop your head like a giant pretzel twist. It took a long, long time each day to get it, well, mounted on my head.

It was a great group to hang out with. Buck Henry was in the cast, too. The movie was so low on funds day to day that if a friend visited the set, he or she would likely end up as an extra. But that gave the production a kind of Spanky and Our Gang, let's-put-on-a-play kind of feel that made shooting it a lot of fun. To say nothing of how cool it was working with David Bowie—he called himself Rock God. I couldn't agree more.

My character, Jeanette, the restaurant's hostess, refuses to speak but does swear in sign language at just about everyone and everything. I appreciated that director Richard Shepard was giving me a chance at comedy; most people just thought of me for dark, dramatic roles. He would go on years later to write and direct one of the cleverest comedies, *The Matador,* with Pierce Brosnan and Greg Kinnear.

AFTER A LONG time hanging out in the Winklers' backyard, I decided to move out and get an apartment of my own. Stacey's convinced that if they didn't have dogs, which meant I couldn't have a cat, I might have stayed. She might be right!

I set up a brief tenancy in an apartment in the Valley on Arch Drive that would have been dreary had David Oliver not been my neighbor and dear friend.

The one thing that sticks in Jack's mind when he describes the Arch apartment is that it smelled like cat pee. My brother Eric, who stayed with me a few days during a trip to L.A., remembers it as smelling rather like cat poop. I remember that I just got used to the smell and forgot about it.

Then my friend Stephanie told me about an apartment near what is now West Hollywood and the Fairfax district. It was on Blackburn, right next door to Laura Dern, another of her friends.

This is a wonderful old section of L.A., just around the corner from CBS, but already jammed with a blend of trendy new restaurants and shops and old Hollywood classics, such as Canter's Deli, which is open twenty-four hours, which in L.A. is a rarity.

There was block after block of huge duplexes, most of them built in the 1930s. The one I lived in was in a traditional style, but with lots of nice detail inside. It had three bedrooms, two baths, soaring ceilings, and hardwood floors—after Jack had the carpets ripped out and the floors redone one time while I was away.

It was a great place, terrific neighborhood. I stood inside it one day and thought and thought about what it needed. I know, it needed Ruthie!

By this time Ruthie had graduated from college and was getting ready to do some specialized research to get ready for graduate study. UCLA was just a fifteen-minute drive. It was perfect.

So I put in a call on a lark and asked if she'd be my roommate. She said yes, packing up her life, which was halfway across the country, and taking up residence in one of the bedrooms. I took the other, and the third was converted into an office for me and Jack.

New chapter of my life to write, and my soul sister was coming to town to help write it.

The Maa-Ruus were on the loose and living in L.A.—watch out!

37

Arsenio Hall was calling.

Michael Jordan—as in Chicago Bulls superstar Michael Jordan—was supposed to be on Arsenio's breakthrough, late-night talk show. But the NBA all-star had to cancel at the last minute.

I was from Chicago, right? Well, yes.

I love the Bulls right? Well, sure.

Then would I come on in Michael Jordan's place? Why not!

I always had the best times on Arsenio's show—it was so loose and fun, as if we were just teasing and playing the entire time. Some people you click with instantly, and that definitely was going on with us. Maybe because Hollywood didn't really know what to do with either Arsenio or me most of the time—so I think we saw the world, at least a little, from the same side of the fence.

That night I showed up in jeans, high-tops, and a Chicago Bulls GETTIN MEAN T-shirt. There was a giant bowl of candy backstage and I grabbed it at the last minute. I was ready to rock.

After he introduced me, I jumped in.

"The reason I brought all this candy . . . everybody here was expecting a big, tall black guy, and instead you got a short, white, Deaf Jewish bitch." And I started throwing candy to the audience—they were roaring. Arsenio was doubled over laughing.

I liked that so much that I got a license plate for my car that read SWDJB. Near the end of Arsenio's run, when he knew his show had been canceled, I gave him that plate as a the-show-may-be-over-but-don't-forget-the-good-times present.

"People expect you to be shy and introverted," he said when the laughter died down that night.

"Well . . . they're wrong!"

Then he told the story of our recent stint on the Comedy Awards. The censors were all set to bleep him, but they ended up bleeping me instead.

He asked me about my glasses—I'd taken a fair amount of public grief for wearing them, the fashion police at it again. I tried to explain. Pointing to the glasses, I said, "I think they're me."

"They say you should wear contact lenses."

"I say, 'They should go to hell.'"

It was definitely me unleashed that night, and the chemistry onstage was just working. Ruthie, who was in the audience, got a shout-out from both of us and some face time on camera.

He closed out my segment by having me do a triple-reverse, spinning slam dunk into the hoop. It was crazy, campy, and I ultimately landed on my butt. I knew people had come to see Michael Jordan, the least I could do was give them a good time.

I would turn up pretty often on Arsenio's show—sometimes when I had a new project, but just as often to simply sit with a friend and talk. We always found some kind of common ground—once it was my newfound love for rap music. I loved the bass, I could feel the beat.

One time when my mom was there with me, he bounded up into the audience, camera following every move, and gathered her up into the biggest hug. Here's Arsenio towering over this tiny woman—my mom barely hits five feet—and she just disappears laughing into his hug. She had a fantastic time that night, and I'm glad I was able to make it happen.

Too often, I'm taken for a serious person—I can be when it's called for, but at heart I love having fun, making jokes, playing pranks. Life is infinitely better when you're happy, and humor is really not a solitary occupation—you need to have people to laugh with you, to share in it, and I love that, too.

I WAS TRYING to milk the Hollywood scene for a little fun, too. I wasn't in the mood for any serious relationship entanglements. Since I'd spent my high school and junior college years with Mike and gone straight from that into two years with Bill, I think I just wanted to play. Over the next few years I would go out with, well, a lot of guys—maybe making up for lost time.

Dennis Quaid, who was just so hot! Timothy Hutton, whom Ruthie and I dubbed Mr. Airport because it never failed, if he called from an airport it meant our date was off. I went out with an absolutely lovely Canadian assistant director, David Till, for a while, but the distance did us in. A short interlude was spent with an ICM agent, Steve Rabineau, who's since climbed to far greater heights in the talent-agency world, most recently at William Morris. There was a terrific surfer dude, Darin Pappas—he turned surfboards into art, seriously—who has since tried his hand at rapping. And there was a night with David Copperfield.

I met David after one of his shows. We chatted for a few minutes, and before I left, he asked me out. Before the date, Ruthie and I hatched a plan. She would show up where we were having dinner, camera in hand, and pretend she was a paparazzo.

The night was strange from the beginning. He's this famous guy and he asked me to pick him up. So I went to the St. James Club, where he was staying, and met his assistant in the lobby. David came down dressed all in black—with his dark hair and dark eyes he looked striking, definitely turned heads when he moved through a room. He looks theatrical, but at heart he's a sweet, genuine, down-to-earth guy.

He got into my black, sporty Toyota, probably not at all the sort of transport he was used to, and we headed to Beverly Hills for dinner. I pulled into the parking lot and reached for my wallet, and he stopped me and pulled out of his pocket the biggest wad of cash I have ever seen in my life. It could have been a scene from a movie—both the cash and my double take were completely over-the-top! I was dumbfounded, but then I thought, *I guess he's going to pay for dinner, too.*

Inside, we were sitting there chatting and I was beginning to feel that we didn't have a lot in common, but then I'm known for making fast judgments about people, so maybe we just needed a little more time. I was also having a hard time understanding him—I couldn't read his lips well—and for me that is always important, particularly when I'm on a date with no one to interpret for us.

But we're talking, or still trying to, and I had completely forgotten about Ruthie. Suddenly there she is, camera in hand, and she's snapping away, the flash is pop, pop, popping.

Oh, I jumped! She scared the heck out of me! But then I started laughing; it had turned into such a bizarre, quirky moment. David was startled, then puzzled, then just confused, even after I introduced Ruthie and tried to explain. *Hmmm*, I thought, *not in sync with me when it comes to the jokes.*

I was done with the date then; it wasn't going anywhere. He was the sweetest guy, but I was bored. The communication wasn't there.

We headed out and I asked him, "Where's your car?"

"I don't drive."

"Seriously?"

"I really don't drive, I've never gotten a license."

That was hard for me to believe. One of the most famous guys around, and he doesn't drive? He's a magician for heaven's sakes, he can make things appear and disappear, surely he can drive!

So I pulled over and made him switch seats with me. He was lost behind the wheel, he really couldn't drive! I guess even a magician has limits to his powers.

We got back to the hotel and he asked me upstairs. I tried to beg off, but he insisted. I was nervous.

It was a penthouse suite and had this beautiful view of Los Angeles—lights twinkling everywhere like a million diamonds had been tossed down. A really romantic setting, but I wasn't feeling anything and was nervous.

We sat on the couch, looked at the lights of L.A., talked a little longer. He reached over to put his arm around me and I stumbled to my feet, apologizing that I really had to go. I had an early call in the morning. It was Saturday night; no one has an early call on Sunday! His face fell and I got out of there as fast as I could. No insult to Mr. Copperfield, he just wasn't my type.

But in the years since, he's always been generous. Whenever he comes to town and I need tickets for his show, whether for my family or friends, he makes sure I get them.

I RAN INTO Billy Baldwin not long ago. We were both headed to the All-Star Legends and Celebrity Softball Game at what would be the final year of Yankee Stadium and managed to get seats next to each other on the bus en route to the game.

It was so great to see him, to catch up. We talked kids—he's got three, I've got four—and it reminded me of our mutual crush years ago.

Billy is one of *the* greatest kissers in the world. He is seriously a wow!-makes-your-knees-weak-and-your-heart-pound kind of kisser. So a hundred years ago we were hanging out, and it was getting a little more serious. One night he stayed over in my apartment and we finally slept together—and I mean that literally, we both fell asleep, nothing more.

When he was leaving the next morning, he gave me the longest, sexiest kiss ever—I somehow knew right then that was the last time we would go out. I'm glad that it ended that way, with just that kiss.

Billy and I ran into each other at JFK Airport last year and sat together in first class. We talked almost all the way from New York to L.A.—about kids and work.

When I saw him again on the bus ride to the softball game, I had been thinking of that last night we had and reminded him. He said he remembered it well. Then I reminded him of that last kiss. He remembered that, too. I told him I was writing a book and asked his blessing to write about us, and he gave it.

I thanked him for ending it between us that way, for knowing that we were better as friends and not ruining that friendship. That I knew with that kiss, it was going to be the last time we would ever be together. He started laughing and said, "Well, I didn't!"

Ah, well, we'll have to save that for another lifetime.

38

In the late eighties, a lot of people around town in the circles I moved in were talking about David E. Kelley, this writing prodigy, an attorney who was currently working on Steven Bochco's already popular *L.A. Law* and, if that wasn't enough, had just cocreated *Doogie Howser, M.D.* with Bochco, too.

L.A. Law was one of my favorite shows. It tapped right into my interest in criminal justice. But as much as I loved the legal tangles, I was completely hooked on the relationship intrigues even more. Because I found the writing so compelling, I was curious about this up-and-coming TV writer and hoped I would have a chance to meet him.

One day a mutual friend introduced us, and I looked up into these amazingly intelligent eyes, a lopsided smile, and tousled hair and was smitten.

David, without question, is one of the smartest, most decent, kindest human beings on the planet. If you've watched any of the unbelievable string of hit shows he's written and created in the years since—*Picket Fences, Ally McBeal,* and *Boston Legal* in particular—you know he's got a sense of humor that is quirky, completely off-center, and remarkably sophisticated all at once. That man never has a simple thought, he's always operating on about five different levels.

We had the strangest first date in history—certainly in my history—the same December night in 1989 that Bill and I went to that final AA meeting together. Jack, who was interpreting at AA for me that night, left before I did to let David know I was running late. When I walked into my apartment, I was clearly showing signs of

just how much that meeting had taken out of me—from my brutally honest recounting of the way drugs, alcohol, and violence had
destroyed the relationship Bill and I had, to Bill's anger that I had
spoken publicly about our situation, even during an AA meeting.

David couldn't have been sweeter when he saw his date walk in
with a red nose, puffy eyes—all the signs of someone who'd been
sobbing. "Let's go for some pizza," he said. And we did. That pizza
tasted better than any I've had before or since.

We started dating a lot, and for the first time in a long time I
looked at him and thought to myself, *This is someone I could see
spending the rest of my life with.*

In David, I also had an avid sports fan, though since he was
from Boston, he followed all the wrong teams. When Boston played
Chicago in anything, it could get pretty messy! He was a terrific
hockey player, too, so I was back to watching pickup games, which
are the best.

Before long I was spending more time at his place than mine,
and when he bought this incredible home at the top of Blue Jay
Way in the Hollywood Hills with panoramic views—I moved in for
good.

His TV series kept him so busy that when he wanted to redeco-
rate the place, he put it pretty much completely in my hands. That
was the first time in my life that I'd ever really thought about how to
create a home so that the space you walk into feels unquestionably
as if it belongs to you.

I tried to make sure everything reflected us and had incredible help from the wackiest but most talented and brilliant inte-
rior designer ever. We even worked on a design for the tiles in our
bathroom that had hearts and our initials intertwined. That's how
it felt inside that house—like hearts and sweet love. When we gave
a housewarming party, I hoped all our friends could see the peace
and fun and joy that filled that house.

WHENEVER I WAS traveling or on location, I couldn't wait to get
David's faxes—they would never fail to bring a smile. They always
started out with his "Heyyy!!!"

One of my favorites, one I've kept for years now even though the paper is fading into purple streaks, is a photo of an angry baby boy, probably around six months old, sitting in diapers, with a little American flag clutched in one hand, his face scrunched up into a squall, with the note *DEK without MBM.*

He sent that one to me in March of 1990 while I was on the set of *The Man in the Golden Mask,* which was filming in San Miguel de Allende, Mexico. If ever I needed a lift in my spirits, it was then. That was an extremely difficult shoot, and the location was so remote—much of it was shot in the tiny village of Pozos, about three hours north of Mexico City—that I was begging anyone who came to the set to come armed with Evian, candy, and board games that Jack and I could use to help pass the time.

Despite his insane schedule, David took a few days to come visit me there—he was like an oasis in the middle of the desert. He could just take my mind miles away.

When his thirty-fifth birthday rolled-around, I wanted to do something special, unexpected. What else but a big surprise birthday party?

I spent weeks contacting family and friends from around the country, planning everything down to the smallest detail. Well, except one . . .

With his success came more and more pressure, and David seemed to be living with a massive writing deadline hanging over his head virtually every day. But the weekend of the party—a yummy dessert party—I didn't realize he was in overdrive. For someone who would come home each night, have dinner with me and catch up on the day, then go work for another four to six hours of writing, that was significant.

The evening of the party I had it all planned out. First we met a friend for dinner. He showed up saying, "Oh, man, my car died. I ended up taking a taxi here, hope you guys can drop me off." When we got to his house, he casually asked, "Come in for a second, I want to show you something." So we walked in—Surprise!—the house was filled with people from all parts of David's life. Man, was he ever surprised!

It was a great party. He couldn't have been more gracious to everyone, and I like to think he did really relax for a bit and enjoy it.

He never let anyone know the kind of crushing pressure he was facing. I realized how bad it was after everyone left and all the out of towners were packed off to the airport. We were both ready to collapse when he said he was going to work for just a little bit.

When we were together, David worked on legal pads, writing out pages and pages of dialogue in longhand. I think he liked the mental discipline of that—no computer with its ability to seamlessly shift everything from words to scenes around in a split second. His method took a different kind of concentration and focus.

I would guess that weekend he worked straight for the next twenty-four hours to get the script he was working on finished in time. All this and, except for a brief, and *very* quiet "Oh, shit" that slipped out when he first saw everyone, not even the whisper of a complaint.

Love and caring in any relationship can be measured in many ways. For David and me, one of those ways was a kitten named Lucy. She was a beautiful white fur ball, a Persian that David brought home for me one day. Now, he is definitely *not* a cat person; still, he got that kitten for me because he knew I was.

We'd only had her about a week when she fell from the top level, where the den was, down to the living room. She was just a little baby. She landed on her feet and at first seemed to be okay, but then she wasn't.

I couldn't bear to take her to the vet alone because I was so afraid of what he would say. David did and came home without her and, when I was inconsolable, took care of me, too.

All this is not to say that David was a saint, though he came pretty close at times.

As our relationship deepened, ironically communication became more difficult for me because we were relying almost solely on my ability to read lips and talk. I needed the person I was going to commit to for a lifetime to learn my language. In the end, I needed him to be more in my world that he had the time to be.

Ultimately that—along with his singular focus on work, which made him such a success in Hollywood—would leave us drifting apart.

The day I packed up and moved out was incredibly sad for both of us, but I knew I had to follow my heart.

Sometimes I think fate decides to intervene, even if it starts in pain, in all the right ways. If David and I had stayed together, neither of us would have found our true soul mates. He met the exquisite Michelle Pfeiffer, whose kind heart and gentleness matches his, not long after we broke up. And I met my own amazing partner, my favorite guy in uniform, Kevin Grandalski.

I will always treasure David and his family. He and Michelle came to our wedding, and it wouldn't have been the same without them.

SAN MIGUEL DE Allende is a beautiful old town in the mountains of central Mexico. Cobblestone streets wind through it, and the city is filled with colonial architecture and baroque chapels, which makes it seem like a little bit of England lost in the Mexican highlands.

But we spent most of the shoot for *L'homme au masque d'or* (*The Man in the Golden Mask*) in Pozos, about forty-five minutes from San Miguel and civilization. The village was dusty, with dirt roads, no running water, virtually no electricity or telephone lines—impoverished.

I had jumped at a chance to work with Jean Reno, who was starring in the film. He had already established himself as one of France's finest actors and was developing a rich, creative collaboration with the great French director Luc Besson.

Unfortunately, Luc Besson was not the director on this film. Instead we had a relative newcomer in Eric Duret, also French, whose only experience was directing a few episodes of a TV series. But he had written the script and was able to parlay that into a deal to direct it.

Jean, who was an absolute delight to work with, played a village priest working with an impoverished orphanage. He begins to make extra money to plow back into caring for the children by donning a gold mask and wrestling in area matches.

Along the way, he gets offered a shot at the big time. Professional wrestling, big money, orphans in need, what's a humble priest to do? My character, Maria, is Father Victorio's sister and helps him care for the children.

Duret's script intrigued me. He had envisioned my character not as Deaf, but reluctant to speak to anyone except the children and her brother. Playing a character who wasn't Deaf, but who had a unique and distinctive way of communicating, was challenging. So many of the scripts I was sent would cast me as the victim, and I wanted to resist the poor-little-Deaf-girl stereotyping as much as I could.

Much of the film took place inside either the orphanage or the church, and Pozos had absolutely nothing that resembled either. The crew, and I think most of the citizens of Pozos, constructed an entire complex to house the church and the orphans.

In what was, I thought, a wonderfully humane gesture, the church/orphanage was built of brick and wood, rather than the false fronts that Hollywood usually throws up, and was given to the village when the film's cast and crew departed.

I think virtually all of Pozos worked on the film while we were there. Roughly forty-five of the village's children were cast as orphans, and I fell in love with one tiny boy with the sweetest, saddest dark brown eyes set off by the most angelic smile. I kept hugging him and holding him throughout the shoot, and I knew that someday, before too much longer, I wanted to have children of my own.

Eric decided that to get deeper into my character I should sleep on the newly built chapel floor one night. Only then would I be in the right frame of mind to shoot a particular scene the next day. I had spent enough time in that church to know that scorpions scuttled across the floor every day.

Beyond that, nights in the high desert were cold and unpredictable. One night a huge storm, with lightning crackling and thunder that I could feel, rumbled through. The electricity went out, and the few lights we had were courtesy of the generators that had been trucked in. The next morning, you could look out and see the desert covered by a layer of ice, sparkling white in the sun.

On every production, large or small, I try to accommodate whatever my director asks of me. I'm always anxious to dig deeper into my experience and my emotions to enrich a character. But Eric had failed to explain how sleeping with scorpions in a desolate church would accomplish anything productive.

There is no nice way to put this. The production was a mess and too many days were ruled by chaos. Sometimes a director's first film is breathtaking; sometime it's a disaster. You always hope for the best.

Making it even more complicated, four languages were being spoken on set—French, Italian, Spanish, and sign. The director and Jean and actor Marc Duret, Eric's brother, were French; the director of photography, Ennio Guarnieri, who had shot for Fellini on occasion, his assistant, the set decorator, and the gaffer were all Italian; most of the rest of the cast and crew were Mexican; and I, of course, was signing.

Day after day the shoot went on at a glacial pace. I got a one-day reprieve from the director and producer to go to L.A. for a Billy Joel concert that I refused to miss! David and I had a great time at the concert, and the time we got to spend together was so unexpected and last-minute, it felt like a gift.

Then it was back to Mexico and the shoot that would take forever. I was desperate for another break, and David couldn't make another run south of the border.

So Ruthie came to the rescue.

She flew down and spent a long weekend with me. I couldn't have been more excited.

The morning after she arrived, I told her to look in her coat pocket—I'd slipped two tickets to Mazatlán in there. We hopped the flight and headed for the beach.

Mazatlán was beautiful and restful, and neither of us wanted to leave, so of course we pushed it to the last minute. Still we were careful, had everything timed right down to the second, and by now we were masters of down-to-the-wire arrivals.

We pulled into the airport in plenty of time—we thought. Turns out when Ruthie looked at the tickets, she didn't realize the Mexican airlines used a twenty-four-hour clock. At a glance our departure time had looked to be 5:30 p.m.—it was actually 15:30 hours, or 3:30 p.m. The ticket agent explained the plane was gone, with no others due for a couple of days.

I was panicked; the ticket agent just shrugged. I couldn't hold up production. Every lost day would cost money. If something else was going to go wrong on this production, I didn't want to be the reason for it.

So, in what has to be the most expensive three-day holiday in my entire life, we found a private jet that I could charter for $2,000 thanks to my American Express card that flew us to Guadalajara. Then we took the taxi ride from hell—nearly four hours of back road to San Miguel and on to Pozos, mostly after dark, at a fee that could probably have bought me a brand-new car.

I still can't quite believe we managed to do it—two chicks, one Deaf, neither of us could speak Spanish—but we were back before sunrise. Or at least before my call time.

In the end, Mazatlán turned into another great memory.

The Man with the Golden Mask, not so much.

It was released in France and Japan, but never in the States. The one videotape I have of the film is in French. But working on the movie did give me a lasting friendship with Jean Reno—and that was definitely worth the price of a misadventure in Mazatlán.

My $2,000 jet ride

39

ONE OF THE few commercials I've done was for Whiskas. It featured my beautiful orange shorthair, BJ (named after Billy Joel, of course), and my black cat, Booty. It was shot inside the Blue Jay Way house, while David and I were still together.

Now BJ and Booty were great cats, and we were close, but they had never been trained—not in the way most animals that are featured in ads or movies are. We spent hours rolling balls of foil over different surfaces to try to entice them to run in certain directions. We tried string: "Chase the string, BJ." "Go after the ball, Booty." They were having none of it!

In the end, the cats cooperated enough, and the ad agency got enough footage to turn it into a beautiful spot with a short story arch that simply said BJ and Booty could understand me as I signed, and I could definitely understand them when they wanted Whiskas.

I loved the creativity of the writers on that ad; it was a perfect example of how if you understand the possibilities, deafness can be turned into an asset rather than an issue. They shot my signing as if it were a ballet—focusing on the beauty of the movement.

Someone once asked what was the greatest barrier I faced in Hollywood. It wasn't my deafness as much as the many closed minds. I remember answering that I hoped that anyone I might work with could see beyond the deafness to everything else about me.

One of the projects I very much wanted to be considered for was Jane Campion's *The Piano*. It was a remarkable script—the story of a mute Scottish widow who with her child is dispatched to a primitive New Zealand in the mid-nineteenth century for an arranged marriage. She communicates by writing and by signing.

Jane and I had a meeting and I thought it went well. I came away thinking the door was open. But Jack drove her back to her hotel, and on the way she told him she just couldn't see me in the part. As Jack tells it, she said that after *Children of a Lesser God,* she didn't think anyone in the audience would be able to forget I was Deaf.

Those are the kind of arguments that drive me crazy!

If you get inside the character's skin, of course the audience will get past anything and believe whoever you are. Al Pacino, blind in *Scent of a Woman;* Patty Duke as blind and Deaf Helen Keller; Daniel Day-Lewis with cerebral palsy in *My Left Foot;* Dustin Hoffman in *Rain Man;* Javier Bardem paralyzed in *The Sea Inside;* ditto Tom Cruise in *Born on the Fourth of July;* ditto Jon Voight in *Coming Home.*

The list is endless, and those are the extremes. On the most fundamental level, that is exactly what is expected of all actors with each role we are given—take the character, slip inside the skin, and make the audience believe it.

In Jane's mind, I could have been wrong for the role for many reasons. I just hated that I was crossed off for consideration for that one.

Holly Hunter would ultimately get the role and win a well-deserved Oscar for an exceptional performance. Jane would take home an Oscar as well for her screenplay, and Anna Paquin would win in the supporting actress category. I loved the film, but I will always regret that it got away.

THAT WAS CERTAINLY not the first nor the last time I would encounter the many misconceptions that people have about what it means to be Deaf. Depending on the moment, it makes me want to laugh, cry, or throw up my hands in sheer disbelief.

In 1995, I wrote a letter to Ann Landers. She had written a column about a reader who was losing his hearing. He'd written to her saying that if he had been given the choice, he would have opted to go blind rather than Deaf, writing, "Sight cuts you off from things, loss of hearing cuts you off from people."

I knew that was not the case. Certainly my own life, which has been so enriched by family, colleagues, and so many friends, is a testament to the power of human connection. I wrote in a letter published that July:

> Deafness cuts you off from people only if you let it. If this were not true, we wouldn't have successful Deaf doctors, lawyers, educators, scientists, businesspeople, and actors. There is even a Deaf Miss America. . . .
>
> It may be true that life is challenging when you are unable to hear, but believe me when I say the real "handicap" of deafness does not lie in the ear, it lies in the mind.

I have dozens of examples, but just consider this one. I'm flying cross-country with Jack, headed to a project on the East Coast. We are in first class, always a nice perk. The stewardess comes along handing everyone menus—this was back in the old days, you know, when airlines still served food.

I was discussing something with Jack, which meant signing. That caught the stewardess's eye. Then I watched as she became flustered, then confident. She walked back to me, smiled, plucked the menu right out of my hands, and scurried away. Back in a minute, looking proud of herself, she handed me a menu with no words and covered in bumps.

I looked at Jack. He looked at the menu, then signed "Braille," before handing it back to the stewardess and politely explaining that I wasn't blind. I simply couldn't hear.

Another time I was set to do an interview for CNN. I was sitting with the woman who was going to interview me, and just seconds before we went live, she leaned over and said, "Marlee, I have to tell you, my dog is Deaf."

Suddenly we were live and I was sitting there looking absolutely stunned—eyes wide, mouth open . . . I guess she thought we had a lot in common now.

In the early years of my career, anytime I went onto a set for the first time, I needed to find a way to quickly break the ice with a lot of people. You may know the director and one or two of the actors, but you're generally facing an extensive crew whom you've never met before in your life.

The last thing I wanted was for them to be intimidated by me—that is death on a set, you need the crew to feel comfortable.

And so I found the perfect icebreaker.

I'd hand out this book called *Signs of Sexual Behavior,* which demonstrated how to sign most of the major dirty words in our language. After that, for the first couple of days, the cast and crew would get a kick out of signing insults and bad words to one another across the room.

Then, as with everything else, people got bored and moved on. But the payoff for me was that they began to feel that I was approachable, just another actor, which I am.

EVERYONE WHO WORKS in this town has a long list of projects that came close to happening, only to collapse along the way. They tend to be moments you meet with either heartbreak or relief. There were several in my life that I so wish we'd been able to make.

Jennifer Beals and I were set to do a film together in 1989 called *A Reasonable Doubt,* long before the TV series *Reasonable Doubts* was even a glimmer in producer Robert Singer's eye. It unraveled, as I remember it, due to financing. It would take about fifteen more years before we would end up working together on *The L Word.* And not only did we have a great time, but it turns out that we mesh well in scenes.

Another project was being developed for me and Jennifer Grey called *Most Wanted.* Jennifer had become a friend and I know we would have loved working together. Our sensibilities and our senses of humor just clicked.

A fantasy-love story called *Fox* was set up at Paramount and was close to a go when it was derailed by the writers' strike in 1988, which ground the town to a halt for five long months. I'm really sorry that one didn't get off the ground.

Fox was set in England—a love story between a gent and a woman who moves between human and animal forms—think *Ladyhawk* only with foxes.

Then I would meet producer/director Robert Singer to talk about a network drama series he was developing. A young, aggressive DA named Tess Kaufman, would be paired with a burned-out cop, Detective Dicky Cobb. Singer hadn't even considered that Tess might be Deaf, but after meeting me, he decided that's exactly what Tess should be.

40

In the summer of 1991 I started getting to know Tess Kaufman, another character who would change my life. I was twenty-six and had snagged a role costarring with Mark Harmon in a new NBC drama, *Reasonable Doubts*.

Series television is its own special beast. I had seen it from a distance, watching David Kelley wrestle it to the ground each week, so I had a sense of how demanding and unrelenting it could be. If you're lucky, you'll get twenty-six episodes a year. It looked as if I was going to be lucky, and I couldn't wait to step into the belly of the beast.

For the first time in my career, *Reasonable Doubts* was going to mean more than a great creative challenge and a huge audience; it was going to be steady work, and just about any actor will tell you what a precious commodity that is.

Press attention swirled around the project since this was the first network prime-time series to feature a Deaf actor in a leading role. I'm sure I told the story a thousand times that year of meeting the show's executive producer, Robert Singer, who had never envisioned the role for a Deaf actress until he met me. He was simply looking to cast two strong actors—one male, one female—and build the show around the conflict, tension, and attraction that could spark as they worked shoulder to shoulder to do the right thing in the weekly courthouse drama.

The series was set in Chicago, but we were shooting on the Warner Bros. lot in Burbank, just a few miles from my house. Something about stepping onto a backlot always reminds me how much I love being a part of this industry. Studio executives, directors, produc-

ers, actors, and crew may be in various stages of sheer panic, but you don't really feel it unless you're in the room.

Walking through the corridors between towering soundstages, or down streets where classic movies have been filmed, I'm always struck by a kind of peace and quiet you can find there. It really does feel a million miles away from the reality that waits outside the gates. But then, of course, you find yourself in the room and everything from exhilaration to panic is waiting for you right around the corner!

The idea of a Deaf attorney might sound far-fetched, but I found a top-notch one in Michael Schwartz, who was living and working as an assistant district attorney for New York at the time. NBC made arrangements for us to meet—flying me to New York from L.A. and Michael up from Washington, where he happened to be. The network put us both up at the Plaza Hotel, and we had dinner together.

Michael remembers, "I was in the appeals bureau. My job was to save the convictions, but NBC was fascinated with the trial bureau. With that in mind, I talked to Marlee about what I did and also what it felt like to work in an aural world where everybody else was hearing. I wanted to help her feel that this job was very doable; that what they were talking about could be believable. I was doing it."

The next day Michael took me to meet his boss, the NYC district attorney, and to show me around his office so I could get a sense of the place where he spent so much of his time. The DA was then and still is Robert Morgenthau, now approaching his nineties. He is arguably one of the most powerful men in Manhattan, with long ties to the Kennedy family. Michael was surprised at how well the meeting went:

"Robert is a wonderful man, but very powerful, a kingmaker. Most people, when they meet him, genuflect. When Marlee and I walked in, she immediately noticed two photographs, one with the Kennedys and one with his children. She started asking about the photos, and Robert was thunderstruck by how at ease she was with him. Marlee was just herself and he took right to her."

Michael and I had been introduced a few years earlier in El Paso at a National Association of the Deaf conference. We had a mutual friend in the legendary Bernard Bragg—writer, actor, mime, and a founder of the National Theater of the Deaf, where Michael had spent a year before beginning his career in law.

Deaf acting pioneer and friend Bernard Bragg

I had first met Bernard when he visited the Center on Deafness in Northbrook, and as with Henry Winkler I talked to him about my dreams of becoming an actor.

Bernard recalls, "It seems just like yesterday when I first became acquainted with Marlee, who participated in my weeklong theater workshop. She was eight at that time and we did some improvisational activities together, which enhanced learning. My first impression was that she was free-spirited and eager. When it was time to say good-bye, she was the last person to leave the room.

" 'I have a question,' she asked. The expression on her face was thoughtful. I said, 'Yes, what is it?' After a moment of hesitation, she signed to me, 'Can I become an actress?' I smiled and replied, 'Why not? Just do it!' And little did I ever dream that I would be looking at her on TV twelve years later when she came onstage to receive her Oscar."

Bernard was a true groundbreaker, the first Deaf person to have a show on television. Called *The Quiet Man,* it aired in the Bay Area and featured Bernard, who had studied with Marcel Marceau, as a mime.

And in another strange coincidence, Jack remembers serving as Michael's interpreter when he argued a case before the New York State Supreme Court in the years before Jack and I met and began working together.

From Michael I got a firsthand glimpse of the pressures on any assistant DA in a big city. Heavy caseloads, tragic stories, lives gone terribly wrong. And always that search for justice.

I'll never forget one scene because it spoke to the way you have to measure your emotional investment in each case. The case on this day was exceptionally prickly, with a man's life hanging in the balance. Mark's character, who worked in tandem with Tess as an investigator, turned to me and said, "You need to care less." I looked at him and shot back, "You need to care more." With Tess, I was always walking that emotional high wire.

Michael still remembers what it was like for him all those years ago watching *Reasonable Doubts:*

"First of all, Marlee is a phenomenal actress, she becomes the role, the character. And what she did in the show was groundbreaking—it helped people to wake up to the idea of Deaf people as professionals. That was a time and a day that I could point to and say on this day people's attitudes and perceptions began to change. Marlee has always played an extraordinary role in terms of breaking rules, changing attitudes, perceptions. She has a historic role and she's also concerned with the actor's life—she has those two things and she's always walking the fine line between the two."

In what was becoming a pattern in my life, some in the Deaf community embraced the show, while others were angered by my signing choice. Rather than use the more common ASL, I chose English signed, which is more precise and doesn't require the interpreter to, well, interpret—the interpreter translates exactly what you're saying in English signs.

My rationale was tied to my character. Since Tess was a courtroom litigator, it was important that the jury or judge hear the exact words she was choosing. But this brought another flurry of outrage and debate within the Deaf community.

Bernard says, "I wrote an article defending Marlee's choice. It was a very good and wise decision on her part. For the role of a lawyer, she needed to use specific and exact words. She proved herself to be a versatile actress by using the bona fide ASL as a Deaf mother in the recent TV movie *Sweet Nothing in My Ear.* I think it's great that she has helped the general public see and appreciate the difference between the two."

THE FIRST YEAR of the series was heaven. But it also changed Jack's role in my life. While he still interpreted for me in my public appearances, he was increasingly focused on building my production company into a solid business.

He never really adjusted to the rhythm of life on a set. You always have long hours of waiting while shots are being set up, or other scenes are being shot that don't involve you. That downtime either drove him nuts or put him to sleep.

I'd get the call that they were ready for me, only to find that Jack had nodded off somewhere. I think he could sleep through anything!

Jack sleeping

The studio brought in a lot of actors who could also sign to read for the interpreter part, and one was an old friend, Bill Pugin. I had met Bill in the summer of '87 during the Very Special Arts Festival in downtown L.A. He did a song/sign workshop every year, and we had a mutual friend in Lauren Tewes, who played Julie McCoy on *The Love Boat.*

Cindy, as we all called her, said she had a friend she wanted me to meet and brought me over to Bill's booth. He remembers, "I had all these Down syndrome kids there and I was in the middle of teaching the song 'Day by Day.' I saw Cindy come up with Marlee, and I waved at Marlee like I knew her. And Marlee is looking at me like 'Who is this guy?' I said, 'Hey, you sign, right? Come over here and help me out.'

"She walked over and I quickly signed, 'Hi, I'm Bill, it's nice to meet you.' And she just played along, got right into it with the kids. And when the workshop was over, we were officially introduced."

Over the years Bill and I would run into each other at other Deaf events—he was a terrific signer, his older sister is Deaf, and he's also an actor. But when I first knew him, Bill was with the National Captioning Institute helping with its closed-captioning work and doing a lot of freelance interpreting, which he has over time built into a major enterprise with 135 interpreters working for him.

I didn't know when I walked into the room to read with the actors auditioning to play my interpreter on *Reasonable Doubts* that Bill was in the group. I wished everyone good luck, then we started reading with each one.

Bill says, "They had Jack there to let the producers know if any of us could really sign. Marlee and I had such great fun that day, and we had what is called matching register. When a Deaf person signs, the person voicing tries to match their register—if they're signing sarcastically or angrily, you match that tone.

"The producers liked it, said they thought the chemistry was right, but also they liked my voice and they said that was important since they knew they'd be hearing it all the time."

In the years since, Bill has been with me on many productions, as my interpreter both on camera and off. It helps that he's one of the most entertaining people I've ever been around, too.

It's important for me to have someone on set that I'm completely in sync with. The person has to relay the cues from the director and the other actors, and to understand what the director wants to convey to me and also communicate what I need back to the director. It all has to be done in a way that no one looking at the series or movie is ever aware of that part of my process.

I also count on my interpreters to make sure no one crosses my sight lines when we're working. Since I need to stay so focused on any visual cues or signs—the foundation of communication for me—a distraction in my line of sight, while it might not bother a hearing actor, can completely destroy my concentration.

THE ENERGY ON the set that first year was great and was exciting to be a part of.

Both Mark Harmon and I are practical jokers, and not necessarily of the highbrow kind. So any number of times the toilets were wrapped with Saran Wrap—both of us were guilty. Or I'd find my glasses had been buttered—yes, the lenses slathered with butter. All I can say on that front is that fingerprints can be traced!

Mark was fond of sneaking up behind me with a fake mouse. I favored launching Silly String attacks. There would be tape-ball fights. My retainer disappeared on a few occasions and turned up in the freezer. And we were always jockeying for the best parking space. Two spaces were near our trailers, but only one was easy to get in and out of—it was definitely the primo spot.

Then there was the executive who looked at an early episode and said. "That Marlee Matlin is terrific. Is she going to be Deaf for the entire series?" Unfortunately he wasn't kidding!

The crew was great—I loved them all. One of my favorites was a grip named Mike. One day he was walking toward me carrying two cups of coffee. I said, "Come on over here."

He said, "I can't, I've got these cups of coffee."

"Well, why don't you drop them," I teased.

And he did. Right there, just let both cups of coffee drop to the floor. I laughed so hard! It became a running joke between us. Whenever he'd see me, he'd drop whatever he had in his hands—a hammer, food—and come give me a hug.

I also got really close to this sweet girl Adrianna, who did my wardrobe. We would always talk, and I found her to be sensitive, straightforward. In a horrific tragedy, she was getting into her car one day on a busy street and a drunk driver hit and killed her.

I WAS SO new to the television side of the business that I didn't realize we wouldn't know until the end of the season whether we were going to be picked up for another year. But as soon as I understood the process, I started saying my prayers.

When I found out that we had gotten picked up for a second season, I was so happy. I loved the show. I loved the people, and by now I was also in love with a guy named Kevin.

41

An old Burbank hospital that had long ago closed down was our first location shoot on *Reasonable Doubts*. Anytime you shoot in Burbank, the city will have a number of cops on the set—to manage traffic and security, that sort of thing. Since I'd wanted to be a cop when I was younger, I always chatted them up.

On this day, I noticed a good-looking guy in uniform standing there and thought I'd just say hi. Who can blame a girl? We talked a little, but he was serious, somber, being very professional.

My day was short as I only had one scene. So when I was finished, on my way out, I said, "Have a good day," and left.

Kevin remembers, "When I work on a set, I'll usually ask who's there. Somebody said that day it was Mark Harmon and Marlee Matlin. I'm not big into the movie scene, so I knew who Mark Harmon was, but I hadn't heard of Marlee, didn't know anything about her except that she was a Deaf actress.

"When she left, I saw her get into her car. It was a Porsche, but I took a second look because I noticed it had a cell phone antenna, and I couldn't figure it out. She was Deaf, why did she have a cell phone in her car?"

I wouldn't see Kevin again until November. During the four months in between, I'd met just about all the cops who worked on the set. That morning I arrived at work exhausted. I went up to Sergeant Tim Stehr, who's now the Burbank chief of police, to say hi. We'd gotten to know each other pretty well. But when I reached to give him a hug, his body froze.

I took another look and realized it wasn't Tim.

Kevin and Tim—they could be brothers

"I'm so sorry, sir." I was so embarrassed, blushing madly as I slinked away. A little later the real Tim showed up. I told him what had happened and he said, "Yeah, it happens all the time. His name is Kevin." I felt a little better. Even now, if you see photos of Kevin and Tim, they look so much alike, they could pass for brothers.

Kevin started working on the set more, and before too much longer I told him I'd love to go for a ride-along—"for research . . ." He said sure.

Another couple of months passed before we set a day. The department sanctions ride-alongs, but a male and a female can't be in the car alone. Perfect, I brought along my gayest assistant, B, who rode in the backseat in the cage.

I wouldn't sit in the back because I didn't want anyone to think I'd been busted. I could see the headlines . . . it would be a nightmare. Besides, I wanted to be next to Kevin.

With B in the back, I started talking to Kevin on my own. He didn't get many calls that night, but when one finally came in, he turned and said, "We're going to a gay bar." I thought to myself, How weird, a gay bar in Burbank.

In a few moments we pulled into the parking lot of a Kmart.

"There's a gay bar at Kmart?"

"What gay bar?"

"I thought we were going to a gay bar."

He laughed. "No, I said Kmart."

I was having trouble reading his lips because he had a mustache!

At the end of the shift, I asked Kevin something, I can't remember what, but he signed yes. I looked at him and said, "Did you just sign to me?"

"No, no, I didn't."

"Yes, you did, you are so busted!"

He told me that he'd taken sign language at Fresno State, where he'd gone to college. Approval had been given to allow students to use sign language to meet their foreign-language requirements, and he'd opted for that.

But with me he was worried that he really only knew a little bit. It was enough. We began to see each other and we began to fall in love.

IT SEEMS LIFE always has complications. I was still involved with David, and Kevin hadn't broken off with his girlfriend—in fact they were still engaged.

One evening when David got home, he came upstairs and sat down next to me. My heart dropped, I felt in my bones what was coming next. He looked at me with such sad eyes and asked, "Who are you dating?"

I knew I couldn't lie to David, but it broke my heart to hurt him in any way. He couldn't have been more kind, more civil, which only made my leaving that much harder, but I knew I had to follow my heart.

Kevin's got such a good heart, and just as I had struggled with ending my relationship with David, he was struggling with how to break it off with his girlfriend. He didn't want either of us to be hurt, which was not going to be possible no matter what.

By now *Reasonable Doubts* was on hiatus and I was heading to Portland to do the film *Hear No Evil*. The night before I left, I told Kevin, I cannot go do a movie knowing you are seeing two people.

He needed to make a choice. And he chose me. I got on the plane the next morning filled with relief and hope for the future.

One of the best things about Kevin is that he is absolutely not interested in the Hollywood scene. As he says, "Other than going to movies and being entertained for a couple of hours, it doesn't have any real fascination for me."

I could coax him to come with me to an occasional premiere, or to attend the Oscars or Golden Globes, but he was always doing it more for me than anything else. Our dates were much more likely to be catching a movie, packing a picnic, hiking or going to his beloved Mammoth Lakes to ski, eating sushi, simple pleasures.

From the beginning, we were really comfortable in each other's company. We talked, laughed, had a great time just being together. We always had wonderful chemistry, too—sometimes it was hard to keep our hands off each other!

As we got to know each other, we found we wanted the same things—a big family, four kids, a dog. We could see building a white-picket-fence kind of life together with a close-knit family at the core of it all.

KEVIN'S BIRTHDAY IS February 13, the day before Valentine's Day. In 1993, it was warm and we decided to go on a picnic to our favorite park in Burbank.

Kevin recalls, "I think we both knew that we were entering that next stage of the relationship that led to marriage. I've always tried to think of the least-expected thing to do whatever the occasion. And I figured Marlee would think that if I were going to propose, it would be on Valentine's Day.

"During the picnic, I had a picture of roses and a picture of a wedding ring. And while we were having lunch, I pulled both out and said something like 'Tomorrow is Valentine's Day. Which do you think you'll want, the roses or the ring?'

"She got all excited and it seemed like that meant 'I want the ring,' so I got down on one knee and opened up the box that had the ring I'd gotten for her and asked if she'd marry me."

◌ ◌

Kevin had just popped the question but we were very much in synch because I got him a ring, too!

I said yes so fast!

We were in jeans, sitting at a picnic table in the middle of a park, and it was absolutely the most romantic moment ever. We started calling people to tell them, and one of the first calls went to Tim Stehr and his wife, Barbara, who is also one of my best friends. If I hadn't mistaken Kevin for Tim that day of the ill-fated hug, maybe none of this would have happened.

42

I'D NEVER WORKED out with a trainer. I was on the go a lot, no couch potato, but exercise was not part of the agenda. And then *Hear No Evil,* a project I'd been working on with director Robert Greenwald for about four years, was finally going into production.

The film was about a woman who's a personal trainer and marathon runner who finds herself caught up in a web of corruption and betrayal that she doesn't begin to understand. What she does figure out pretty quickly is that if she can't untangle the web, she will likely pay with her life.

I went through three months of training before we began shooting, cutting fats, oils, sweets, and red meat completely out of my diet. When I showed up on the set, I was seventeen pounds lighter, and as lean and buff as I would ever be until years later when I landed on *Dancing with the Stars* and found movements and muscle tone I didn't know existed!

As I headed up to Portland in the spring of '92, I was excited about the project and absolutely infused with the glow of being newly in love, and that made everything around me feel like warm sunshine.

Portland in May was amazing, what a beautiful city; it remains one of my favorite places. I had a terrific apartment, a penthouse overlooking downtown. Kevin would fly up a couple of times during the production, and we would disappear behind its doors, in our own little world, until I had to be back on set.

This was the first film I'd done since *Children of a Lesser God* where the character's deafness was key in a way that played very much into the core action driving the film.

We went through a number of writers to get a script that both the director and I were happy with. The film had echoes of *Wait Until Dark,* the thriller starring Audrey Hepburn as a blind woman trying to evade a killer, but was very much its own movie.

The central thread was how vulnerable you can be in certain situations if you're deprived of a key sense. And then, how you fight to compensate and overcome the jeopardy you find yourself in.

Jillian, my character, was definitely the target of the bad guys, but I still wanted her to be infused with an inner strength. She becomes very much a part of her own salvation.

One powerful scene in the film, when I'm out and being chased and desperate for help, was particularly emotional to shoot. I'm running for my life, desperate to find help, when I see a phone booth. It looks to be my only chance. I grab the receiver and begin desperately calling 911—but since I can't hear, I don't know that the call hasn't gone through. I fall to my knees, sobbing and screaming into the phone. I let myself just collapse into the terror of that moment—I let my mind wander into exactly what that would feel like, and it was a dark, dark place.

Getting swept up in that scene reminded me uncomfortably of my own vulnerability, which most of the time I keep completely locked out of my thoughts. I hate the notion that I would ever be at greater risk than someone who can hear, and I don't like the idea that I ever need help to navigate the world, even when I do.

For part of the shoot, we moved out to the Timberline Lodge in Mount Hood, Oregon. It's beautiful there, fir trees rising to impossible heights, the gorgeous lodge set in this pristine landscape. They also shot a good bit of *The Shining* here, which made it hard not to imagine a menacing Jack Nicholson lurking in the shadows.

Our film had a lot of darkness, Robert did his best to lighten things up. As a director, he had a deft hand and a keen sense of humor. Oh, he could be funny. His favorite line was "Screw continuity," which is scary since continuity ensures that even though you shoot the film out of sequence, all the scenes match up when they're edited together.

I kept telling him, "But I was there in the scene and now I'm here."

He'd just laugh and say, "Screw continuity!"

He was good about getting me to the emotional ledge I needed to be on throughout the film. "Marlee, remember why she's here," he'd say as Jillian moved through a range of crises trying to outwit her pursuers. We had talked a lot about the different "whys" as we developed the script, so I could lock in and get there quickly.

I grew to adore many people in the cast. Martin Sheen, though he plays a scary bad guy, Lieutenant Brock, was terrific and such a professional. D. B. Sweeney's character, Ben, who becomes my ally and falls in love with my character, is so funny and so charming that it made work a joy. At least for me.

One day Kevin was visiting the set, and D.B. and I had a pretty steamy scene with a long kiss. I looked over at Kevin after the scene wrapped and noticed he looked stunned.

"What's wrong?" I asked.

"I didn't know you were going to have to *kiss* him!"

"But that's acting."

Later that night when I covered Kevin with kisses, I promise you absolutely no acting was involved.

John McGinley plays a down-on-his-luck journalist who seems to be a friend, but in a surprise twist betrays me. He is a fantastic actor, has a great wicked smile, and is a supernice guy. Of course, I have to watch *Scrubs* now, so I can follow his pitch-perfect turn as the cynical Dr. Perry Cox. I am so proud of him.

It was a cool cast and crew to work with. Bill Pugin was there as my interpreter, and when they needed someone to step in and play a doctor for a scene or two, they grabbed Bill.

Bill was going through such a difficult time then, I was grateful that he was able to be there during any of the production. He stayed only half of the time, flying back to L.A. to be with his partner, who was on his deathbed from AIDS. Watching Bill go through the excruciating pain of losing someone who meant so much, and being completely unable to do anything to help him beyond just being there, was one of my hardest times.

ᖇᖇ ᖇᖇ

HEAR NO EVIL was, without question, the most physically demanding film I had done. My work with the trainer focused primarily on running. Before I hit the set, I was averaging about six miles a day. I loved it.

Running created just the right rhythm and space for my mind to work through all sorts of issues and problems. Whether it was life or a scene I was struggling with, if I went running, I had it figured out by the time I got back. I even ran an 8K race while I was there.

The more time I spent acting, the more I was able to understand and tap into the ways in which my deafness could enhance it. If you're Deaf, you learn early on to use your face and your body language to communicate instead of your voice. As with just about everything else in life, as you get older and more experienced, you get better. That life experience fed into my acting. David Kelley used to call my eyes my weapon of choice in front of the camera. My eyes are my ears and I put that into my work.

All that is nuance; this role also demanded that I be concrete and visceral, too. I had to be able to run long distances for many of the scenes; some days it felt as if I were running most of the day. When it was on big, open boulevards, it was easy. Much more difficult were the scenes when I had to run through woods with thick underbrush in the middle of the night.

Before we wrapped, I had to run, get attacked, get knocked over, and scream over and over. I've never screamed so much in my life! And I was covered in scratches and bruises throughout the shoot.

Most days ended with my edging toward exhaustion, but in a good, this-body-had-gotten-a-serious-workout kind of way.

It was a long shoot—we started the first week in May and wrapped at the end of June—but was a light, bright time for such a dark, dark thriller . . . except for one serious tiff with the director.

In one scene, I'm in a bubble bath when something startles me and I begin getting out of the tub. My body was not supposed to be exposed. When I saw a rough cut of the film, the camera had captured far more than I wanted revealed.

I was furious! Absolutely no artistic reason justified it: nothing in the narrative demanded it. It was a cheap shot, a bid to show a little skin. When the skin in question is mine, I care deeply.

I had a few days of extremely testy exchanges with Robert over this. He wanted to leave it in. I wanted it completely cut.

In the end, the scene was trimmed, then trimmed a bit more. It was still more of me than I wanted out there, and it wasn't pleasant to have that fight. All of my contracts in the years since have been tightened significantly on this front. No nudity, and no body double either—at least not without my knowledge and consent.

IF THE FIRST season of *Reasonable Doubts* was heaven, the second season was not quite hell, but a long way from heaven. The show was struggling in the ratings, and what had been a really good working relationship with Mark began to sour. I began to feel isolated, as if I were an outsider in an old boys' club.

It began to feel as if the production revolved around Mark. On too many days I'd get called to the set, then be left waiting with the rest of the cast and crew until he showed up. I felt his character was getting more of the focus and mine was receding. Virtually all of the publicity for the show was falling on my shoulders.

Signing never came easy to Mark, and trying to learn pages of dialogue and signs each week was wearing him down, too—you could just feel the energy deflating. Our time slot didn't help the mood on the set either. NBC had put us head-to-head with *Roseanne,* then the number-one-ranked show in prime time. It was hard not to feel that was a battle we had no chance of winning.

I was still so new at all of this. The writers would come in and observe, but never really talk to me. I tried throwing a few ideas their way and got a few story lines added that brought in other Deaf actors for an episode or two. But there was no real collaboration.

At one point Bill heard one of the producers say, "Keep Marlee's dialogue short, we don't want so much dead air."

You cannot write for me or shoot me exactly as you would a hearing actress. There are differences, not impossible differences, but ones that you need to understand. *Children of a Lesser God* was a prime example of how to make it work.

It always starts with the script, and in *Children* there is almost no air—as I was signing, dialogue kept running, translating everything for the audience but in a way that felt natural. It was written so that you are hearing Bill Hurt's character's reactions as well as seeing them. Randa spent hours planning, adjusting shots in different ways, to catch the action between me and the other actors.

Here's a simple way to think of it. If a director is shooting two people talking, they typically do a lot of over-the-shoulder shots. The person who is speaking is shot from the back, over his or her shoulder, so that the audience hears the voice, but is watching the other person's reaction.

If one of the actors is Deaf, that pretty much kills the over-the-shoulder shot for at least half of the dialogue. So the director has to be more inventive in staging the action.

Another mistake that's often made in writing for me is to over-explain, to be too literal with the dialogue for the character translating my signing. It's a delicate balance between telling the audience too much and not telling them enough—but that's really the case with all dialogue.

It is definitely an art, but one that the best writers seem to know how to do intuitively. The brilliant Aaron Sorkin, who would write me into *The West Wing,* was one. *Seinfeld*'s incredible Carol Leifer, one of the show's core writers, absolutely got me and my humor. She wasn't afraid to use my deafness as comic grist.

On *Spin City,* I was lucky to work with the legendary Gary David Goldberg; Bill Lawrence, who went on to create *Scrubs;* and Kirk Rudell, who helped sharpen tongues later on *Will & Grace.* And the always clever David Kelley, who, years after we were just sending each other family Christmas cards, wrote me into *Picket Fences* in a pretty remarkable and crazy way.

You can look at any of those episodes and they flow seamlessly; the dialogue between me and the other actors feels organic, believable. As an actor, those are the qualities you're looking for.

∾ ∾

THE SITUATION ON *Reasonable Doubts* continued to deteriorate. The ratings continued to drop, despite the fact that both years I received an Emmy nomination for Best Actress in a Drama series.

On one particularly difficult day when tempers were already short, I muttered something under my breath about Mark's attitude—unfortunately he overheard it. Things turned nasty and we didn't speak for weeks unless it was the dialogue on the page. Given the number of scenes we had together, that made for an extremely tense set. It reminded me a little of the high school standoff Liz and I had had years ago—not good for anyone.

We got no feedback from the show's producers on what they did or didn't like about any of the performances. I would have loved being a part of discussions on how to improve the show. It seemed the only way they thought I could help was to hit the publicity trail. I was a good soldier on that front. I did endless interviews and I think I hit every talk and late-night show in the universe.

When I found out the series had been canceled, I was both relieved and devastated. Relieved because I wasn't going to be fighting with Mark anymore—because at heart I know he's a good guy and I hated that we were at such odds—and devastated to lose the work. Now what?

It was time to move on, but whatever I did career-wise, I also had a wedding to plan.

43

In THE SPRING of 1992 I was looking for a house to buy. It would be my first, and though I didn't know exactly what I wanted, I always trust my gut instinct and knew when I saw the right place, I'd just know it.

In late April, the Realtor called about a house in Hollywood that he thought was ideal. It had the space I wanted and the price was right, I should try to see it right away.

The house was in the hills above the Chateau Marmont Hotel on Sunset Boulevard, where I had stayed in 1986 when I went to the Oscars for the first time. It was not far from the apartment where I was living so I knew the neighborhood well. It was much closer to Le Dome, where I loved to treat myself to dinner, and Nicky Blair's, where I had a favorite chopped salad that was the best ever, and a friend in Nicky, which was better still. And it was just about eight miles from the lot where *Reasonable Doubts* was being shot.

It sounded perfect. I was due to fly in for a quick break from *Hear No Evil,* I was missing Kevin, and so I thought I'd come see the house and see Kevin. Since Jack was already in Hollywood, I dispatched him to take a look first.

The day quickly turned disastrous, though I wouldn't realize how disastrous until I landed in L.A. many hours late after my plane was rerouted from LAX to Burbank Airport after shots were fired at police helicopters in the skies above the city.

It was April 29, the day the Rodney King verdict came down, with a Simi Valley jury acquitting four police officers caught on tape beating the black motorist after a high-speed chase.

For six days the city would riot and burn. National Guard troops would start filling the streets in South Central L.A. and span out from there. Guards wearing fatigues holding rifles could be spotted on rooftops, tanks rolled down the streets I was used to cruising.

One of the Tommy's Hamburgers that Ruthie and I used to hit when nothing else but their famed chili burgers would do when we couldn't concentrate—she on her studies, me on a new script—was in Koreatown on Beverly and Rampart boulevards in one of the battle zones.

Just as my life was coming together, it seemed the city I lived in and had grown to love was coming apart.

Jack was trying to deal with my flight change and didn't realize what was happening until he went to his bank on Wilshire Boulevard, and saw the Big 5 athletic store across the street under siege and then a wave of looters running down the street holding TV sets still in their boxes.

By the time I landed, I knew there were riots, but it all seemed surreal and I couldn't quite imagine what that meant. Kevin had left his car at Burbank Airport for me, so I was headed from the Valley back to my place. I realized just how bad it was when the car in front of me started swerving wildly—back and forth, back and forth—as if the driver was making sure no one could pass. I just tapped my horn and the car ahead slammed on the brakes. Four gangbangers piled out, shaking their fists and shouting at me. I can read lips; I knew just how scared I should be.

I used signs, gestures, anything I could to communicate that I couldn't hear them, I was Deaf. I kept telling them over and over. My heart was racing and they were looking at me, deciding whether to believe me. I was trying to calculate how quickly I could squeeze through my window and start running. But then they turned and walked back to their car.

The rest of the drive home was a nightmare. Most of the streets were a maze of panicked gridlock, people driving on sidewalks to keep moving, and the faces in the other cars looked either frightened or angry.

The city was locked down, and everyone I knew was lying low, waiting for things to break. But Kevin, my new fiancé, was working nonstop. Like every other cop in the area, he was pulling long, frightening hours. At least they were frightening to me.

Kevin is careful, I know that, but he also never hesitates to step in and do whatever is necessary to carry out his job. We are both perfectionists in that way. So my heart would sink every time he walked out the door in those days, and I would worry until he was home safely.

It really hit home for the first time what I was signing on for in falling in love with Kevin. This is the reality that I try to push aside to help me cope, knowing that each time he walks out that door to go to work, I never know what kind of danger he could step into or what he will face before the day is done.

He loves his job, has never wanted to do anything else, and he loves working the streets. But I was thrilled in the summer of 2008 when his latest promotion meant he'd spend more time at the station and far less on patrol.

The riots passed, though scars linger. For all of us, I hope we never see that rage rise up anywhere in our country again. I hope that we keep searching for ways to eliminate the anger and replant it with hope.

THE HOUSE IN the hills turned out to be perfect. It had the look of an English country house with four bedrooms and views that did not stop. On clear days I could look west and see the ocean and Catalina Island. Below me was the basin of the city, with downtown rising to the east.

The two best times of day were the quiet early mornings, before the hum and buzz of Sunset Boulevard penetrated the trees, and the evenings, when the lights of this living, breathing city turned on.

As soon as I bought it, I dove into redecorating it. I wanted it to be cozy and warm. When I was asked by photographer Michael McCreary to participate in one of his projects to help fund AIDS research, I immediately said yes.

He envisioned a coffee-table book filled with photos not of celebrities—many of whom he shot as part of his day job as a top photographer—but their favorite rooms.

I didn't have to think about which room in my house that would be—what Whoopi described in the introduction as "that room that lets you be you."

For me it was the family room, though at the moment that meant just me and Kevin. It had a fireplace that we stoked up when the nights grew chilly, walls lined with bookshelves, and a great de-stresser, Galaga, the classic arcade game in which my spaceships shot down more than their share of flying insects.

But the pièce de résistance was a huge wraparound, blue denim couch, as comfortable as your favorite pair of jeans, and big enough to easily seat twenty. It was covered with huge throw pillows, and in the middle of it all sat a weathered wooden coffee table that wasn't happy unless feet were propped up on it, with a bowl of popcorn within reach. I could just sink into that couch and not move for days!

A lot of our wedding would be planned on that couch.

SUPER BOWL XXVII in 1993 was at the Rose Bowl in Pasadena—Cowboys versus the Buffalo Bills. I love football; I also love Garth Brooks, who was slated to sing the national anthem that year.

That's something I'd always wanted to do, sign the national anthem at a major sporting event. Jack put in a call to Garth to see how he'd feel about me signing while he sang. He loved the idea.

It was great watching as they set up the stage on the floor of the Rose Bowl—it might look small when you see it, but up close, it's massive. We were getting ready to do the run-through when Garth had some words with the producer and walked off the stage.

The dispute was over whether the network would also air Garth's video "We Shall Be Free," which I'd participated in with lots of other actors the year before. An agreement had originally been struck, but now someone up the food chain was getting cold feet.

The song is a moving portrait of Garth's hopes for this country. The lyrics beautifully weave together the notion that once we end poverty, war, prejudice, injustice, all the things that divide people and countries, only then will we be free. There's no condemnation, just a prayer for a better day.

But word had come down that someone at the network thought it was too political; the network would not air the video after all. Well, Garth told them, then he would *not* be singing the national anthem. The one thing to know about Garth is that he's a man of his word, and he expects other people to extend him the same courtesy.

Someone with the production came over and talked to Jack, alerting him that I might be signing the national anthem by myself. This was definitely not what I had had in mind. I was terrified of stepping out there by myself, Garth-less, in front of that huge stadium, packed with fans, to say nothing of the biggest television audience of the year.

How desperate were the producers? They saw Eddie Van Halen there and asked if he would step in and sing. He declined. At some point they even asked if Jack could sing. No way!

I tried to steel myself, all the while praying that the network would relent and air Garth's video. At the last second peace was declared!

Garth sang, I signed, the video aired, and the Cowboys won. It was a great day.

My bridesmaids

ဢ ဢ

WHEN IT CAME to a wedding, I wanted the perfect blend of elegance and comfort. We were going to be surrounded by all the people we loved, and I wanted the evening to be like a great party for everyone, the kind that you remember years later.

The first question, where to hold the wedding, was once again answered by the Winklers. Just as they had opened their hearts, then their Toluca Lake home, to me many years ago, they opened up their beautiful yard for the evening in late August that Kevin and I had settled on as the day we would marry.

As in all things, they were incredibly gracious. When the wedding planner I worked with wanted to cover their pool to create a dance floor that night—even though it would mean removing the fencing around the pool—Stacey and Henry said absolutely.

The invitations were hand-painted and my dress was white silk taffeta—off the shoulders but with sleeves capped just above the elbow. The rusching of the fitted bodice opened up into beautiful open folds of the skirt that draped to the floor. Amazing beading was at the neck and the waist. The only jewelry I wore was a pearl choker, and my four-carat diamond engagement ring.

My wedding planner convinced me to tone down my love of purple a little, so we used pale lavenders and lilacs. The bridesmaids wore plum.

The tables were covered in chintz and lace, with enough food to feed probably twice the 250 guests who came to celebrate with us.

The ceremony was short—performed by a priest and a rabbi. Kevin and I signed our vows, so in a sense we married in silence. A good friend, Jann Goldsby, signed the ceremony for my many Deaf friends who had come from Chicago to share the night with me. Liz was my matron of honor and Ruthie was my maid of honor—I couldn't have done it without my best friend and my soul sister!— along with the other important women in my life: my bridesmaids Barbara, Barb, Gloria, Kevin's sister Kim, and my niece, Arielle.

All my family was there, aunts, uncles, cousins. I asked both of my parents to walk me down the aisle—which had been created out of rose trees—and give me away.

Just before the ceremony, my brother Eric slipped me the coolest, funkiest pair of sunglasses that he and my brother Marc had come up with. They were white, then covered in rhinestones with a little bride and groom on each corner. Just as Kevin and I turned around to greet everyone as husband and wife for the first time, I slipped on the sunglasses and grinned. Not to be outdone, Kevin and the groomsmen showed off the hot-pink socks they were wearing under their black tuxes!

The rest of the night was filled with fun and food and dancing. We had seven food stations and the most amazing cake. Henry and Stacey were such gracious hosts, but the entire time they were greeting guests, Henry was worried about the "dance floor" that covered the pool that night—people were dancing wildly on it. Funny sight.

The final song before we left just around midnight was and is our song, "I Cross My Heart." And I still do.

44

I WAS IN NORTH Carolina; my destination was Cherry Hospital, an inpatient psychiatric facility where they house those who have, for the most part, lost complete touch with reality. It's what we used to think of as an insane asylum.

At times when you are researching a character you find yourself looking in the face of some terrible tragedy that was the starting point for the story you're going to be telling.

For me, Carrie Buck's tragedy, which we would be telling in *Against Her Will: The Carrie Buck Story,* was that she never had a chance at life. As a baby she'd been abandoned by her mother and placed with foster parents. For a while she went to school, but she dropped out, taking on many of the household chores for her foster family. At seventeen, she was raped by their nephew.

It was 1923, and whether the family was motivated by shame or something even darker, Carrie was institutionalized and deemed both "feebleminded" and promiscuous. Her baby was taken away from her and handed over to her foster parents. In the months after, doctors went to court to test the Virginia Sterilization Act, which allowed them to sterilize Carrie after a court hearing. The Supreme Court affirmed the law, and Carrie was sterilized under the theory that if she was mentally incompetent, her children would be as well.

In a chilling decision, Justice Oliver Wendell Holmes wrote, "It is better for all the world, if instead of waiting to execute degenerate offspring for crime, or to let them starve for their imbecility, society can prevent those who are manifestly unfit from continuing their kind."

Carrie would ultimately be released from the Virginia Colony for the Epileptic and the Feebleminded and marry. Those who interviewed her over the years found a woman of normal intelligence.

Even more than sixty years later in what one would hope to be a far more enlightened time, the facility I toured was depressing, claustrophobic. Walking through the hallways, I could feel a weight of hopelessness pressing down, filling the corridors, sucking up all the air. You just knew these people would never leave, would never be able to live on their own.

I couldn't help but think of my own situation—what if someone had mandated that the Deaf couldn't have children, or the blind? It was that sense that anything outside what is deemed "normal" is automatically bad, something to be erased so that it doesn't have to be faced or dealt with, or, more important, accepted.

So I took this character into my heart. If the times or the circumstances had been different, I wondered what doors might have been closed to me forever. I might make a mess of my life, but I wanted those choices and those decisions to be in my hands.

Carrie was the first character I would play who was hearing, who also speaks. That was entirely new terrain for me. I had to be able to react in scenes as if I could hear. I had enough play in my voice that I was able to sound like someone who was intellectually just a little slow.

I also studied Dustin Hoffman in *Rain Man,* with the sound and captioning turned off. If you're an actor, hearing or Deaf, it's a great lesson to watch a movie with no sound to see how an actor's body language and face are communicating. By that measure, Dustin's performance was a master class.

For the first time I was working with my friend Melissa Gilbert, who'd been acting professionally since she was a small child and was only ten when she took on the iconic role of Laura Ingalls on *Little House on the Prairie.*

Melissa would play a young attorney who works on the case and becomes convinced that what is happening to Carrie is inhumane. We were already close, but the two of us completely bonded on this film.

*A different type of role for me. I played a hearing woman in the
film* Against Her Will: The Carrie Buck Story *opposite my good friend
Melissa Gilbert. (Credit: CORBIS/SYGMA)*

I find that I learn something from almost any actor I work with.
With each experience I try to keep myself open for what I might
discover—good or bad—from my colleagues. I was intrigued by
how Melissa could seemingly just flip a switch and be in whatever
emotional peak or valley the script called for. She knew how to get
there in an instant.

It was about the acting process—learning how to bounce off
the energy and intensity of each other in any scene, many of which
were highly emotional.

But it was also about the downtime, when we could just kick back and be girlfriends. We talked about important things, we talked about silly things, and, boy, did we have a great time gossiping!

The challenge of acting and reacting like someone who hears means so many tiny things: the tightening of the muscles in your back at the sound of a car door closing outside; the slight tilt of your head as the mail drops in the slot. All the physical and verbal changes that happen while carrying on a conversation with your back turned. All of that I needed to be able to do believably, even though I couldn't hear the door close, the mail drop, or when dialogue began or ended.

I always work closely with my interpreter, but in this case Bill Pugin and I worked overtime to develop cues that he could give me off camera so that I could make my reactions look effortless.

I was proud of my work on this film, which is unusual for me as a perfectionist, and pleased when the performance earned me a CableACE nomination. But more than anything, I felt grateful that after all these years I'd been able to give Carrie a voice. She had passed away in 1983, in her later years saying that one of her chief regrets was that she and her husband were unable to have more children. She was buried next to her daughter, an intellectually normal child, who died at eight of an infection while still in foster care.

SOMETIMES THE ROLE brings the tragedy to you, but at other times tragedy pushes you to seek out and fight for a role, as when I heard they were casting for the AIDS drama It's My Party, starring Eric Roberts.

I had met the remarkable Elizabeth Glaser at one of Swifty Lazar's post-Oscar bashes. Not long afterward, she called and asked if I'd be willing to help raise money on behalf of AIDS research for children. She was setting up what would become the Elizabeth Glaser Pediatric AIDS Foundation, and I immediately said yes.

This woman had a resolve of steel that I have never stopped being humbled by. She had been given so much to bear—contracting AIDS through a blood transfusion when giving birth, facing her own illness, then that of her children, losing one and desperate to save the other.

It was heartbreaking, but Elizabeth had no time for tears, she had too much to accomplish before she couldn't. I am so grateful for the time I had to know her and work with her. She was the definition of the word *selfless,* and the foundation that is her legacy continues to touch so many lives.

I think she must be smiling down as she sees how much progress has been made, that AIDS is no longer an automatic death sentence, but also impatient that much is left to do.

Ryan White and his mother, Jeanne, also came into my life. In July of 1988, I worked with Elton John and Charlie Sheen to cohost the Athletes and Entertainers for Kids fund-raiser "For the Love of Children." Elton, who had become close to the Whites, brought Ryan and six-year-old Jason Robertson, who was also struggling with the disease, onstage while he performed. I would occasionally stay in touch with Ryan and his mom over the years.

Both Ryan and Jeanne were such compelling examples of grace under fire. Most people I'm sure remember Ryan's story. As an infant, he had contracted AIDS through blood products used to treat his hemophilia. Jeanne became nationally known when she pushed for Ryan's right to attend school on the days he felt well enough.

So much fear surrounded AIDS in those years. People were convinced they could catch AIDS just by being around someone who was infected.

In Jeanne I saw a mother lion, a blend of faith and strength, attacking obstacles fearlessly. She did whatever was necessary to see that Ryan and his life were not marginalized.

It was impossible not to fall in love with Ryan; he was such a charming, brave kid. He had a really funny sense of humor and loved movies and movie stars. He used to say he was in awe when he was around celebrities. Like many others, I was in awe around him.

Like so many people, I lost friends who were not on the public radar to AIDS. They were loved, then far too soon, they were lost. One that hit me particularly hard was the death of David Oliver.

David and I had gotten to know each other in 1988. He was probably best known for playing Sam Gardner in the Emmy-winning miniseries *A Year in the Life,* opposite Sarah Jessica Parker, but I met him through Young Artists United, the political action group of actors that worked in the trenches for voter registration.

When I was without a boyfriend that year, he went with me to Hawaii to compete as my partner in a series of sporting events held just off the coast of Kauai. I don't think we won a single event, but David and Jack and I had an absolute blast, especially on the days we toured the island.

David was smart and devilishly funny, and if a piano was anywhere within reach, he would sit down and get lost in the music for a while. We did an *US* magazine shoot with Helen Slater and Craig Sheffer—"Dressed to Kill," four young Hollywood stars show off holiday party clothes to die for—that ran in November of 1988. The look was sort of French aristocrat, and we spent a day changing clothes and moods and scenes and it seemed as if nothing could stop us.

Over the next couple of years, we lost touch. I heard that he was sick, very sick, and I called and we talked. He was so weak, and he didn't like his friends to see that. He asked me on his deathbed whom I was dating. I told him about Kevin—that he wore a uniform—and David smiled and said, "You go, girl!"

David died in November 1992. He was thirty, and no matter how AIDS ravaged his body, he was still as beautiful as when we first met.

So when I heard about *It's My Party,* I wanted to get involved. The film followed the last days of Nick Stark, the role Eric Roberts was playing.

When Nick went from HIV-positive to full-blown AIDS and finally to lesions on his brain, he chose to end his life before the disease could run its horrific course. But before he goes, he gives a final party for his family and friends.

Randal Kleiser wrote and directed the film, which was loosely based on his own experience, as his partner had contracted AIDS and ultimately committed suicide.

Lee Grant played Nick's mother, I was Nick's sister, Gregory Harrison the lover who had left him after the diagnosis, Margaret Cho a close friend. Olivia Newton-John was in it, too. Many others were in the cast, all of us dealing with the losses that AIDS had exacted in our lives. Everyone worked for scale.

It's hard to explain what it was like during that shoot. There wasn't a day when someone's emotions were not on edge, as a scene would touch the raw nerve of experience. But it brought out the best in all of us, with such support for one another, such love on that set, such healing.

The reviews were largely gentle and sad. A few criticized the film's sentimentality. The box office was barely there. But it was one of the best experiences of my life.

The critic Roger Ebert wrote, "Watching the film is uncannily like going through the illness, death, and memorial service of a loved one." In my mind, that was the true measure of its power.

Left to right: George Segal, Eric Roberts, Lee Grant, and Dimitria Arliss on the set of It's My Party. *(Credit : CORBIS/SYGMA)*

45

THE OUTER LIMITS, with its mix of the unexplained, seemed like the kind of series that we could pitch ideas to. Jack did, they bought one, and before I knew it, I was on my way to Vancouver to shoot an episode titled "The Message."

In the story, a young Deaf woman, Jennifer, gets cochlear implants, but her doctors tell her the surgery has failed.

Despite the doctors' assessment, Jennifer starts hearing something—a series of numbers. Everyone thinks she's crazy except for the mysterious hospital janitor, who, Jennifer discovers, is really an astrophysicist quite possibly able to unlock the meaning of the binary code she keeps hearing. Okay, I said it was *The Outer Limits.*

A number of Deaf children were cast in the show, and normally I love spending time with children, but I was feeling sick. I was really hoping it wasn't the flu.

The shoot wasn't long, just a little over a week, but as the days went on, I wasn't feeling better. It took everything for me to get through the days—even indulging in my favorite junk food wasn't helping. I was so cranky to the cast and crew—and so unlike myself on the set—that I apologized to everyone before I left.

Toward the end of the week, I started wondering if I might be feeling sick for another reason.

Kevin and I had been trying for about a year to have a baby. We were both incredibly healthy, so I couldn't imagine that anything was wrong, but I talked to my doctor. That's when I learned all about the rhythms of my cycle—Kevin's the Catholic in the family, he should have known all about that!

We'd just recently gone from the make-love-anytime-you-feel-like-it approach to paying a little attention to the timing. Could it have happened that quickly?

I started thinking about buying a home pregnancy test, but I didn't want to wait until I got back to L.A.—someone might see me, and any information in Hollywood seems to be fair game for the tabloids.

I wanted to keep this under the radar for two reasons. First, it would be so sad for us if it wasn't true; and second, if it was, I needed to keep working and it's far harder to get the next film or the next TV episode if you're pregnant. Sad, but true.

So I slipped out one day, all alone, and went in search of a pharmacy in Vancouver. I found one, found a pregnancy test, and packed it. I didn't want to find out the answer so far from Kevin and from my doctor.

I got home on a Wednesday and Kevin was still at work. I was exhausted, and not just from the travel. I couldn't sleep the night before, I couldn't keep anything down, and I couldn't stop thinking about taking that test.

As soon as I walked in the door about eleven thirty that morning, I dropped my bags, rummaged through them for the pregnancy test, and headed to the bathroom. I was shaking.

I took the test, counted the seconds, then checked. There it was—a plus! I was over the moon; I had a plus! But it was early; if I was pregnant, I was just barely pregnant. I wanted to be sure. A call to Dr. Schapira's office and a plea—"I need a blood test right away."

"Why?" he asked. I didn't answer. "Okay, come on in."

Since he was not my ob-gyn, he had no idea what to think, I'm sure.

When I walked in, it was still the lunch hour. "I'm here for a blood test." The nurse asked why. "I got a plus on a home pregnancy test." She smiled. They drew my blood, then I asked to please, please let me know that very day. They explained that normally it takes two days. No, no, no, I wanted to know now. I kept insisting, asked to talk to the doctor. Dr. Schapira listened, sighed, smiled, and told me to come back in a couple of hours. Did I mention he has the greatest smile?

Now my mind is going crazy. If I'm pregnant, really pregnant, how am I going to surprise Kevin? I headed to a nearby Rexall, right across from the Beverly Center, and went to the baby section to look around.

When I got back to the doctor's office, the nurse said. "The doctor wants to see you in his office."

"Can't you just tell me?"

"No, sorry, the doctor wants to see you."

Sitting in his office, I was nervous. I kept waiting and waiting and waiting. I was beginning to wonder if they'd forgotten I was in there. Finally he walked in, looking serious. He sat down and took a deep breath and said, "Congratulations, you're pregnant."

I started to cry and cry and cry.

"What's wrong?"

"I don't know, I'm just happy, so happy. It's taken a year!"

I laughed, blew my nose, and he hugged me.

Then I went home to wait for Kevin. He remembers, "I came home from work around six and looked around for Marlee. I finally found her in the kitchen. She was standing there with a pacifier in

Preggers with our first child

her mouth. I looked at her kinda funny, then she pulled the pregnancy test out from behind her back. And I grabbed her and just held her."

We hugged and cried and hugged some more. We started talking about all the things that we needed to do to get ready for this baby. Kevin finally said, "We've got to go get something to eat." So we went to this little Italian place on Third Street, nothing fancy, it had a little red awning and served home-style Italian food. Simple place, the best dinner of my life!

While we were eating, Kevin said, "Well, I have a surprise for you, too. I bought tickets for the two of us to go to Hawaii for your thirtieth birthday."

Now, I'm an actress, I should be able to pull off the thrilled-because-your-husband-surprised-you-with-tickets-to-Hawaii reaction, but I was having a hard time of it. My birthdays are usually not two-person affairs. They range from crowded to massive. I honestly didn't know how to tell Kevin I was really hoping to have a big party at home. So I didn't.

Besides, I tried telling myself, we were still getting used to this whole baby thing, so maybe a quiet getaway with just the two of us would be perfect.

GETTING PREGNANT WAS definitely worth it—*they* are definitely worth it, my children. But with all four I had the worst morning sickness for the first three months. I could not keep much of anything down. Just the smell of chicken would send me flying for the nearest bathroom. The nose-stomach connection for me was so intense that if I was even downwind of a chicken restaurant, I would know it—my insides would start churning.

One day in August during my first pregnancy as I was nearing the end of my third month, I threw up. It was worse than usual and the barf was so violent that some splashed back up on my face from the toilet. Yuck!

After that, I washed my face, brushed my teeth, looked myself in the bathroom mirror, and said, "That's it! I am not doing this anymore!" And that was the end of it. The morning sickness stopped.

In case you're wondering, yes, I tried it with the three pregnancies that followed, hoping it was just a mind-over-matter thing. But, no. It would only work when I was heading into that fourth month. I guess I just got lucky that day.

That was a good thing because Kevin and I were due to head to Hawaii in a few days for the birthday trip he'd planned. Jack was already on his way to Italy to attend the baptism of a friend's kid.

We headed first to the island of Lanai. It's so beautiful there; if you get the chance, you should go. I had a great time relaxing, swimming, reading on the beach, eating, which thankfully I could do again. Jack called from Italy to wish me a happy birthday. It was the first birthday of mine he'd missed since we started working together a decade earlier.

On the last day we were in Lanai, I got flowers from Henry and Stacey wishing me a happy thirtieth. I was thrilled, but thought it was so strange that they knew where we were. Then we were off to Maui, with no time to second-guess.

The weather in Maui was miserable, cold for Hawaii, and I was miserable. On my birthday, Kevin left and said he'd be back in an hour. He didn't come back for three and a half hours—I was not a happy camper. It was my birthday, I was pregnant, I was alone, I missed Lanai.

He finally got back about four fifteen and said, "Let's hit the showers, I've gotten a car and made a reservation for us to go to a different hotel for a luau." I didn't understand why we had to be in such a rush, but he said we had to be there by five. "I told them it was your birthday and they want to sing, so we really have to go."

I was not moving fast, or at least not fast enough for Kevin. He was gentle but he kept hurrying me along. It seemed as if nothing was going right, the shower didn't work, I didn't really have anything I wanted to wear. My hair was wet. Finally he said, "Just put your hair in a ponytail, there's no time to blow it dry."

When we got in the car, Kevin floored it! I'd never seen him drive so fast. "What are you doing? We're having a baby, slow down!" When we got to the hotel, the valet seemed to recognize

Check out Jack's coconuts!

him and took the car right away. We got out and Kevin started run-ning; he ran, I walked. When we got there, we found a bunch of empty tables, and I thought to myself, *Great birthday, I just want to go back to Lanai.*

Then the show started. The hostess said, "Okay, everyone get up, we're going to learn the hula." I'm thinking, *Thanks a lot, Kevin.* But I got up, and the next thing I saw was Jack onstage wearing a coconut bra and a grass skirt doing the hula. Then everybody from my family started pouring out onto the stage.

And so began my thirtieth birthday party, with dozens of friends and family who'd flown in to celebrate with me, including Jack, who clearly wasn't in Italy at all.

It was the most incredible birthday ever. Kevin had managed to keep it a complete surprise—and I thought I was the only actor in the family.

He and Jack had been planning it for months. The present I treasure most is a big book filled with birthday memories from all my friends and family. They'd asked everyone to send in a page—writing as much or as little as the person wanted.

I look through it now and am reminded of how rich I am from the love and support I get from the friends I've made over the years. The book is about two inches thick, and if I'm ever feeling down, I only need to pull it out and open it to any page and I know I'll feel better.

Every page is a favorite. Many recapture moments that are incredibly special to me. Some from those who are especially dear to me I won't share, but here are snippets from a few that made me laugh or made me cry:

From my friend Janet: "I've learned many things from you. Below I've listed just a few: 1. Choose your friends carefully and only show your tattoo to those who are worthy."

From my friend Kirstie: "Dear Marlee, I love you madly, however, you are now too old for me."

From my former accountant Gary: "Dear Marlee, You **do not** owe City National Bank $1,000,000 by the way."

From Arsenio: "Would you give me one of your cars to put my 'SWDJB' plate on?"

From Billy Joel: a "Happy Birthday" and a sketch of the piano man as a piano! It's amazing how a face can fit into the shape of a baby grand.

From my friend Kathy: "You know, Marlee, one of my very first auditions as an actress was for the movie *Children of a Lesser God.* And you got it. Thank God! Cause if I had to swim naked in that pool I know I would have gotten a chest cold. But then again at least something would have been on my chest."

From my dearest Henry: "To watch you become the woman you are today gives me a sense of pride, touches me deeply and brings the hugest smile to my face."

And finally, from my mom and dad, who wrote possibly the longest poem known to modern man, thirty-three stanzas in all, ending with:

Thank you for the happiness and also, Yes,
The tears you've brought to our lives.

It hasn't all been fun but,
The bottom line when all is said and done,
The rewards are there. . . .

So now, I'll close with best Wishes,
And Happy Birthday and Always . . .
Our love and Kisses,
Mom and Dad

For other reasons, also, I'll never forget this birthday. It was a difficult time for us; an early blood test had indicated our child could possibly be born with Down syndrome. I had an amino before we left, but the results would take a while and we had left still not knowing the outcome.

One morning the baby stopped moving. I couldn't feel a kick or a push or anything. I went down to the pool by myself and lay there and talked and talked to this baby. When I patted my belly and the baby kicked, I ran up to the room, opened the door, looked at Kevin, and said, "Yes!"

It was terrifying, wondering what would happen, but I was praying that we wouldn't be faced with deciding what to do if the baby had Down syndrome. We wanted this baby very much.

We called the minute we got back home, and the doctor's office said he would get back to us in a couple of minutes. After what seemed like forever, the phone rang.

"Can I see you smile over the phone? We have good news, the baby is healthy."

After that, everything else was a snap.

46

W ITH *REASONABLE DOUBTS* canceled, I was once
again a struggling actor. One of the most intriguing opportunities
opened up with *Seinfeld*. They were playing around with the idea
of lipreading and deafness for an episode and asked if I would be
game.

That's like someone asking if you'd like to win the lottery. This
was my first chance to really show what I could do with comedy,
and it was *Seinfeld*, smart, funny, unconventional, and such a remarkable collection of actors with Jerry Seinfeld at its center.

I said yes right away, but as the day approached for me to show
up on set, I was intimidated. This was season five and the actors had
worked together from the beginning. I knew they must be so close
by now, able to play off one another completely organically. I wasn't
sure how it would feel walking into that group.

But it was great!

Jerry, George, Elaine, and Kramer—I mean Jerry, Jason, Julia,
and Michael—could not have been more welcoming. We had such
fun on the set and I loved the way the script was so irreverent. There
were no sacred cows, especially the Deaf.

I realize I'm biased, but I still think "The Lip Reader" is one
of the series' classics. Whether it's Jerry and George discussing the
relative merits of PABA in sunscreen or Elaine pretending she can't
hear so she doesn't have to talk to a limo driver; Kramer as a disaster of a ball boy at the U.S. Open; or George saying that having a
lip-reader is like having Superman for a friend.

In one of my two favorite scenes, Jerry, George, and I are having dinner, and George starts to hatch a plan to have me read the

lips of his ex-girlfriend at a party. He and Jerry begin assessing the pros and cons, and a crazy conversation unfolds behind their hands, drinks, napkins, food, anything they think will keep me from using my superpowers on them. It was funny dialogue, but even funnier physical humor.

In my other favorite scene, Jerry and I are working out the details for our next date. I turn my head away just as he says we'll be taking a car service. When I look back, he's asking, "How about six? Six is good. You have a problem with six?" A series of my reactions mirror his dialogue—an arched eyebrow, a gasp of disbelief, a look of disgust—enough to clue anyone watching that I've mistaken what he said for "How about sex? Sex is good. You have a problem with sex?"

That's one of the things I've always loved about *Seinfeld,* the writers expect the audience to get it. And they did. That freed both me and the other actors to play the moments for all they're worth.

A few months later it was great to hear that I'd been nominated for an Emmy for that performance. Icing on the cake. I did actually bring a cake to the set for everyone on the day we wrapped.

Emmy-nomination day was a particularly good one when it finally rolled around in 1994. I was nominated in two categories, Outstanding Guest Actress in a Comedy for *Seinfeld,* and Outstanding Guest Actress in a Drama for a *Picket Fences* episode called "The Dancing Bandit."

WHEN DAVID KELLEY heard I was looking to do more television as I coped with losing *Reasonable Doubts,* he decided to write me into an episode of *Picket Fences,* the quirky drama/comedy about the folks in small-town Rome, Wisconsin.

And so the Dancing Bandit was born. In the bandit, David had created a character that had so many little bits of my life stitched into it, the episode will always be one of my favorites.

First there was the bandit, who is Deaf. Her MO, which the FBI has been tracking, is charming. She truly "stages" robberies—complete with specific roles that her cohorts play. She's delightful, mischievous, entertaining; after she's finished a heist, boom box at the ready, she takes a moment to dance for bank patrons on her way out the door.

David knew my history—I'd grown up signing songs. He knew I loved to dance, so it was a nice touch, and I'm sure he was one of a handful of people who wasn't surprised in the least that I turned up nearly a decade later on *Dancing with the Stars*.

In one of the episode's plot twists, he has me and three others in my gang walk into a school disguised as the characters from *The Wizard of Oz*—Dorothy, the Tin Man, the Lion, and the Scarecrow. So just as the role of Dorothy was a career changer when I was eight, it was again when I was thirty.

To cap off this totally surreal escapade, when my character needs to be airlifted to a hospital for a special procedure, the only hospital able to do it is located in Chicago—so at the end of the episode, David airlifted me safely back home.

The Dancing Bandit was never intended to be anything but a one-shot appearance. But as David explains, "There's a lot of humanity to Marlee that comes through even if she's holding a gun or kicking down a door. She's profoundly intuitive, which makes her a great actress, she always finds the truth within the character.

"As the Dancing Bandit, she played a bank robber, who ended up being mayor of the town. . . . Even for that series, that was a big character arc, but she's so truthful she was able to take the audience with her on a believable ride."

The episode of *Picket Fences* that is always at the top of my favorites list is "Snow Exit," which aired on January 19, 1996.

By then, I had become an occasional guest star as Mayor Laurie Bey. The Dancing Bandit had morphed into one of Rome's upstanding citizens, but then she was a Robin Hood–style bandit even in her criminal days.

I'd also become pregnant with my first child. By this time David had moved on to focus on *Chicago Hope* and was getting *Ally McBeal* under way, but the writers decided to write my pregnancy into the script.

We shot it a couple of months before it was set to air, when I was around seven months pregnant. In the episode, the town is hit by a blizzard and I go into labor at the police station—I have to deliver there. So I give birth—breathing and sweating and pushing and pushing. A nurse/midwife was on set to monitor me to make sure my acting wasn't so good that it induced real labor—and Mayor Laurie Bey gave birth on a cold winter day.

MY BABY WAS due on January 15. The day came and went and no baby. My doctor told me not to worry, first babies are often late. I remember asking, "When will it come?"

"Oh, you'll know when you're ready. You'll have contractions and your water will break. Don't worry about it."

Don't worry? Me?

Kevin and I went to sleep on the eighteenth, but I was soon awake, pacing the floors. The doctor was right; I knew it was happening.

I waited until daylight, then woke Kevin up. He remembers, "Marlee was sitting up in the bed. She told me she'd been up all night having contractions, but she didn't want to wake me. She said, 'I thought I better let you sleep because I think we are having the baby today.'"

You couldn't have found two happier people anywhere that day than the Grandalskis as we grabbed a suitcase and got ready to drive to the hospital to have our first child.

One of the few things Kevin has always insisted on is that we not know the sex of our children before they are born. This despite the technology, despite the amnio, the sonograms, all the ways it's possible to have that question answered long before the birth. He says, "My feeling is that it's the last true surprise left on earth, that if God wanted you to know what kind of baby you were going to have, there'd be some sign, *you'd* turn pink or blue. . . .

"Marlee kept saying, 'I don't know what color to paint the room, I don't know if I should get boy's clothes or girl's clothes.'"

"I said, 'When the kid pops out, we can paint the room and buy some clothes because they aren't going to need anything right away, and they don't care about what color the walls are anyway—at least not until they're twelve.'" (The kid who popped out was twelve as he was recalling this story. Sarah turned thirteen in January.)

How could I not fall for that argument? My husband, a romantic at heart?

Now you might think that's easy to do—keep the sex of the child a secret. But it's really tough in the delivery room, when I have a baby, there's usually a crowd. At a minimum there's the doctor, the anesthesiologist, the pediatrician, the nurses, Kevin, an interpreter—someone I can't do without. Kevin can sign, but a new father in a delivery room has a few other distractions—Liz, when she can make it, and often one or two more family members.

Jack faints at the sight of blood, so he's always with the waiting-room contingent. For baby number one, I got Bill Pugin to interpret. By the time I had the other three, I'd met Connie Schultz, a mother of seven. We met at a Baby and Me class, where she was interpreting. She's become a good friend, is an expert signer, and besides being at my side for births, has come to sets more than a few times to work with me, too.

I'd planned to deliver the baby naturally, but I just wasn't dilating, and after about fifteen hours the doctor said we needed to do a C-section—now. And so Sarah Rose Grandalski entered this world. Kevin walked out into the waiting room, grinning from ear to ear, but not saying a word. We'd come equipped with two buttons—a blue one that said BOY and a pink one that said GIRL. When the assembled masses finally noticed the pink button, there was much laughing and crying.

A couple of hours later, with Sarah in my arms, we watched Laurie Bey give birth on *Picket Fences*. Forty-three years earlier, on January 19, Lucille Ball had given birth to Desi Arnaz Jr., and on that night her character, Lucy Ricardo, had given birth on *I Love Lucy* to the child we'd come to know as Little Ricky, on the same network, CBS. I loved that Sarah became a little bit of history that day.

47

For a few glorious months I did nothing but feed, change, bathe, dress, coo, cuddle, and play with Sarah. I loved this baby girl beyond measure and I adored being a mother.

People say you can't imagine what you will feel about your children before you hold them that first time, you can't understand that it's something that is so much bigger than anything that has come before in your life. They're right. It was magical even through all the sleepless nights, the endless diaper duty, and the desperate attempts to lose all that baby weight.

Ahhh, the baby weight. With my pregnancies, I didn't count calories at all. Depending on which child I was carrying, I gained between fifty-one and sixty-three pounds. For someone who is five feet three inches and usually weighs between 98 and 110 pounds, that's a lot. It worked out well for the babies; I had strong, healthy, perfect kids. But getting that body back into shape—well, I had my work cut out for me.

A new baby also meant more financial responsibilities. Schools, college funds, pediatricians, clothes, toys, tutors, all the things a growing child needs. I needed to go back to work—needed to find work.

Salvation came in the form of a TV movie with James Garner titled *Dead Silence,* based on the novel *A Maiden's Grave.* It would shoot in Toronto, and by the time production started Sarah would be about six months old.

Signing on for a few months to shoot in Toronto or Portland or wherever was no problem when it was just Kevin and me. Now with a baby, we had to figure out how we were going to handle things. Kevin says, "I remember the discussion, it went something like this: 'I would like Sarah to go with me.' 'No, you're leaving her at home.' 'No, I'm taking her with me.' She won because she was breast-feeding."

On that trip, I'm sure I was way over the airline's limit on bags—I packed enough stuff for Sarah to get her through first grade. I'd had some help finding a nanny who lived in the Toronto area to help me through the shoot.

Sarah and I and our three thousand bags checked into the Four Seasons Hotel, where the producers had decided to house some of the cast. It was a terrific place to stay as a new mother—if I needed something, no matter what time of the day or night, no matter how crazy the request, the Four Seasons' staff would find it. Thank you, Randy!

As a perfectionist, I'm sure I drove the nanny up the wall—everything had to be perfect for Sarah, and just a few months into this mom gig, I wasn't sure from day to day what perfect was. I glommed on to anyone on the set who had kids, especially young ones, to grill them for tips on how they were raising theirs.

While I had a baby in the hotel, I had a handful of kids to work with on the set. *Dead Silence* tells the story of a twelve-hour siege—three escaped prisoners take a busload of Deaf schoolchildren and their teachers hostage. In a tense showdown between the bad guys and a hard-boiled hostage negotiator, the role Jim Garner played, one hostage is to be killed every hour until all the demands are met.

My character was Melanie, a teacher at the school and one of the hostages. We're being held in an abandoned slaughterhouse, and I'm not content to wait for a rescue and start looking for a way to sneak the children out.

It was interesting to shoot something that takes place over just one day. We had no different looks or styles to our wardrobes, just a single outfit each, which got dirtier or ripped or wet or shot through with holes and splattered with blood, but that was it. Same thing went for hair and makeup.

Sometimes things that seem so simple when you're watching them are the toughest to pull off. Rarely are scenes shot in the exact sequence in which they unfold on-screen. Since the clothing, makeup, and hair needed to undergo small changes during the siege, continuity was critical over the eight-week shoot. If I ran through a muddy drainage ditch at 4 p.m. and the bottom of my dress got dirty, the dress couldn't be dirty during a scene at 3:59, and it had better be at 4:01 and every minute and hour after.

James Garner was a hoot to work with. He's a great storyteller and had hundreds of Hollywood tales. I loved working with the Deaf kids as well; they were sweet and talented, and I got to know their families a little bit, too.

Entertainment Tonight came on the set to shoot a segment about our show. Jim said no way was he doing it, he was boycotting *ET,* but I was certainly free to go ahead. I wanted to know why he did that—had the show done something terrible to him in the past?

Sweet Jim Garner

"They announce everybody's birth date and their age," he growled. "I don't like it."

Just about anyone can find out how old an actor is pretty easily. On the other hand, I was thirty-one and Jim was around sixty-eight, so maybe I'll feel differently about it in another thirty or so years.

Like Jim, I want any assessment of me to be about the work, not my age, not whether I can hear. There's always an x-factor lurking around in the background, shadowing all of us, something that can shift the focus away from what is really important every time you step on a set or a stage.

KEVIN DID NOT like being away from his new baby daughter any longer than he had to, so he made a couple of trips to stay with us in Toronto. Babies can change so much in just a few days.

One morning all three of us were in the room. Sarah was teething on a piece of cold cantaloupe, when I saw her put her little finger to her mouth and her thumb to her ear and fold the rest of her fingers neatly down.

"Look, Kevin, it looks like she's signing 'telephone.'"

But he was already headed over to grab the phone. Sarah had said her first word—in sign language! And we were both there to witness it.

On another day, Sarah had been eating baby food—apricots—and suddenly Kevin said, "Don't look at Sarah."

"What?"

"Just don't look at Sarah."

So of course I immediately looked and gasped—big red blotches covered every inch of my baby's pink, smooth, beautiful skin. We got the doctor on the phone right away; he said to give it ten or fifteen minutes and see if it went away. He suspected it was just a mild allergic reaction. Which is what it turned out to be, one that she eventually grew out of.

But until you know everything is going to be okay, your heart is racing and your mind can conjure up the most horrible things. At these times a vivid imagination is something I'd gladly give up.

At the end of the production, I started packing to go home. Sarah was so cute that day and being so good, she'd fallen asleep sitting in her little car seat on the bed while I was finishing up. I couldn't resist; she was sleeping so peacefully and her little toes were just as still as could be.

I grabbed some hot-pink nail polish and painted her toenails in a flash. When I got home and Kevin saw them, he freaked out! I let a few years pass before I painted Sarah's toenails again.

The flight home should have been exhausting, but I was in luck. Goldie Hawn was on the same flight, and she came over and asked to hold the baby. I was so grateful for the break and thought I'd have about a five-to-ten-minute breather, but Goldie held Sarah for more than an hour, talking to her, rocking her, completely engaging her. She didn't miss her mom at all. An hour's rest when you have a six-month-old is heaven. Thank you, Goldie!

Babies are just hard not to love and be charmed by. In 1998, when I was at designer Nolan Miller's being fitted for a dress for the Oscars, Sarah was playing on the floor. Nolan asked if he could borrow Sarah for a minute while I was changing.

When he came back, I asked where he'd been. He said Sophia Loren was there and had caught sight of Sarah and wanted to hold the baby for a few minutes.

"Sophia Loren? Do we get a picture?"

But the legendary Italian actress had already disappeared into a waiting limo. I sighed. How I would have loved to have a photo of Sophia with Sarah.

THE WORK WAS coming in fits and starts. Nothing steady. I got a call about doing an episode of *Spin City,* working with Michael J. Fox. Once again I was thrilled to be doing comedy and to be back on prime-time television.

In television, it's easier somehow to think that whatever role a person plays in a comedy or a drama is really pretty much how they are in real life. Sometimes that's the case—the show will build off the energy and essence of the person—but just as often it isn't.

If you think that Michael J. Fox is anything like his TV persona, I'm here to tell you you're wrong. He's actually nicer, more decent, kindhearted, and has some of the best comic timing I've witnessed.

Like *Seinfeld, Spin City* was filled with actors who'd been together for a while. They were blessed with terrific writers/producers, and the episode, written by Sarah Dunn and Kirk Rudell with me in mind, was called "Deaf Becomes Her."

One of the best scenes is when the temp who's been hired as the sign-language interpreter for the mayor's State of the City address hasn't a clue how to sign and just starts making it up as he goes along. In a couple of scenes I get to flirt with Michael J.—who wouldn't like that? The show was an absolute blast to work on, completely irreverent.

I also got to do a scene with Brooke Shields on *The Larry Sanders Show* with Garry Shandling, which was a lot of fun.

Then a handful of smaller film projects started casting me as the seductress, the villain, the con artist—I liked playing against the good-girl stereotype.

In Her Defense with Jeff Fahey was just downright steamy. I think 90 percent of my wardrobe was different cuts of black leather. Then in *When Justice Fails,* an affair ends in murder—did she or didn't she?

The most interesting project to come along during this time was *Freak City,* in which I played an adult who was intellectually and emotionally about nine years old.

Samantha Mathis's character is at the center of the story. She's a young woman struggling with multiple sclerosis and finds a different sort of family in a group of us who have all been relegated to the same nursing home. It was one of those great sets where everyone just clicks. Natalie Cole played an injured blues singer. Peter Sarsgaard was already crafting his ability to portray infinite layers of cynicism, and Jonathan Silverman played a blind man to perfection.

This bittersweet story was about finding hope in the place you least expect it.

In 1999, I was in production in Portland on *Where the Truth Lies,* another courtroom drama. My character is accused of murder, and my attorney is blinded by his feelings for me.

I liked the challenge of this film, but it carries such sad memories for me. We were in midproduction when news broke of the plane crash that took the life of John F. Kennedy Jr. and his wife, Carolyn. John and his sister, Caroline, had been so gracious to me over the years.

I'll never forget how they helped me navigate an uncomfortable situation in August 1987. They had invited me to the Special Olympics being held on the Notre Dame campus, and Bill Hurt was also attending. It was all coming just a month after our horrific July break up, and it was beginning to feel as if every time I turned around, he was there.

For the duration of the event, John and Caroline gathered me up and kept me close, and I was so grateful for their friendship during that difficult time. One of the funniest moments came when we all went out for pizza. When the check came, everyone kind of looked around—none of them had cash or credit cards—so I picked up the bill.

John's death, so unexpected, so needless, was such a loss for the country and especially painful for those of us who had experienced his kindness firsthand.

Elaine on Seinfeld *would've been very jealous:*
I spent a lovely day with John F. Kennedy Jr.

As Kevin and I headed down to San Diego with Sarah in 1998 to celebrate Christmas Eve with his family, it felt as if everything was coming together for us.

We had decided to sell the house in the hills and move to a quiet neighborhood outside L.A. where we could raise our kids away from the Hollywood scene. Though there was much to love about our house, it was expensive, and one Sunday when we were doing our loop walking Sarah, as we rounded the corner on Sunset Boulevard, we walked right into a hooker fighting with a john. It was 10 a.m. and Kevin said, "You've got to be kidding me. That's it, I'm done."

Besides, we had another baby on the way.

On Christmas Day I told Kevin I had seen a little blood and said we had to drive home from San Diego right away. On this solemn ride, we were quiet; there wasn't much for either of us to say. I dropped Sarah off with Jack the next day, and Kevin and I went together to the doctor.

This was the one time in my life I didn't want to be right. I was praying that I was wrong, that everything was going to be fine. It wasn't. The doctor confirmed what I had feared.

The miscarriage hit us hard. It took about a year to mentally and emotionally recover. Then we faced a terrifying scare with Sarah.

She was about three and a half and was in child care during the day. On a Monday, she came home with a big bruise on her wrist. One of the kids at school had accidentally hit her with a plastic dinosaur. On Tuesday she came home with a few more bruises. On Wednesday she came home with even more. Now Kevin and I were alarmed.

We talked to the child-care center, and on Thursday an observer watched Sarah throughout the day, recording everything that happened to her, especially anything that could cause bruising. It was all ordinary stuff, such as at 8:35 Sarah bumped into the arts-and-crafts table. Everyone was mystified. By Thursday night, she also had some little red dots—they looked like tiny pinpricks—that were barely visible along the back of her neck.

On Friday, Kevin headed off to work with my worry level rising. I decided I had to get Sarah to a doctor. The doctor took one look at her and said, "Go get a blood test right now." I got to the lab and it took five people to hold Sarah down, she was screaming bloody murder, so much I could see the veins bulging on her little neck. It was killing me.

The doctor said they'd call with the test results that night. The call came at 9 p.m. Sarah was asleep, I was lying down. Kevin, who was livid that I hadn't told him about all this from the start, answered the phone.

He remembers: "The doctor said they had the results back from the lab and that they'd called ahead and the hospital had a bed waiting, she needed to go to the hospital now. 'Right now?' I asked. 'Right now.' It was a hospital we hadn't heard of, but we got Sarah up and headed out. When we drove up, the first thing we saw was the sign: CITY OF HOPE CANCER RESEARCH CENTER."

We went from worry to absolute terror. We got inside, and as soon as the doctor walked in, he began looking over the test results. I asked if it was leukemia. He said it wasn't. He told us, "This is the kind of case I enjoy. At the end of the weekend she'll be going home. And she'll be fine."

Sarah had a serious case of idiopathic thrombocytopenic purpura, or ITP. Mild cases are not that uncommon in kids and usually clear up on their own. Essentially, as they explained it to us, Sarah's platelet count was extremely low; her blood was so thin that if she broke the skin in a fall, her blood had no ability to clot. Also, internal bleeding that we wouldn't be aware of until the situation had become life threatening was possible. All of it was compromising her body's ability to fight off infections.

The doctor who treated Sarah was a visiting specialist from Oregon. Dr. James Miser, who was the hospital's chief medical officer at the time, also got involved and was so filled with compassion and patience. He was great with kids. None of us will forget the Donald Duck puppet he used to explain what was going to happen—I'm not sure whom Donald reassured most, me and Kev, or Sarah.

Kevin and I took shifts staying with Sarah that weekend. He stayed the first night—I was so afraid something would happen and because of my deafness I might not understand, or the doctors and nurses might not understand me. I took the days, and we did that through the weekend.

Sarah quickly adjusted, and she still remembers clomping down the hospital corridors in a pair of princess high heels, pulling her IV behind her. Over the next year, we had to take her in for weekly, then monthly treatments until the platelet count was stabilized. I don't think we have ever felt such anguish as we did going through that experience—and we were so lucky that ITP was so treatable and that Sarah is completely healthy today.

When Sarah was in kindergarten, she had a birthday party and asked all the kids to bring unwrapped gifts to donate to the City of Hope toy room. The hospital has a toy store, and each child patient gets to go in each day and pick out a toy. Sarah wanted to fill up that room. Sarah's birthday netted about forty-five toys, and we had another fifty toys we took from our closet. Then we headed over one day to donate them.

Sarah wanted to give the toys herself to the children there. But hospital policy forbids a child who could have an infection so slight he or she might not even be aware of it to be around children whose immune systems are already so weak. But Sarah was adamant—she had to give at least one toy to one child.

The staff found a two-year-old who had Down syndrome who was being released the next day. Her name was Sarah. And so my Sarah, with a big, purple dancing Barney in hand, got to hand him off to another Sarah and see her smile and giggle with delight. It was one of the best days ever.

With Sarah healed and bouncing back, I was anxious to throw myself into work again. I needed a role that would really challenge me.

The role didn't come overnight, but finally arrived courtesy of the brilliant Aaron Sorkin.

48

By November of 1998, I was already hooked on the new Aaron Sorkin series, *Sports Night.* It was so sharply written and so unexpected, and considering my love of sports, I had to watch this show.

But then he wrote an episode called "Dear Louise," which aired on November 10.

In the episode, Jeremy, who was played by Josh Malina, is writing to his Deaf sister, Louise, a college sophomore. He's telling her all about his new job at *Sports Night* and everything that's been happening over the last few days.

"Dear Louise" was funny, poignant, and I dropped Aaron a note just to let him know how much I'd enjoyed it and appreciated the shout-out to the Deaf community. I wanted him to know we paid attention to that sort of thing, that even a simple gesture like that meant something.

That note soon led to a completely unexpected lunch at Mandarin in Beverley Hills. Aaron and I had such a good conversation and found that when it came to character and story and ideas, we thought about things in many of the same ways.

Sports Night was canceled at the end of its second season in May of 2000, long before it should have been. But by then Aaron already had a new series on the air, *The West Wing.*

Some TV series take time to build an audience, others just hit. *The West Wing* landed in prime time with gale-force winds. Critics loved it, the Washington power brokers became immediately addicted. Not only did it draw big audiences—it was consistently one of the top ten prime-time series in its early years—but its viewers ranked among the best educated, the most affluent, the most influential.

When Aaron said he wanted to write me into an episode, I was thrilled.

On December 16, 1999, I got this fax: "This is your first scene. There's obviously more to come. Aaron."

It was enough. Five pages that rocked my world!

MY FIRST LINE—DELIVERED to a hung over Josh Lyman, played by Bradley Whitford—was "Are you the unmitigated jackass who's got the DNC choking off funding for O'Dwyer's campaign in the California Seventh?"

Meet Joey Lucas, my character on *The West Wing.* She was high octane, feisty, and no-nonsense—I immediately liked her.

I also liked the way Aaron mixed things up, really capturing the way I communicate. Sometimes the dialogue was words I signed

Working on The West Wing *was one of the most difficult but rewarding jobs I've ever had. I loved Aaron Sorkin's brilliant writing and having the chance to act opposite Bradley Whitford and a great cast. (Credit: Warner Bros./Getty Images).*

and an interpreter translated, other times it was words I spoke, and still others it was words I signed that weren't translated.

Frankly that's usually the way it is, and somehow Aaron managed to do it so that it rang true—the character's voice sounded completely authentic.

Here's one bit from the first scene that was just masterful in moving from one voice to another—the first is signed and translated, then I speak the italicized words:

JOSH

You're O'Dwyer's campaign manager?

JOEY

Yes. And I have three sources, two at the DNC and one at the Leadership Council, that say the reason why I'm running a campaign on spit and tissue paper is—*what the hell are you wearing?*

Aaron constantly changed the rhythm and texture of my dialogue in that way and, as a result, built a real flesh-and-blood character that just happened to be Deaf.

When I showed up to shoot my episode, I was hit with waves of nausea. This time I knew exactly what was causing it—I was pregnant again.

I didn't want to jeopardize this shot at *The West Wing,* and after the miscarriage I would take a long time before trusting that this pregnancy was real. So I tried to find discreet ways to not look green, and I fought my need to throw up as much as I could.

The West Wing cast and crew were all terrific and were the hardest-working group I have ever seen in my life. The dialogue was complex and you never had enough time to feel that you absolutely had it, but you absolutely had to have it nailed.

One reason the show worked so well is that sense of reality Aaron gave to all the characters, not just mine, and the stories. For the audience, it felt like a window into the real West Wing. When Aaron left the show, I felt a lot of the playful nature of my character left with him. I went from sharp-witted, tough, funny, possible love interest to smart lobbyist, period.

ONCE I WAS past the morning-sickness phase, I had a great pregnancy. I felt great and the show found a way to work around it since I was not a regular, but they kept asking me back and for that I was grateful.

One of the best times I had was in the spring of 2000 going as part of the cast to the annual White House Correspondents' Association dinner. It's one of the major events in Washington, with the White House press corps, politicians everywhere you turn, lots of politically active stars, and of course most of the time the president—all showing up at the Washington Hilton the last Saturday in April.

As Jack and I headed out from my hotel around six, the strap on my shoe broke. I was five and a half months pregnant and I couldn't hobble along. I needed stability, and I had nothing else with me except a pair of tennis shoes, which didn't really seem as if they would do. The hotel concierge said a Nine West was a few blocks away.

The clock was ticking because in about twenty minutes the streets would all be closed for the president's motorcade. Thankfully our driver knew a shortcut that would get us within about a block of the store—but we'd have to walk that block.

So I'm in formal wear and sporting an already very pregnant belly, Jack's in his tux, and we're half running and half limping down the street toward Nine West—people must have thought we were crazy.

The store was packed—I walked in and felt as if I were at the back of a rock concert—all I could see were shoulders and heads.

Jack stepped in front of me and started pushing through, sounding very official as he announced, "Move aside, move aside, she's seeing the president in twenty minutes and she needs a pair of pumps." If I weren't so panicked, I would have died with laughter on the spot.

But a saleswoman took us seriously and ran to the rescue, asking, "Are you the actress?"

"I don't have time, I'm late to see President Clinton!"

Pregnant feet swell, so I had to buy two pairs of shoes—slipping a 6½ on one foot, a 7 on the other.

Suddenly other Deaf people were in the store. My worst nightmare. "Don't sign, don't sign," I said under my breath to Jack. I had no time for casual conversation, and I knew from past experience that if I didn't take time with a Deaf fan, I'd have the entire Deaf community up in arms again.

Finally, as the saleswoman rang up the bill, I said, "Yes, I'm the actress, and thank you so much!"

Outside again—no car to be seen. Jack started yelling the driver's name: "Anthony? Anthony?" and running up and down the street.

People on the sidewalk kept stopping, asking if I was the actress in *Picket Fences.* I didn't want to be rude, but I was in the middle of a crisis and didn't have time to chat, sign autographs, shake hands. So to anyone that felt slighted that night, my sincerest apologies.

Suddenly Anthony drove around the corner and we hopped in. We had eight minutes to get to the Hilton before they closed the streets down. By the time we got near the hotel, traffic was at a standstill—the president had arrived, no one was moving anywhere.

Once again Jack and I hit the streets. Inside we were directed to the *US News & World Report* reception. It was packed with unfamiliar faces. I was rescued by a woman from *People* magazine, who whisked me off to the *People* party.

Inside I ran into John McCain, who remembered me from my day testifying to the Senate committee on behalf of closed-captioning, and he thanked me again for coming to Arizona a few years earlier to speak at a charity benefit that his wife had been involved in.

Heading into the banquet hall a bit later, I ran into Martin Sheen, who gave me a big hug.

"Come with me," he said. "Let's meet the president."

With the Clintons at the White House Correspondents' Dinner

We headed into the VIP party, but were stopped at the door. My name wasn't on the list.

"But I'm the president." Martin said, "and she's my guest!"

That wasn't enough. Even with Martin in my corner they weren't going to let me in. The security guy at the door promised he'd check on my status and waved Martin on inside.

"Nothing doing," he said. "I'm staying here until Marlee gets in."

President Clinton might have been the main attraction, but everybody wanted Martin's President Bartlet in the room, too. A woman came over to see what the problem was, and within minutes we were all inside.

Walking into that room, you could feel the power just radiating off people. Alan Greenspan and Andrea Mitchell. Madeleine Albright stopped me to say she was a fan. But wait—I was the fan. Then someone announced the president was on his way.

The door swung open and there stood the president and the first lady. I'd first met the Clintons in 1994 when President Clinton appointed me to the Corporation for National Service board of directors, which I had been so honored to be involved in.

I went over to speak to the first lady, who looked at my belly and said, "I see there's a baby on the way." We were smiling and Jack snapped a photo. Then I shook the president's hand—another snapshot. He told me, "I have so much respect for you," which always just makes me feel so humble that I've found myself in a position to hopefully make a difference along the way.

Then the cast of *The West Wing* gathered around the president—snap, snap, snap, more photos!

After the dinner everyone was off to another party. I got separated from the rest of the group and slipped into a quiet room that had a fireplace and a couch, where I could rest for a few minutes. It was so restful there, candles everywhere. A couple of attorneys came over to meet me, then suddenly one said to Jack. "You're on fire!"

He was—literally—a spark from the fireplace had landed on his jacket. It was put out with little damage—although Jack was trailing smoke for a while. As the parties were winding down, we walked out with Rob Lowe, Martin Sheen, and Aaron Sorkin. As late as it was, a crowd was waiting outside, cameras and autograph books ready. I expected the fans to scream for one or all of the guys, but a chant started rising: *"Blue's Clues, Blue's Clues."*

The guys looked confused, I looked shocked. We had walked into a crowd filled with mothers who recognized me from the popular kids show on which I occasionally made a guest appearance. Sometimes what touchs the fans are things you least expect.

I finally made it back to the hotel around 1 a.m. with a flight out just a few hours later—all in all, an absolutely grand night.

LATER THAT SPRING, David wrote me into an episode of *The Practice,* the newest of his prime-time series. The drama put him back in the courtroom, where he is a master storyteller.

I played a woman who kills the man who had raped and murdered her seven-year-old daughter. It's one of my favorite pieces of work, also one of the toughest.

I was seven months pregnant and the script was emotionally heavy all the way through. I was terrified of doing it.

Knowing that David had written it, I wanted to do a great job so that he would be proud of my work and glad that he had featured me in the episode.

In this script, he pushed me to tap into all the darker emotions—anger, hatred, remorse, sadness, pain, retribution.

In one scene, Camryn Manheim, who plays one of my attorneys, and I have a heated argument. Camryn, like my husband, Kevin, had learned sign language in college. As a starving actor she would pick up extra work interpreting at hospitals, usually in delivery rooms when one or both of the parents were Deaf, so she is fluent.

In the scene, neither of us ever speaks, we're both signing furiously, faces and bodies expressing everything that needs to be said. The silence made the exchange even more potent.

But the most difficult scene for me was in the courtroom. Bill Pugin, who was interpreting for me on that set, remembers, "In the script it says that Sally Berg, Marlee's character, breaks down on the stand and cries. Marlee said, 'I'm not going to cry here. I mean, there are not going to be tears here.' And the director said, 'But it would be great if you could.' She said to me, 'I just can't do it; I can't give them what they want.'

"I looked at her and said, 'You are not going to like what I'm going to say.' She looked back at me and said, 'Then don't say it.'

"All I said was 'Sarah, Sarah. When you do it, you have to think of Sarah.' She got onto the stand and it was one of the most amazing things I've ever witnessed, her ability to break down on that stand, in that way. There was not a dry eye. Grips. cameramen . . .

"Oh my God, when they called, 'Cut,' Marlee couldn't stop crying. Tears were streaming down *my* face. Camryn turned around

David E. Kelley knows how to write for me. I earned two of my four Emmy nominations, one for his show Picket Fences, *and one for this episode of* The Practice. *Here I am opposite my friend Camryn Manheim in a tense courtroom moment. (©Vivian Zink/American Broadcasting Companies, Inc.)*

and called for makeup and said, 'Thank God the camera wasn't on me.'"

One take. It was a wrap. They got everything they wanted and more. I was nominated for an Emmy for that performance for Best Guest Actress in a Drama Series.

Aaron Sorkin sent me the sweetest e-mail the day after that episode aired. Here's a bit of what he wrote:

> The scene in the holding room with you and Camryn demonstrated a level of communication and emotion that spoken words usually only serve to reduce, and your scene on the stand, of course, was as honest as it was gut wrenching. I can't imagine there was more than one take of that. It's still very much with me today.
>
> I can't wait to get you back on *The West Wing*.

I couldn't wait either—but a baby was about to be born.

49

With my second child, I wanted to have a natural delivery, Lamaze, breathing, no C-section. I talked it over with my doctor and he told me, yes, it was absolutely doable.

With Sarah, I'd gained fifty-one pounds; with this second pregnancy, I had gained sixty-five pounds. Too much—and I'm lucky that I didn't develop diabetes or other complications.

I was ten days past my due date, enough that the doctor called his office over the weekend asking if they'd heard from me. He told me it was time for this baby to come, so we picked a day to induce labor—September 12, 2000.

Liz got on a plane and headed to L.A. Connie, an incredible interpreter whom I'd first met at a parent/infant/toddler group and who was my on-set interpreter for *The West Wing,* said she'd meet me at the hospital. My mom and dad flew out, Kevin's mom and stepdad drove up. Jack was there. Other friends kept arriving. We could have fielded a baseball team!

This birth seemed completely different from the first; everything went much faster and I hardly felt the contractions. I was so tired at the end I could barely stay awake, and I was so uncomfortable. Someone bumped the bed and I must have looked as if I would tear his or her head off because Kevin immediately said, "I did it, I did it." He was protecting my mom, who'd accidentally hit the corner of the bed.

I started to push. And I pushed. And pushed. And pushed until I couldn't push anymore. It wasn't going well. Everybody in the room was tense, including the bunch of medical students who were observing. At one point the doctor whipped around and snapped, "Quiet, peds!" in their direction.

The doctor came around to huddle with Kevin and me and said, "You have thirty seconds to decide—C-section or forceps."

I looked at Kevin. I was exhausted but we'd gotten this far. I looked at the doctor and said, "I'll push."

"Okay, forceps it is."

I had no time to ask what risks might face the baby with a forceps birth. It felt like an emergency and I just put all my trust in the doctor.

And boom, the baby came out and Kevin was bawling. He said, "It's a boy. It's a boy. Brandon, Brandon." It was 6:09 p.m. when Brandon Joseph came into the world with a lusty cry. A healthy baby boy, my Brandon was fine.

I wasn't doing so well though. I looked over at the doctor and saw he was covered with blood. It was all over him, on his shoes. I lost 1,300 cc of blood, and they came close to having to give me a transfusion. Kevin recalls, "It was hard for me to tell how bad things were because I was by Marlee's side, trying to comfort her. It wasn't until after the birth that I saw the huge mess on the floor that they were trying to clean up."

After a frenzy of activity, everybody left the room but Connie. Everything felt as if it was moving in slow motion. I was having trouble concentrating. Connie told me later I was as white as a sheet and she was trying to keep me distracted. I remember Connie leaving and my father-in-law coming in and talking to me, then a nurse came and whisked me up to intensive care. My blood pressure had gotten dangerously low.

I spent five days in the ICU. The first few times I tried to get up, I felt so faint I couldn't do it without support. The doctors would later start me on Synthroid, which helps boost the thyroid, and I'll be on it for the rest of my life.

The pain was excruciating—I'd never experienced anything like it, it felt as if my insides had been ripped apart. The medication they put me on to help with the discomfort was so strong that the doctors were constantly monitoring me so that I wouldn't become dependent on it.

The birth was extremely hard, and the doctor said if I had other babies, they would have to be by C-section, no debate. But Brandon was an easy, sweet baby; maybe he knew that I was too weak for him to be anything else. When the American Red Cross asked me to aid their blood-drive efforts, I was more than honored to lend my name, my time, and my support. I had come so close to needing a transfusion and couldn't imagine how frightening it would be for anyone whose life is hanging in the balance not to have access to lifesaving blood.

When Brandon was about six months old, I was suddenly offered a film. When I say suddenly, I mean they told me if I accepted the role, I would have to get on a plane the next day, *the next day,* to fly to an animal preserve in South Africa where they were shooting.

It was insane, but the project sounded interesting and I knew we could use the money. So I got on the plane.

Not too many hours later I learned one of the cardinal rules of breast-feeding—you have to stop it gradually or you will suffer. Oh, did I suffer. I hadn't had any experience with breast pumps yet, and I had planned to just take a break for the three weeks I would be shooting.

Thanks goodness Bill Pugin was with me. He could keep a goose entertained, and that's just about the challenge he was facing with me. Bill says, "If you are going to fly to South Africa, fly first class on South African Airways. They make up a bed, a flat, beautiful bed with down comforters. We're side by side and Marlee is in pain, tossing and turning. Finally she turns to me and says, 'There's too much turbulence, I can't sleep. . . . Tell the attendant to tell the pilot to do something about it.'

"I looked at her, rolled my eyes, and said, 'We're flying over the Atlantic Ocean, there is turbulence, you are not at the Four Seasons—deal with it!'"

That story always makes me smile!

Africa was absolutely beautiful, and depressing. Once again, extreme poverty was everywhere you turned.

In *Askari* I played one-half of a couple tracking the behavior of elephants and struggling to save them from encroaching poachers. At first I was petrified to be around the elephants—they looked massive at a distance. But then, standing next to one and just looking up, their power and their size can just take your breath away.

The trainers were there all the time with the five or six elephants I was working most closely with. They were well trained and well cared for, and soon I began to relax around them and enjoy the experience.

Most of the time when we were shooting around the elephants, it was on an open plain, which made things easier. But in one scene near the end, the poachers are trying to shoot the elephants from a helicopter. The elephants begin stampeding, heading right into the sights of the poachers' rifles, and I run out in front of the elephants trying to scare them into turning and also to keep the poachers from firing.

In the leadup to the scene, I'm in a van and my niece and I jump out of it to run in front of the elephants. Bill had a walkie-talkie in the van, and he's crouched down, ready to give us our cues. Bill will never forget what he calls our *Jurassic Park* scene:

"I just remember seeing the elephants—they were totally panicked and racing by. I'm looking out of the window thinking that just one little movement by their trunk and they could knock this van over.

"I remember thinking how much it looked like *Jurassic Park* to me—the elephants' eyes were huge and looking right in the window of the van. I have done a lot of scary stuff, but this really scared me."

We found out on the day we were to fly out that one of the workers had been killed by one of the elephants. The wranglers had told us never to touch the elephants if they weren't around, no matter how calm they seemed, and that this sort of tragedy could so quickly happen.

෨෨   ෨෨

KEVIN AND I had always talked about having four kids—we thought that number would be the perfect size for us.

Not long after Brandon was born, Kevin told me if we wanted to have more children he wanted to do so before he hit forty and ran out of energy. So the Grandalski baby boom began.

Brandon was born in September 2000, and by December of 2003 I'd had two more babies. Tyler Daniel came along twenty-two months after Brandon on July 18, 2002—it was Connie's birthday, too. She stayed to interpret through Tyler's birth, then we all sang "Happy Birthday" to Connie in the OR, then sent her off to celebrate with her family.

Finally, Isabelle Jane arrived on December 26, 2003, just seventeen months after Tyler.

I remember when I found out I was pregnant that last time. Kevin had taken Sarah on a father-daughter weekend to Mammoth with another neighborhood dad and daughter, John and Casey. It was Oscar weekend and I was due to attend. On Saturday afternoon, Kevin and Sarah were zooming down one of the runs when the sled went off track and was heading straight for a tree.

Kevin says, "I could see a low branch on the tree and thought I could just put my foot out and stop the sled. What I hadn't figured on was the block of ice underneath it."

Kevin stopped the sled all right; and Sarah, who was sitting in front of him, was safe. But his ankle snapped. He was transported to the hospital there, but he wouldn't let anyone call me—he knew I'd drop everything to get there.

The doctors in Mammoth stabilized his ankle while John took the girls for dinner. On Sunday, I headed to the Oscars with no idea what had happened, and Sarah, Casey, John (behind the wheel), and Kevin, his ankle wrapped and elevated, began the long drive back.

When I got home that night, I walked in and found Kevin already in bed, watching TV, the remote in his hand. I was standing in the doorway in my gown and he looked up, smiled, and said, "You look pretty."

That's my sweet Kevin, but I knew something wasn't right. "What are you doing in bed?" I asked. He flipped off the covers—

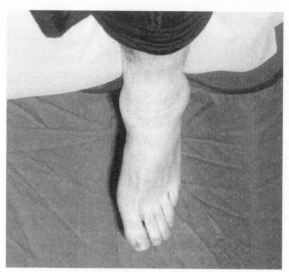

Kevin's broken ankle

his foot was propped up and it looked awful. I was angry that he hadn't called—and relieved that he was okay.

A few days later, he was due to have surgery to repair the ankle. Just before he was rolled into the OR, I gave him a box with a little pregnancy-test stick in it. My final plus. I wanted to make sure that he knew a baby was on the way.

My Isabelle. I remember walking into the hospital the day after Christmas thinking, *What kind of childhood are you going to have with Christmas and Hanukkah and your birthday and New Year's all at the same time?*

This time the kids were all with me. Finally it was time and the nurse told me I could walk to the OR if I wanted to, but the doctor said only one person could go in with me—my husband or the interpreter.

"But I need them both!"

The doctor said he would compromise—only one person with me while they did the spinal injection—"We can't deal with two people in there who might faint."

So I said, "You both wait, you both stay out." I had requested a nurse who had been there for Sarah's birth whom I just loved. She held me and talked to me, and the spinal wasn't as bad as I remembered, though I did ask the doctor as the numbness set in. "Are my legs still there?"

As always, strict instructions were for no one, including the interpreter, to tell me the sex of the baby. I would hear that only from Kevin, and he told me the baby was a girl. Sarah chose her name—Isabelle—and the Jane is in memory of my uncle Jason, who was so dear to me.

Usually after each baby, Kevin and I would look at each other and say, "Yeah, I think we could to this again." After Isabelle's birth, we looked at the baby, just cleaned up and wrapped in a blanket—such a beautiful baby—then looked at each other and said almost at the exact same time, "We're done!"

Photographers at red carpet events were convinced I was constantly pregnant for four or five years, and they were close to right!

Aaron kept fitting *West Wing* episodes in between the pregnancies, but it was almost impossible during those years for me to do much of anything except care for our growing family.

Gap asked me to do a print ad for them when I was pregnant with Tyler—with a photo that I love. I'm in a white, tailored shirt with my big belly peeking out. It was just a beautiful shot, great lighting—the sort that make you appreciate the great photographers of the world.

AFTER TYLER WAS born I got what ranks as my most difficult project of all time—*What the #$*! Do We (K)now!?* It tried to blend the story of Amanda, a Deaf photographer that I played who is going through life-changing events, with real-life experts from scientists to psychics talking about quantum physics and the notion that we're all connected in this world.

I still had my postbaby body. I was pumping breast milk every day, freezing it, then sending it off to California by FedEx, three days a week, so it would be there for Tyler. It was expensive, but it worked and was worth it to me. And, more important, Tyler was content.

In one scene my postbaby self has to stand half-naked in front of a mirror in front of a crew, and of course ultimately an audience in a movie theater.

I don't think I slept for a week before that scene was shot. But I told myself, this is what the scene is about—there is no such thing as a perfect body. Still I wanted to make sure everyone was off the set except the cameraman, the sound guy, and the director.

They had to shoot it over and over—they kept shooting with different types of underwear to see which one would cover my butt the best.

Ironically, everything that I had to go through to shoot the scene made the opposite point—I couldn't have ended up feeling much worse about my body than I did after shooting that day.

I remember asking for body makeup. When I was getting smeared with the makeup, one of the girls who thought I couldn't read lips kept pointing to different spots saying, "Get that spot there." Maybe she was trying not to hurt my feelings, but she did. I would rather she had just said something to me.

I've always had issues about my body. My kids tease me because they never see me in shorts or bathing suits. I don't want to tell them it's because I don't feel comfortable with my body. That's not a message I want to send them, particularly not my daughters.

It would take *Dancing with the Stars* to help heal that part of my psyche.

50

In sifting through all of the boxes that hold bits and pieces of memories and moments in my life, I unearthed an old letter from my mother. She sent it in April 1995. There's no clue that any particular event triggered the letter, it just feels that she wanted to tell me something that had probably been on her mind for years. Make it official. Here's part:

"I am sixty-four years old and whatever I am, whatever my personality is, not much is going to change it. If I could change it, I would have to unwind my mind, much like a movie reel and start over again."

She talked about her role as Jewish mother, adding that it wasn't all "chicken soup and eating, but working your butt off trying to instill a real sense of values."

Then she got to the heart of what she wanted to say: "I want my children to accept me as I am and not attempt to change whatever I am today . . . to sum it up, please don't try and change me."

It got me thinking a lot about family—the one I grew up in and the one I am trying to build with Kevin. I never want to write a letter like that to my children—closing the door on the possibility of changing our relationship. It felt like a replay of all the times as I was growing up when the door closed and she retreated to her bedroom if she was having a bad day.

I'm working to cherish my kids but also to really know each of them as they grow and change. I want our relationships to grow and change, too; I never want that evolving to stop.

I learn something every day, and I spend a lot of time thinking about my relationship with my mom as Kevin and I make decisions about our kids' lives. I hope that whatever path I choose along the way, whatever choices I make, something positive will come out of it.

I know in my heart that parenting is a lifetime of work, and with four kids it is forever a blend of joy, discovery, and chaos—lots of chaos. Here's a snapshot of my family and our life.

We are a well-oiled machine. When morning comes, and it comes early, everybody is up and getting ready to go—to school when its in session, to classes during the summer. Breakfast is simple, from cereal and juice to eggs and toast. A nanny helps during the day, but Kevin and I are hands-on parents, from making treats for their classes, driving them to school, guitar lessons, football practice, dancing lessons, making school lunches. No overnight nannies unless I'm out of town.

My favorite time is picking them up from school. I love it when they pile into the car with stories about the day spilling out all around me. I want to scoop up and save all of those moments—knowing who their friends are, how Brandon's math test went, what picture Isabelle drew in art class, what joke Tyler played on his best friend.

It is amazing to watch these four personalities emerge—each so different, so unique.

Sarah, my oldest, is MIT—Marlee in training. She is a free spirit, extremely friendly, and everybody she meets falls in love with her.

She'll be thirteen by the time you are reading this, and I'm already starting to feel the pressure of those teenage years. There's a boy she likes, but thank goodness it is all still innocent. I try not to take the teenage rants personally—I know this pulling away, this clash with me, is the natural order of things.

Maybe because we had Sarah to ourselves for her first four and a half years, she's both a mommy's and a daddy's girl. Both Kevin and I are extremely close to her, but she's very independent. Always has been. No crying on the first day of school—that was me with the tears!

I just love seeing her bloom, whether it's watching her swim (she's an absolute fish in the water with natural ability) or dancing (she loves hip-hop) or singing, playing guitar, and especially writing songs, something that she's gravitating to more and more as she grows older. She is also an incredible soccer player and has a wicked sense of humor . . . like me.

She's very much a cross between a tomboy and a girlie girl. She has the most beautiful lips—Angelina Jolie lips—that most people would kill for: but she is a teenager, so of course she hates them. She is a social butterfly, adores clothes and loves shoes as much as Carrie Bradshaw. I think about two hundred pairs are in her closet!

Brandon is Kevin in miniature—all he needs is a mustache. He's calm and steady, centered, which is remarkable to see in an eight-year-old. Yet he's sentimental and caring and absolutely such a handsome little boy.

Brandon has the two most beautiful dimples you could want a child to have. When Sarah was born, the first thing I noticed was the dimple on her right cheek and her beautiful hazel eyes. When I saw Brandon, he had these two deep, deep dimples, dark hair, and dark brown eyes.

In Brandon, I got my sports fanatic. I wanted to take the love and devotion for the Chicago Bears in my head and plant them in his—I didn't have to try too hard. He lives and breathes football. He plays flag football, and you'll hardly ever find Brandon without a football in his hand. He even takes his football to bed with him at night, and the helmet is always close by. On Sundays during the season, if I'm not right there beside him, he'll come running in to give me updates on the score. We'll high-five with each score and moan over every setback.

Brandon is such a sweet boy, reserved, polite, and loves school almost as much as he loves football. He's a natural at all sports—he plays baseball, soccer, football, and loves basketball, too. He hasn't tried hockey yet, but I'm guessing that he'll get around to that, too. I can see him having his heart broken by his first love (grrr!).

Tyler is mischief with a killer smile. We are alike in many ways. If you put one of my baby pictures next to Tyler's, it's almost impossible to tell them apart. He's my total entertainer! He has blond hair, aqua-blue eyes, and is 100 percent Matlin.

When he was younger, he loved to rummage around in the closets and dress up and use his imagination in the most creative ways. Tyler is very much my out-of-the-box thinker.

People love him because he'd so engaging, funny—he calls me Sugar Mama and shimmies his shoulders! He's definitely a handful! He's a gymnastic whiz, and though he was a little slower to take to water, now, like Sarah and Brandon, he's a fish and loves it.

I remember how much I hated being away from him when I was shooting *What the #$*! Do We (K)now!?* When I got back, I was so worried that after those weeks away he wouldn't remember me.

I flew in, and as soon as I got to the house, I jumped into a shower—I wanted to wash away anything that wouldn't seem familiar to him.

Then I walked in his room. He was lying there and looked at me and gave me the biggest, toothless grin. I picked him up and held him so close and sat down on the bed and nursed him. It was one of the most special moments, and I knew then we had a bond that nothing—not time, not distance—could break.

All of my kids are close, but Tyler and Isabelle are just about inseparable. They're just seventeen months apart, so Tyler was still such a baby when Isabelle arrived that they've really grown up together.

Where Tyler is so outgoing, Isabelle is my shy one. Nothing, but nothing, gets past Isabelle—she's very observant. She'll check everything out before she approaches anyone or anything.

She's so pretty, she naturally attracts attention. We are forever having people, strangers really, coming up to gush over her. But she's like a little cat—she wants life on her own terms and sets the boundaries. Get too close and you'll hear Isabelle's infamous *Noooooooooo;* it arches like a cat's back into highs and lows.

But Isabelle trusts Tyler. If it's a new situation, she'll get behind him, feel his vibe, and if it's okay, then she'll approach. While most of my kids love the camera, Isabelle has never been too keen on it. She doesn't like the attention. But when school started in the fall, the pictures came home this year with Isabelle's beautiful smile—like Tyler's, with two dimples.

When Isabelle was born, we had a crowd at the hospital. I was in the recovery room for a couple of hours, so by the time they rolled me back to my room, everyone had seen the baby. Just as I got there, someone teased, "So who's Isabelle's daddy? Where's the UPS guy?"

Isabelle had a head of jet-black hair, and the UPS guy, whom I had a huge crush on, had black hair, too. Cute, funny, not my baby's daddy!

I got a visit from my longtime friend Bernard Bragg not long after Isabelle was born. He's done something special for each of my kids, but let him tell you:

"Here is this story, our favorite. When Marlee had her first child, Sarah, I bought a U.S. savings bond to help open the baby's first bank account. A few years later when Marlee gave birth to her second child, Brandon, I had to follow suit. Before long, Tyler, the third, came along. I sportingly helped open his account in the bank. For her fourth darling, Isabelle, I mustered up a smile and said to Marlee, 'Here is yet another bond to open her bank account, and I'll have to close mine for good.' To this, Marlee vowed not to have any more so as to save me from a life of poverty."

Four is definitely a full house. So many days I wish for one or two more hours, there's so much to do. For a while Sarah was in a pre-school for both hearing and Deaf children to help her learn sign language, but over the years we've developed a sort of hybrid language of our own to communicate. So I don't feel left out of their lives.

Still, one of the hardest things for me as a mother is not being able to hear what's happening in another room—it makes it almost impossible for me to know who started what, the daily back-and-forth that comes with four kids. Kevin is good at monitoring that sibling back-and-forth, so he plays cop all the time, during the day, then at home, too. Kevin is one of the most involved fathers you could imagine. He is very much a part of their lives every single day. He is my rock; he is theirs, too.

Dinner in our home starts at five thirty because it's never hurried and then it takes an hour and a half to get them all ready for bed. Unless I'm out of town, we always have dinners together. It's fun and loud and messy—I love it! Kevin finally got a toy microphone so that when it gets too rowdy with everyone talking, we can pass the microphone to one of the kids—he who has the microphone controls the floor!—then after a few minutes the child has to pass it along to someone else.

The china cabinet in the dining room covers most of one wall. It is filled with art the kids have made over the years, and to us everything in it is priceless. We've saved everything they've ever made for us—from the smallest crayon doodles on a scrap of paper to elaborate collages. We have boxes and boxes already, so I guess we'll have to expand the storage unit before they're all grown up.

I try in vain to teach the kids to clean up after themselves—do their chores—and just be themselves.

Nighttime, bedtime, is all about reading—they read to me or Kevin, or we read to them—and talking. Kevin is always there, and we make sure everyone gets tucked in and kissed good-night.

Here I am at the Oscars 1998 wearing an exquisite Escada gown. And on my arm is my leading man for life, my husband and best friend, Kevin Grandalski. (Credit: Time & Life Pictures/Getty Images)

∾ ∾

We don't live in the Hollywood dream machine—that was a decision Kevin and I made long ago, and we've never doubted that it was the right thing to do for our children. Our neighborhood is like any other family suburb you might drive through: nice homes, no mansions. We have a corner house with a big yard where lots of the neighborhood kids congregate to play. Most days you'll find a couple of Razor scooters on the front walk, and there's a jungle gym out back.

I try to avoid the image of the Hollywood mom—it never felt natural to me. When treats need to be baked for school, you'll find me in the kitchen with the kids mixing up oatmeal/chocolate-chip cookies, one of my specialties, or slathering frosting on cupcakes.

When it was my turn to handle the reading circle for Isabelle's pre-K class, I changed it up a little. When the kids asked why I "talked funny," I explained to them I was Deaf and that I had another language, but it was one they could learn. So they started throwing out words, and I'd teach them the sign. "Red." "Spider." "Monkey." The kids had such a great time that two other classrooms asked if I could come in and teach them, too.

Saturdays around our house are sports days all day. We spend most of it going from one game to another. I'm like any other parent, standing on the sidelines cheering my kids on. Some of the parents are scared to approach me; others treat me like another parent, and that's the best because that's what I am.

I do have to admit, while I love being involved with my kids and their various activities, and I loved almost everything about Sarah's time in Girl Scouts, I didn't do so well with the mother-daughter campout. It wasn't the cooking or the cold showers or the bathroom facilities, it was the claustrophobic attack that came about 1 a.m. when I woke up and felt the tent was going to close around me. I ran outside into a night as black and as claustrophobic as the tent.

Luckily the campground was about five minutes from our house. One of the other moms called Kevin, and he came and rescued me—not particularly happy about it, but he came. One of the other moms took over Sarah. The next morning when we picked up a not-too-happy Sarah, I said. "Look, Mommy got a little scared, now get over it."

Our extended families go a long way to keep all of us grounded. My children know that I'm an actor, but it's something they are all humble about—they've found a way to be proud of what I do without being arrogant.

Besides my immediate family to help keep egos in check, there is Kevin's clan.

Since his mom, Charlotte, and stepdad, Dan, live close enough to be around the kids a lot, Gramma and Papa Dan have been very much a part of my kids' lives, and they make it possible for me to juggle my home life and my work. They have so much energy it never ceases to amaze me, and I know the trips they take the kids on to the mountains or the beach, the arts-and-crafts projects they undertake, are making memories for a lifetime.

Gramma Charlotte and Papa Dan

I don't know how we'd do it without their help. When I have to go out of town for work, sometimes for several months, depending on the production, it's such a relief to know we can call on them.

Charlotte says, "I don't want someone else raising my grand-kids. Besides, we love being with the kids so it's not a chore, you get to see things all over again through their eyes. And I feel very lucky that they want us to be here."

Charlotte underestimates her impact. At times she's moved in for as much as six months so that both Kevin and I could work without any worries that the kids weren't in excellent hands.

Of course even with Gramma around, when something happens, it's really hard not to be there. The summer that Isabelle was three, I was in Vancouver shooting *The L Word*. Kevin was at work when he got a call from his mom. He remembers, "My mom was on the phone and she said, 'Isabelle is okay, but she fell and hit her head and I think I should take her to the hospital.' Isabelle had fallen backward and hit her head on the corner of a concrete step. When my mom picked her up, she had one arm around her, and one hand on the back of her head. When she set Isabelle down, she saw that her hand was covered in blood."

Kevin raced to the hospital, and about that time I was in the elevator going up to my room at my hotel when I got a call from one of the neighbors that Isabelle had fallen and was okay but on her way to the ER. When Kevin got to the hospital, Isabelle saw him and said, "Daddy, you're in your costume," which is what she used to call his police uniform.

She wasn't crying, and she was barely talking, but otherwise she seemed fine. The doctor considered, then decided against a CAT scan, Isabelle had just stitches to face. To keep her still, the nurses told her they had a special princess dress for her to put on—and they wrapped her round and round in a sheet that was more straigt-jacket than anything else.

Kevin knelt down beside her while they got ready to put in the stitches and says, "She was looking at me, and when the doctor put the needle into her scalp to inject the anesthetic, she barely reacted. Not a peep, not a cry. I thought, *This is not good.*"

The doctor was concerned as well. After the stitches were in they did a CAT scan after all. Thankfully there was no damage, and Isabelle pretty much just giggles at the memory today.

KEVIN IS THE oldest of three, with a younger brother and sister. And the clan just keeps extending out with all sorts of aunts and uncles and cousins. My favorite time is Thanksgiving, when just about everyone decamps for Charlotte and Dan's house near Yosemite. It's on about five acres, and by the time everyone arrives, there are about thirty-five of us. When everyone is inside, we're like sardines, and if you find an empty spot, that's where you sleep.

Every year there's a theme—sometimes it's who has the best hats, or the sixties, or pajamas, or togas. Games go on inside and out, with more food than you can imagine. The party goes on for five or six days, and it always feels like such quality time just hanging out with people we love.

Christmas is a close second. A Santa always stops by for the kids with a big bag of toys, and my kids have countless cousins to play with. We make the trip to San Diego for the day each year. Every Easter we go back to San Diego for egg hunting, with each kid getting his or her very own colored egg to hunt for—with new toys after the hunting is done. There's Hannukah at my cousin Lynne's too every year. All these traditions make the holidays feel complete.

And really, I think that's why we have holidays—to give an excuse for families to get together and remember where they're from, who they are, and the people who will always be there for them.

51

BEING AROUND TY Pennington and the gang at ABC's *Extreme Makeover: Home Edition* is like finding yourself dropped inside a beehive—although instead of bees buzzing there's a crazy man with a megaphone! *GOOD MORNING, TY!*

I have *never* seen so much movement and activity compressed into such a short time in my life—and I say that as the mother of four young kids!

This show I love—it has so much heart. Even though it's essentially the same story every week, it never fails to leave me reaching for Kleenex by the end of the show. Week after week, a family's life is transformed.

Admit it—is there anyone out there who hasn't secretly wanted to stand in that crowd at the end of the week and yell at the top of his or her lungs, *"BUS DRIVER, MOVE THAT BUS!"*

It's as if the bus is powered by the sheer sound and energy of all those voices.

I knew I wanted to be there at least once, watching as the bus rolled away to reveal a new home and a new life for one lucky family. So when the network asked if I'd be on one of the episodes, I couldn't say yes fast enough.

But before I met the family for the first time, there was that bus. It is huge, and it takes a while to get used to moving around inside while the bus is rolling down the road.

Oh, yes, they do really ride in that bus. It's like a mobile headquarters for the army Ty leads into battle each week against rotting floors, leaky roofs, defective plumbing, and, most important, hopelessness and despair.

The Extreme Makeover: Home Edition *demolition derby*

The families that make it onto *Extreme Makeover* are always facing incredible hurdles, usually with remarkable strength and grace. That was certainly the case with the Vardon family of Oak Park, Michigan.

Stefan was in high school when he wrote to *Extreme Makeover* about his family—his parents were Deaf and his only brother was blind and autistic. Stefan was the family's communicator whether it was interpreting for his parents at the store or explaining what someone was saying to his brother.

That's a heavy load for a kid to carry, but Stefan did it with humor and charm.

I stood on the Vardons' front lawn with Ty and the design team as he screamed into the megaphone—for the first of many times that week. With "Good morning, Vardon family," the controlled chaos began.

The design team, the builders, the volunteers, everyone worked at warp speed, seemingly flying in a million different directions, but somehow it all came together. In between everything else I was responsible for that week, I had a thing for that megaphone. Anytime Ty put it down or looked away for just a little too long, it was mine!

The Deaf chick had volume—I could rev up the volunteers with the best of them.

In the world of *Extreme Makeover* the impossible happens—a house comes down, and a week later in its place is a new, state-of-the-art home equipped to enrich life for everyone under that roof. In the Vardons' case, the Starkey Hearing Foundation, which I'd been working with for a few years, gave Stefan a college-scholarship check worth $50,000.

Often by the time Ty and the designers show up, the families are just hanging on by a thread. If you are ever feeling sorry for your own plight in life, or down if you've hit a rough patch, *Extreme Makeover* is a good reminder of how good life is for most of us.

Even in that world, the Llanes were a heartbreaking case. So when I got a call to be on the show again in 2006, I was there.

Vic, the father, was blind from a hereditary disease that he'd passed along to two of his three children; daughters Gueni and Carrie who were now going blind. His other child, Zeb, was Deaf due to a case of German measles his mother, Maria, had had when she was pregnant.

Vic's mother, Isabel, who was also blind, lived with the family, too. Maria, who served as the main interpreter for her son, Zeb, and was the rock of the family, had battled thyroid cancer.

The house was a nightmare—a small, fifty-year-old split-level with dark, narrow corridors that would have been difficult to navigate if you had perfect vision. It was not nearly enough room for six people. This family definitely needed the help of Ty and the design team.

Once again the army was mobilized. More than two hundred volunteers and a lot of innovation conspired to create what was dubbed the "Z home," because of its A-to-Z technology. When the bus rolled away from Bergenfield, New Jersey, we all knew that life might never be easy, but it would definitely be so much better for this great family.

So once again I kicked the dust off my work boots, packed up my tool belt, reluctantly handed the megaphone over to Ty, and said good-bye to the design team and the bus, until the next time.

ᙡ ᙡ

ONE OF THE best things about the career I've built is the chance I get to be a guest on many TV series that are among my favorites, working with actors and writers that I so admire. Andre Braugher and Ruben Blades on *Gideon's Crossing;* the *Law & Order: Special Victims Unit* crew, in another performance that would earn me an Emmy nomination; Gary Sinise at *CSI: NY;* and *The Division,* five female cops try to figure out life—how much did I love that!

While I thrive on the dramas, it was a kick to be on the lighter side—well, the lighter/darker side—in *Desperate Housewives* and *Nip/Tuck,* two of the most smartly written, beautifully acted, cynically perfect series around.

Though they are very different series, a kind of high sheen and intensity about both *Nip/Tuck* and *Desperate Housewives* sets them apart, and both have a Swiss-watch precision in their execution that's remarkable to witness.

Then there's Earl. Something is so appealing in watching Jason Lee bumbling along trying to make things right in *My Name Is Earl.* And Jaime Pressly as Joy is my kind of in-your-face, take-no-prisoners woman.

All the characters that writer Greg Garcia has created have this great quality of unvarnished truth that is as compelling as it is funny. I love the un-PC-ness of the show and have had a great time whenever they've written me into it.

As much fun as it can be to watch, it's even more fun on the set. It was all I could do not to crack up when Jaime as Joy stood there, popping her gum, explaining why she didn't want me as her court-appointed attorney:

"I would let you buy me groceries, I would let you greet me at Wal-Mart. I would even buy pencils from you at an unreasonable price, but this is my third strike and I really don't feel comfortable putting my life in your Deaf hands."

But Greg is an equal-opportunity offender, so before the episode ended I got to call Jaime "white trash" and a few other choice things, too.

∽ ∽

WHILE I LIKE the challenge of dropping into lots of different shows—each with its own style, texture, and tone—it makes for a pretty nomadic and unpredictable life.

I wanted to create more opportunities for myself and have more control over my future—and the future I wanted to build with Kevin and our children.

In 2003, Jack came up with an idea for a kids' movie to pitch to the Disney Channel. Unlike other projects we've developed, this didn't star me. Instead, I would be the producer.

Eddie's Million Dollar Cook-off was about a fourteen-year-old who was the star player of his baseball team, but who also nursed a secret desire to be a chef. The conflict comes when Eddie must choose between helping his team win the play-off or participating in a cook-off. Guess which his dad wants him to do.

Disney liked the idea and so we produced the family movie together. *Eddie* felt like a solid start. Producing has been an entirely different sort of education for me, learning the nuts and bolts and the business side of making a movie. To take an idea and follow it all the way through to the end has made me appreciate the suits in the business.

I wanted to be more hands-on with *Eddie* and was set to travel with Jack to New Zealand, where we shot the film. But I had a terrible scare. My mother called to let me know that she was going to have open-heart surgery to repair some damage. No way was I going to leave her side. Jack went to New Zealand to handle the producing duties alone.

After the operation, we were all anxious to see her, but only two family members were allowed in the room with her at the same time. My dad and Eric went in first, but when they came out, they didn't tell us what to expect. Marc and I walked in, and we were like "Oh my God" and both stepped back for a second. She looked dead—her skin looked ashen, gray.

I think the color must have drained out of our faces, too. The nurse looked at us and quickly said, "No, no, no—this is normal." My mom woke up then, still groggy from the anesthesia, and started fighting the tubes and they ushered us out. It was a long night of waiting and wondering.

By the next morning when we came in, mom was sitting up in a chair. Progress. But she was so thirsty. The nurse gave me something that looked like a giant Q-tip, with a spongy end that I could use to wet Mom's lips. The first time I tried it, she bit down and wouldn't let go. I realized she was so thirsty she was sucking all the moisture she could out of that sponge. I thought, *Okay, good, she's feisty, that's a good sign.*

My dad was, of course, charming everyone at the hospital. He started bringing in chocolates for the nurses and any of the steady stream of friends and family who came to visit. Well, my mom loves sweets—I got that from her. She was supposed to stay in the hospital for five days. On the fifth day she got up in the middle of the night, walked over, and started eating all the chocolate. She paid for it—between diarrhea and heart palpitations, she had to spend another five days.

I sat with her for hours each day, to make sure she was okay. We'd chat, but only about the most innocuous of things. We never talked about the past. We never talked about anything important. But I'm so glad I was there.

PUSHING MYSELF IN different creative directions is in part why, several years ago, starting with *Deaf Child Crossing,* I began writing children's books. I wanted to create stories, based loosely on my life growing up, that would be fun and entertaining. I also wanted to help kids see how someone a lot like them learned to face everything from challenges in life when you are different—and we all are different in some way—to living with friends and bullies in your own backyard.

Part of the fun of writing the books has been creating characters who are a lot like many of my favorite people. I get to live out a few fantasies I had growing up.

In my second book, *Nobody's Perfect,* Megan, the young Deaf girl who is at the center of all the stories, throws herself a Positively Purple Party. Finally I get my purple dream day, or Megan does, with everything saturated with my favorite color from purple party invitations to purple games to purple cake. A total purple haze and I loved it.

I love that the books are connecting with children both hearing and Deaf, but I think what has been the most special for me is reading the books with my own kids—helping them in a gentle way understand where their mom came from, what it was like when I was growing up.

52

I WAS ON THE phone to Henry—career-advice time.

The L Word, Showtime's racy drama series about a group of lesbians living and loving—a lot—had called.

Heading into the fourth season, the creators wanted to introduce a new love interest for Bette, played by Jennifer Beals. The character was an artist they described as fiery, an independent spirit—and they wanted me to play her.

This would finally give me a chance to work with Jennifer. I just hadn't expected that it would be as her lover. But the show was edgy enough—lots of steamy sex scenes—that I wanted to at least run it by a trusted adviser to see what he thought.

Henry says, "Marlee called and asked me, 'What do you think, should I do it?' And I asked her three questions: 'How does your husband feel and are the kids taken care of? Could you use the money and will you make a living? Would you enjoy it?' And her answer to all of the questions was yes.

"The great thing about Marlee is that when that door does open, when an opportunity presents itself, she grabs it, throws it to the ground, and beats it into submission. She can't even stop it, it is this life force in her, this commitment in her."

So I headed to Vancouver, where the series is shot, to join the world of *The L Word* and learn how to be a really fantastic lesbian lover.

The writers/producers of the series were great, some of the best I've ever worked with. In talking to Ilene Chaiken, the show's creator, about my character, I asked if we could rename her Jodi. I'd had a friend named Jodi who was a lesbian and a mom, who

L Word *creator Ilene Chaiken and Jennifer Beals*

passed away, and I wanted that touchstone as I thought about this new role.

They've also been sensitive to make sure they are portraying this character accurately as far as her deafness. Over time they've brought in other Deaf actors and have asked me to help with story lines. I couldn't have asked for a more supportive and creative environment.

As welcoming as everyone was, I was still nervous and stressed in the beginning—this was a significant role for me and I wanted to get everything right. I called Liz and asked if she'd come spend some time with me in those early weeks while I was getting my bearings, getting grounded in this role.

Maybe my nerves played into it, but we had the worst fight of our lives in Vancouver. It was so horrible I wasn't sure how we were going to recover, if we could recover.

When I look back at the arguments or disagreements we've had over the years, most of them are over silly things, the kind of fights you have with your sister or best friend, and Liz is really both to me.

This fight was over just a few words—"you have to understand" —that I said one too many times to Liz.

Although it was the last thing that I intended, she was hurt; she felt I was patronizing her. Near the end of what had been a great sushi dinner with another friend of ours—the three of us laughing and talking for hours—Liz slammed her hand down on the table and said, "Stop saying that to me! You're saying that like somehow I'm dumb. I *don't* have to understand."

So we got into it, and I think we scraped open every wound of our friendship, dredged up every slight from thirty-five years. We said terrible things to each other.

It was the first time in all these years of friendship that I remember Liz saying any of this, really telling me how she felt about some of the tougher aspects of our relationship. Or maybe it was the first time I really, truly heard her. More than anything else, it felt completely one-sided—Liz never let me tell her how I felt. She refused. We were both shaken to the core.

Then things got worse.

When she got back home to Chicago, Liz wrote me a letter that just cut me to the bone. She said, "I'm willing to give up, to sacrifice our 35-year friendship if you don't change." Other things she wrote in the letter seared my heart, which I thought were terribly unfair— I didn't think it was possible that I would ever feel that kind of pain from Liz.

I was devastated. I wanted to understand how Liz felt, but I was confused by the depth of her anger. I didn't want to see our friendship crumble, and I couldn't believe it had come to this. I also wasn't ready to believe that it was just me.

I think when Liz looks at me and watches how I go at the world, what I've made of my life, she sees a fearless, intense person who wants to be in control of everything, including her.

What she doesn't seem to see is that I'm like everyone else, I'm human, I get scared, I feel insecure, I worry, I fail, I hurt, I cry.

Maybe I do, as Henry says, tend to grab life and wrestle it to the ground and beat it into submission. Maybe that's the only way I know to protect myself and those I love from all the sharp edges of life, the ones that can damage you, scar you forever.

For a few weeks, it was rough, so rough between us. We were like two boxers badly bruised and beaten, collapsed in opposite corners and not eager to go back into the ring.

In the end, we both found ways to get past that fight, to patch things up. These days we're a bit more careful with each other, I think, as we work to heal the pain that fight inflicted.

Liz says, "I am very, very lucky and Marlee is very, very lucky, too, that we have each other—we have both earned our friendship." That's just how I feel, too. We have earned each other, for better or worse, in love and in pain—and whatever happens, we will find a way to survive it together, stronger than before.

In the first scene of the first episode that introduces Jodi on *The L Word,* I'm holding a power drill, working on a metal sculpture, sparks fly—literally and figuratively.

The scene actually was electric. Jennifer and I had a natural chemistry, and the way the characters were written, this amazing range of emotional and physical interplay occurred between Bette and Jodi.

But sooner or later I knew we'd get to a love scene. It was sooner.

Love scenes are hard to do—there's so much to the logistics and angles so that the camera can actually shoot them. The result is you often find yourself in the most unnatural of positions to achieve a final look that is completely believable.

There's that.

Then there's the fact that Jennifer and I have known each other since we were in our twenties. In those years we've stayed in touch, both got married, had kids, put wilder days behind us.

So in the early episodes, when it came to actually pulling off those love scenes, it was almost impossible for us to do it without completely cracking each other up. Along the way, I mastered the art of completely breaking her concentration by arching one brow just so.

I think we had to get through the teasing to finally shoot with the level of passion, intensity, and sexuality that we needed to make the scene work.

Now nearly thirty episodes in, we're comfortable and so in tune with our characters—whether it's love or laughter, a quiet conversation over coffee or emotional fireworks—we can slip into that sexual place really easily.

I have to admit I've found it so much easier to kiss a woman than a man. I love men and I am a huge flirt, and with cute, handsome guys, well, I can get nervous about that kiss.

Make no mistake, I am absolutely in love with and committed to my wonderful, handsome husband. But that electricity that comes with a first kiss with someone attractive and new, well, I may be married, but I'm still human!

ONE OF THE best things about the relationship between Jodi and Bette that Ilene and the rest of the writing team have created is that it is completely unpredictable. I probably like finding out what's going to happen next as much as the audience—and the fans are rabidly devoted.

They analyze every episode in incredible detail and debate just about every decision the writers make, which is what you always hope for, that those watching the show will be as emotionally invested in the outcome as you are.

I cannot begin to say how extraordinary the acting talent on the show is. Jennifer is truly one of the finest actresses in the industry today. The out-of-nowhere girl we were all first mesmerized by in *Flashdance* has grown into the most remarkable professional at the top of her craft. She just takes my breath away.

The series has been such a fantastic, happy experience. We're finishing shooting the final season as I write this, and I'm struck by how unlike the final days of *Reasonable Doubts* it is. You might think with so many women in the cast that there would be feuds and infighting, egos out of control—there aren't. Everyone is working to keep the quality of the show at the highest level, and the internal support we all extend to each other is pretty unusual.

One unexpected side benefit of the show has been how it has strengthened my relationship with my brother Marc, who is gay. We've always been close, but I think the show has helped me see even more clearly that we've both struggled with being outsiders, having so many stereotypes to overcome.

Marc came out when he was in college. He remembers, "Marlee was too young to really understand it—but immediately it wasn't an issue, she's always been very supportive. My parents were role models; their reaction was just fabulous. . . . I came home and my mother had gotten a new car that day. It was raining out and we sat in the car and she asked how it went with the doctor—I'd been to a doctor for stress-related stomach issues. She said, 'I think you might be gay.'

"I told her what was going on in my life. I felt really good telling her, but asked her not to tell Marlee or Dad or Eric yet.

"A few minutes later in the house, my dad comes down the stairs and says, 'What are you doing tonight? Let's go to Marshall Field's and buy a couple of cashmere sweaters.' Mom says to me, 'I told him.' They both dealt with it in their own way, but they both accepted it immediately."

I've also come to understand the struggle for acceptance and understanding will never completely disappear—it may have peaks and valleys, but it is never-ending. I know we can never allow ourselves to become complacent, to get too comfortable—it doesn't take much for public opinion to suddenly shift and in ways you never anticipated.

But Marc and I had good role models on tolerance in our parents. Just as they accepted my deafness, they accepted Marc when he told them he was gay. In our family, it just doesn't matter; underneath it all, the love is always there.

NETWORK TELEVISION HAS almost gotten out of the TV-movie business these days. So I was excited when I learned that Hallmark was going to produce a prime-time movie for CBS based on the play *Sweet Nothing in My Ear.*

Stephen Sachs would adapt his play, which examined the use of cochlear implants through the prism of a family—the mother was Deaf, the father hearing, the son Deaf but an excellent candidate for implants. The parents' argument over whether their son should have the implants turns into an angry, sad custody battle over an issue that continues to divide the Deaf community.

When word first surfaced, the rumors were not good—the producers supposedly wanted to cast a hearing actress to play the role of Laura Miller, the mother. The thought alone was so depressing—I really wanted the role because the story was so important and I knew it would be creatively challenging in all the right ways. But more than that, I really wanted a Deaf actress, even if it wasn't me, to get cast.

After much back-and-forth on casting for both of the leads, they asked me to take on Laura, and Jeff Daniels would play my husband, Dan. I could not have been happier.

Jeff Daniels is one of the absolute best actors around, and I'd never gotten the chance to work with him. He can move from heartbreaking sensitivity to wry humor to sharp anger in a remarkably seamless way.

This would be a hugely complicated, demanding project for him. In addition to his dialogue, he had to do an incredible amount of signing. Basically he had to act, interpret, sign—all of it.

His performance was not only amazing, but he was a dream to work with, which helped because the three weeks that we shot were really intense. I'd been a fan of his for a long time and am so grateful that I got the chance to work with him.

That said, I was dying to nail him on something, just for the fun of it. We'd been working on the movie for nearly three weeks and Jeff started saying, "I have three more days, then I won't ever have to sign again." Next day: "Only two more days, I can retire these hands." "Today's the last day—I don't ever have to sign again for as long as I live!"

We still had two days of court testimony to shoot, but he didn't have to sign for the scene. So he did his last scene signing and everybody applauded. That's when I started plotting.

I grabbed director Joe Sargent, explained the situation, and asked him to do me a favor. "Could you please tell Jeff that things have changed and he's going to have to sign his entire court testimony?"

The next morning, Jeff and I were in hair-and-makeup together, which was unusual. He's in one chair, I'm in the next. Joe comes in at eight, bright and early. He's never done that in the entire three weeks of shooting. He walks over to Jeff, who's so happy about the signing and still bragging, "No more signing, I'm done!"

Joe leans over to Jeff and says, "Really sorry, I just got a phone call from the head honchos at Hallmark, and they really think you should be signing in court."

I'm watching all this in the mirror, and you should have seen Jeff's face! He just exploded: "No way! You're kidding me! That's insane. How can I possibly learn this script in three hours . . ." All of this laced with more four-letter words than I'd heard Jeff use during the entire production.

I was in tears.

Just then Jeff caught sight of me in the mirror, laughing my head off, and it clicked. "Payback is a bitch, Marlee."

"Oooh, I'm scared of you."

It was really just too funny. But for the next two days, every time we saw each other, I was just waiting, trying to figure out what he could possibly do. Time was running out and I started to think I was safe: I'd escaped!

The next day, Connie, who was interpreting for me, and I rode to work together. As we got to the set, everybody was acting really strange. I looked over and my trailer's gone.

I mean gone. A big honking trailer and it has disappeared.

In its place was a makeshift tent that looked as if it'd been grabbed from under a freeway.

When I walked in, the shower was a fake hose, a toilet was just sitting there, and some really horrific dress from wardrobe was hanging on a wire. An ice chest held my drinks, and a cardboard sign had a big star drawn on it and said MARLEE MATLIN TRAILER.

All I can say is, Jeff Daniels is the king of payback!

53

THERE ARE SHIMMIES, shakes, swings, and spins. There is hip action and whip action. There are spiral turns, cross turns, pencil turns. There are the heels to balance on, get blisters in. There are the skintight barely-theres with enough sequins sewed on to blind you—so, so tight they require another shimmy and shake to get into and out of.

There is, of course, the chance to take home the coveted mirror-ball trophy and the *Dancing with the Stars* title.

But what really hooked me on joining the cast of *Dancing with the Stars* when I was asked—my kids.

Only a few things that I can do these days will impress them, particularly my oldest daughter, who was twelve when I did the show—get my hands on tickets to a Jonas Brothers concert and do *Dancing with the Stars*.

Most of the time when I hear a chorus of "Oh, please, Mom" from four angelic, upturned faces, it's followed by things like "stay up late," "sleep over at . . ." "watch television," "have more candy," "more cake," "more popcorn," "more gum" . . .

Who knew I could take my forty-two-year-old, yes-I've-had-four-kids body—to say nothing of my Deaf ears—and with one little yes be transformed into "the cool mom."

As soon as I agreed to do the show, I started wondering who my dance partner would be. You really are in the dark until that first day when you walk into the studio and meet the person.

So on February 11, 2008, just about a month before season six of *Dancing with the Stars* would premiere, I walked through the doors to meet Fabian Sanchez, the 2006 Mambo World Champion—tall, handsome, great smile, warm eyes, and hips that can swivel so fast they make your head spin! It was his first season on the show.

Fabian says, "I had heard that Marlee might be one of the contestants, and when the producers told me that's who I would be working with, I was excited, I couldn't wait to meet her.

"When Marlee walked in, she looked so sweet and so nice. I could see she looked a little nervous, but then she was walking into my world. I knew right away, it was going to be a challenge for me. I'd never taught a Deaf person before and I wanted to see what we could create together because I knew all eyes would be on her."

As far as my eyes went, they were trained on Fabian. If I could see the step, the move, I could start to teach my body how to replicate it.

Fabian made a few adjustments to his teaching style to help us move beyond the fact that I could not hear the music. He used a lot more eye contact. Once I'd learned the mechanics, I was following his eyes and his body. In one of the interviews I did for the show, someone asked me what I heard of the music, and I told them, "Fabian is my music." That really was true.

A candid moment from behind the scenes at Dancing with the Stars. *Fabian and I thought it was hilarious that Maksim Chmerovskiy actually believed he could whisper sweet nothings in my ear.*

He also quickly shifted the speakers to the floor and turned up the bass, so that I could feel more of the vibrations. Bill Pugin came along as my interpreter, which turned out to be such a lucky break since Bill had done quite a lot of dancing years ago. He knew the language of swivels and pivots, and that helped in translating Fabian's instructions to me.

The days were long—often twelve hours of dancing straight. By the end of rehearsals, we'd both collapse on the floor. Many days I wasn't sure I could drag myself back up. Muscles I didn't even know I had were screaming at me, "Don't move, please don't move again."

Without even noticing, I lost twenty-three pounds before the series ended and gained the most toned body I've ever had. Thank you, *Dancing with the Stars*.

I'M USUALLY MY own worst critic, and on *Dancing with the Stars* I made no exception. Long before we were in front on an audience—or the judges—I felt that I wasn't picking up the routines quickly enough.

Fabian, who was my ultimate cheerleader, didn't agree: "When Marlee started out, I remember thinking, for me she is an average student—has good rhythm, is picking up the steps. But all of sudden, everything was coming faster and faster. I could throw new choreography at her and she was retaining it faster, reacting to the music faster.

"You could see her personality go into the dance—the way she would do her mouth, she has this gorgeous smile, when I saw it, I could tell she was comfortable with that movement. And when she puts that smile on, you can't help but know that girl is having a good time!"

Our first dance when the show kicked off in March was, as Fabian described it, "the red-hot cha-cha-cha baby." With Fabian, I quickly figured out that everything was *baby*. "No, no, no, baby." "Like this, not like that, baby." I got it, baby!

To dance the red-hot cha-cha, I wore a red, sparkly thing with slits here, and more slits there, all designed to enhance the moves you're making. Creating the lines of the costumes is equal parts art and science, and the wardrobe team for the series are really geniuses.

Fabian and I were the last couple to hit the dance floor. Performing live is, at least for me, always terrifying. On film sets you have multiple takes to get it right. When it's live, it's one shot, then it's over. You are done, finished, kaput. No second chances.

Since we were the last ones on the floor, my stomach had a lot of time to tie itself up—instead of butterflies, I think I had mad, crazy bats!

My daughter Sarah and my husband, Kevin, were in the audience that night, and as soon as I stepped out onto that stage, I could feel their smiles and good thoughts just wrapping around me.

So Fabian and I cha-cha-cha'd until we were breathless. Even though you rehearse ungodly hours and by the time you start performing your stamina is so much stronger, doing that dance in prime time takes all your energy and breath. It's like a three-minute extreme workout.

When I finished, the applause was thunderous. I could feel it from my head to my toes—it was just electric in that room. As I looked over at Jack, who was coming to the stage to interpret for me, he was wiping away tears, and that touched me so.

It felt as if Fabian and I had done well, but my heart was pounding as we walked over to the judges' table. If performing live is terrifying, having to face Len, Carrie Ann, and Bruno is a million times scarier. They started talking, Jack started signing, but it took a second for it to sink in—it was good news.

Carrie Ann: "That was almost unbelievable."

Bruno: "You may not hear, but the music is running through your blood."

Of course, once you make it through the dance, the judges, and the scores, then you have to spend the next night standing under the spotlight of death waiting to find out whether you'll be back for another week or going home.

The first week I made it through! And it was on to the quickstep.

Now the quickstep, in addition to being extremely, well, quick, with lots of changes in the footwork, is also a dance you are to perform with little eye contact. Ack! I need the eye contact! Ack! I need the eye contact!

And the judges' scores: 8, 8, 8.

Yeah!

Back in the greenroom, Samantha Harris was conducting the postdance interviews. She's a sweetheart, but she just never got it that putting a microphone in my face doesn't work.

If you watch *Dancing with the Stars,* you always look for certain moments. One of those is a performance that will bring Carrie Ann to tears. Some people never reach that. I was so happy that I did.

During week four, Fabian and I did the Viennese waltz. I was particularly worried about this dance since it has lots of twirls and being Deaf can play havoc with your balance, I wasn't sure how well I'd pull it off. Yet I did.

And I got my Carrie Ann moment: "You made me cry, something about that performance truly touched me."

By week six, I needed a lift. Week five was the samba, and I got really frustrated with myself. I nailed it in dress rehearsal, then missed a step when we went live.

When I'm just being Marlee Matlin the person, you can read my moods pretty easily, and I know the audience and the viewers could just see my energy drop, read the angst in my face. I wanted to go back into the dressing room and beat my head against a wall.

For week six, we got the mambo. Now Fabian is the Mambo King and I didn't want to let him down. I was already being tough on myself because of what I felt was a less than perfect samba. I needed to get my head out of the bad place.

Calling Henry Winkler! If anyone could shake me out of it, it was Henry.

He stopped by as Fabian and I were rehearsing and gave me a great pep talk to use as part of one segment for the show. But the string of e-mails I got from him through the next days and nights were the best. Not always easy to read—Henry pulls no punches—but exactly what I needed to hear. Here's a sample of Henry's tough love:

"Dear Marlee, The audience is with you, but they will start to pick up your sense of doom. You are a very good actress. You are a very good dancer. You have to put the two together and cry only at home unless they are tears of joy. . . .

"No more long faces. Smile. Enjoy. Catch your breath. And be grateful to the Mambo King.

"PS I looked very good in my blue shirt."

Other e-mails would come, most of them starting with "I had another thought . . ."

"The distance between the negative and being positive is as thin as a piece of thread."

"You are a champion. You are a winner in life already. Show THAT to the world."

"You have to make a decision. A big life decision."

And then the PS: "PS I think I have to wear that blue shirt more often."

I tried to drink in all of his advice. I tried to absorb all the amazing love and support that had began pouring in starting in week one from the fans. I tried to lean on the love of my family. But in the end, during the mambo, I lost focus for a second.

In ballroom, just the blink of an eye, just a second of lost concentration, and you can lose a beat—you lose a beat and you lose a bit of movement and it's extremely hard to recover.

Fabian says, "From the samba, there was a small mistake, but she couldn't shake it off. I could see it running through her mind: 'What if I make another mistake?'

"At the beginning of the mambo, she was supposed to turn to face the audience. I went back that night and watched it over again, and as I'm watching it, she stops turning a quarter turn less. As she was turning, Bruno had his hand going up and down, counting the beats, and I've seen him do it with other people. That moment, her eye caught his hand going up and down, and she lost the beat.

"She was just heartbroken, she was so down on herself. I was glad we had to go to New York right away for *Regis and Kelly*. They wanted us to do the mambo and she did it perfect! She nailed it. And when we performed it on the finale, she nailed it again!"

As hard as we were all working on our dances each week, you really do grow close to the other contestants. Everyone really does support one another. But the guy who always had my back was that sweetheart Christian de la Fuente. Going into week six, Christian bet me a hundred bucks that I wouldn't get voted off. He was absolutely sure I'd make it through. Unfortunately he was wrong.

With the verdict rendered, I walked over to stand in front of the judges for the final time. Tom Bergeron, who hosts the series and stitches together so many loose moments with his gentle humor, came over and took my hands.

He has been a friend for many years, and when he told me how proud he was of all that I had done on the show, it was all I could do not to break down in tears.

Even though I didn't make it all the way to the finals, I look back on it as one of the great experiences of my life. Everywhere I go, even now, I'm swarmed by fans that supported me during the show. I was overwhelmed by the number of e-mails I received from ordinary people telling me how much what I had done had inspired them. Many had stories of how life had dealt them a bad hand, but they'd been afraid to fight back, and now, after watching me, they weren't.

As an actor, you always want to touch the audience. I just had no idea that I could do it on the dance floor.

Fabian, the fabulous Mambo King, became a great friend, one I know that I will have for a lifetime. We had an absolute blast doing the show, and I'm the luckiest gal on earth to have had Fabian as my partner.

In December, I pulled out my dancing shoes, practiced my moves, and headed out on the *Dancing with the Stars* tour with Fabian, the man who first taught me the groove and move! A cross-country road trip with my dancing buddies, and all my glittery barely-theres to shake and shimmy into . . . I couldn't wait.

54

Nᴏᴛ ʟᴏɴɢ ᴀɢᴏ, I took Fabian on a tour of my old neighborhood.

Our house in Morton Grove, Illinois, where so many of my memories were made, looked smaller somehow. The trees, newly planted when my family first moved in, are towering now. Kids still play football and baseball in the street.

It brought back a wave of memories—meeting Liz, playing Dorothy in *The Wizard of Oz* at seven, meeting Henry, falling in love with Mike, fights with my mom, seeing the world open up with closed-captioning, slipping into another world of drugs and addiction, being cast in *Children of a Lesser God,* leaving my childhood and my family for New York, then L.A., all the characters that have come into my life, all the opportunities, the challenges, building a family of my own.

I have traveled so many miles and done so many things that I never dreamed I would do in the years since I left Morton Grove. Like the house, I am both the same and different now.

One thing that hasn't changed, I want to experience as much of life as I can, pile up moments—good and bad—as if there were no tomorrow. No stopping, no regrets.

I have been given an extraordinary life thus far, and I am nowhere close to done with it yet.

Every day brings new challenges, creative juices that keep churning inside me, characters whose lives and whose stories I want to tell, new chapters to write.

No matter what I do next in my career, acting will always be my first choice, my first love.

I think back to the time I stood on a stage when I was seven and began telling a story through sign and movement and felt the applause and saw the smiles. That moment—that connection—touched something deep inside me, a hunger that will never go away.

And though I am Deaf, it is not as if I live in silence. Thousands of thoughts are always buzzing around in my head.

That's what defines a life, or at least my life—emotions, feelings, ideas—having them, but also sharing them.

Telling my children I love them each day. Calling Liz or Ruthie or Jack or another friend to share a funny moment. Walking on a warm summer evening hand in hand with my husband. Seeing my brothers and their families, my parents or Kevin's, who've become like my own second family.

As I look at my life, one of my greatest challenges has been my relationship with my mother. I know, without question, that both of my parents absolutely love me. I've never doubted that, and it is the best gift that any parent can give his or her child.

But I also look back and search my mind and my heart for the moments with my mom that are not colored by the fights that have dogged us for a lifetime. In the distance I see myself as a child sick with the flu, spending the day under the covers with a fever and my mom bringing hot soup to my bed. Driving me through a snowstorm to see Liz. My mom always in the audience at the theaters of my life, applauding but fearful it will all go up in smoke and a little envious that she didn't get cast in the starring role.

I have a handful of faded memories like that—both sweet and sad.

I look at the wall that I see separating us, my mother and me, and wonder if maybe it was my first and most important lesson in life: to face that wall and not back down. To find my way despite it—push through it, jump over it, run around it—so that all the other walls that I would face afterward would never seem insurmountable.

In recent years, I've tried to get to a place where I simply accept that the closeness I've wished a lifetime for with my mom is probably beyond us now. She and my dad are both growing older and are not all that well.

Many of the things that used to send me spinning into anger, I just set aside these days. Instead I try to focus on the love that is there and believe that she is giving me all that she can. And I try to make sure both my parents know how much I love them, how much they mean to me.

My life is rich and I am blessed, and I am grateful. That I am Deaf is just a footnote. It is a part of who I am, but far from all of who I am.

And the dark secrets that I kept locked away in my heart for all those many years are now out in the open.

Today, I can face those old wounds head-on. I know they cannot defeat me—the drugs, the babysitter, the teacher, the actor, the deafness, and the rest. I am stronger than all of it.

Looking into all those dark corners has been a little like giving birth—despite much pain, if you breathe and let yourself embrace it, absorb it, you'll come through to the other side and the payoff is spectacular.

So I find myself now, not at the end of my story, but at the beginning of a new story, and I can't wait to see what life has in store for me. Bring it on . . . I'm ready.

ACKNOWLEDGMENTS

THIS BOOK HAS been forty-three years in the making. For me it was about telling the truth. My truth. It was just time. And though I strived to tell the truth about myself, there are so many people I must thank because I couldn't have done it without them.

Betsy Sharkey—thank you for your brilliance. This absolutely could not have happened without you. When can we start on the sequel? Kidding!

Jack Jason—you came into my life at the perfect time and I can't imagine what I would have done without you. Thanks for believing in me. Thanks for putting up with me. You are simply a saint. I know I would *not* be where I am today without you. *No pork!*

To my agent Alan Nevins—thank you for all you've done. Your encouragement, your nagging, your words of wisdom. You rock!

To Jen Bergstrom and Tricia Boczkowski at Simon Spotlight Entertainment—you've made writing this book a breeze; the best publisher and editor ever.

Evelyn Caldwell—I bow to you. Thank you for looking out for me everyday when it comes to my piggy bank.

Carol Bruckner—what can I say but thank you CWAA? You are the only person who can swear better than me but make it sound more palatable. I heart you.

Steve LaManna and the crew at Innovative—good show. Thank you for keeping my dream alive.

Howard Bragman, Brad Cafarelli, and Lisa Perkins—thanks for twenty years' worth of fifteen minutes. You guys give the best PR.

To Mom and Dad—how could I be anything but a Matlin? I love and am proud to be your daughter. For all your patience in all that I put you through, I love you.

To Eric, Glo, Zach, and Arielle—nobody could ask for a better family. Thank you for all your love and support over the years.

Marc and Jay—I've kept a secret all these years: Apples was Catholic. I love you so much.

Lynne Smith—I love you and the whole family.

Samuel Block—thank you for introducing me to the wonderful world of Sign Language.

Liz Tannebaum—you are my sister. I love you.

Mike Lundquist—I will always cherish the good times together.

Bob Michaels—if only . . . oh, never mind!

Patricia Scherer—I couldn't have been Dorothy without you. Thank you for all you do for Deaf children everywhere and their dreams.

Henry Winkler—thank you for helping me to follow my dream. I love you.

Stacey Winkler—I promise I'll clean my room tomorrow. I love you, too.

Sister Mary Elizabeth Endee—you were the best teacher ever.

William Hurt—despite the good times and the tough times, I could not be where I am without having known you.

Randa Haines—you never let me give up. Thank you.

Christine Vericker and Betty Ford—what can I say but that you saved my life. Thank you.

Ruthie McCrary—my soul sister forever—Maa-Ruu rules!

Wendy, Mark A., Barb, Amy M., Danielle, and Cyrani—ILY.

Stephanie Matlow—thank you for introducing me to Los Angeles.

Carla Hacken—I'd laugh very hard if you became my agent again.

Jann Goldsby—I owe you sushi many times over—cranberry!

Bill Pugin—if I could put in words that face we always make together, I would! You are the best!

David E. Kelley—that's mine!

Barbara and Tim Stehr—good thing Tim doesn't look exactly like Kevin!

Charlotte and Dan Culpepper—you are both a Godsend. I couldn't be in two places at once if it weren't for you. ILY.

Benny Jason—thank you for Jack and all the scrapbooks you collected over twenty-three years. Hugs!

JB—what a feeling. I love you.

Fabian—*serra siempre mi musica!*

Mary and Phil—you are both lifesavers. Your carpooling is the best!

Angie Warner—a new friend with an old soul and the best tour manager ever. I only wish I could play the guitar and sing like a rock star so we could hang out more.

BPD—always be safe.

Dr. Robert Gallo and Michael Schwartz—thank you for your invaluable input.

Dr. Miser and the staff at City of Hope—thank you for saving our Sarah's life.

My Sarah, Brandon, Tyler, and Isabelle—you are my light and my loves. Thank you for being patient with me, whether I was right here with you or working half a world away.

And finally, to my better half, my husband Kevin—I can't imagine life without you. As father, husband, and best friend, no one compares to you. I love you forever.